CENTURIONS

A Manchester City 2017/18
Season Review

Howard Hockin

Introduction

Hello. Thanks for purchasing my Manchester City 2017/18 season review book.
Or borrowing/stealing it.
Whatever, thanks.

After selling 37 copies of my ground-breaking work "Manchester City 2014/15 Season Review: Standing Still", I vowed never to do a season review book again (thanks mum for buying 18 copies). However, this season made me rethink, made me want to write again.

I think we can all agree it was some season. Scintillating football, records broken, rivals apoplectic at the skill shown by this merry band of oil-funded mercenaries. If Duncan Castles had hair, it would have fallen out through sheer rage.

It wasn't perfect, and there was a week when some began to wonder if the previous six months would be eclipsed by three bad results, but in the end I think the season can be viewed as a success. Not just because of what was won, but because of the way it was won. That end of season DVD is going to be one hell of a watch.

The importance of the league win cannot be underestimated. This already felt like a make-or-break season for Pep Guardiola, the weight of the world on the shoulders of a man you would imagine psychoanalyses what dressing to have on a salad. Half the world wanted him to fail. The other half wanted proof that the Premier League could tame anyone. The other half wanted his vision to be stamped on the English game. This season the last half got their wish.
I've never been good at maths.

This book is a look back at everything that happened. Well, almost everything. Thoughts on every match (but no "reports"), a few parody pieces, a look at the wider game, a journalist Q & A, squad ratings, memorable moments and much more.

Something for everyone, except United fans, people who hate spelling mistakes and people who can't read - they may struggle with this book. I couldn't afford a proof reader.

I hope you enjoy reading it as much as I enjoyed writing it.

Thanks to Paul Johnson for his wonderful illustrations on the cover of this book.
Paul is a graphic designer/illustrator, and you can check out more of his wonderful work at studionorthandsouth.com, or follow him on Twitter (@northernmonkee1).

Before we look at the 2017/18 season, I always find it interesting to revisit the end of the previous season. It ended nicely, with the not-that-rare thrashing of Watford, to nail down that 3rd place finish, should there have been any doubt. This is what I wrote, on a day that seems a lifetime ago. City had beaten Leicester 2-1 and West Brom 3-1 at home in the preceding week, Leicester suffering from one of those rare penalty double-hits that proved costly come full-time.

And so another stressful season draws to a close, the "typical city" part of my brain still anxiously eyeing the league table and its goal difference, waking up in a cold sweat having dreamt City were 3-0 down at Watford as Arsenal put Everton to the sword. I'll never change.
Let's hope the staggered substitutions in the West Brom game do not come back to haunt us, unlikely as that is, as goal-difference wise we could have put the season to bed on Tuesday night. Well the top four at least – better to go straight to the group stage, and whilst we would be seeded in a potential qualification tie, Liverpool would not, so could face a tricky tie such as Borussia Dortmund. Again, the odds are unlikely, but it's a risk neither team wants to take.

Still, the past week has given us some tears at the departure of a true legend, given the send-off he richly deserved, of which many, including me, have written and spoken about elsewhere, and we could have quite a few emotional goodbyes in coming years, but Zabaleta will be right up there because of the connection he had with the fans that is so rare. He should make us remember that there's more important things in the world than not winning a league, or a few bad results.

Elsewhere, we've also had a tough-hard-fought victory and of course some of the most enjoyable bleating from opposition fans of the whole season – yes the outcry at the correct decisions given in the Leicester match was truly a joy to behold – from a team that pulled, tugged and dived its way to a league title last season, remarkable as it still was, the bleating became even more enjoyable, if that is possible. I mean, fancy having the nerve to correctly disallow a penalty whereby the striker hits the ball against his other foot, when in the past such occurrences have not been spotted by match officials and thus allowed? I mean that's just not fair is it? Just like the numerous encroachments during Leicester's 17 penalties last season weren't acted upon either, but I'm guessing Gary Lineker didn't bother to flag them up on Match Of The Day. There probably wasn't time, packed programme and all that. Funny that. Much in the same way Alan Shearer was raging about that time Newcastle had a goal disallowed against City as a shot whistled past an offside player, yet was happy to argue Silva's goal should not have stood last weekend. Funny that. Yep, funny how rules that are perfectly fair only become contentious when Manchester City benefit from them or poor little Leicester City fall foul of them. They've never been the same since dragging opposition players to the ground at corners became an offence.

Still, football just isn't fair a lot of the time – money talks, a referee's call can be crucial, as can the spin on a ball. Fairness is not applying coefficient scores linked to past success, success from 30 years ago, fairness is not seeding teams to avoid shocks and dwindling TV audiences, fairness is not having a United fan with his fingers in every pie on every table of every football governing body in the game, fairness is not the FA charging players due to a Sky Sports rolling news campaign, fairness is not found in the brown envelopes that allegedly swirled round our governing bodies offices, it's not bribes for hosting World Cups, ignoring human rights or homophobia, fairness is not financial fair play, despite what the name suggests, fairness is not Wayne Rooney earning £300k a week, fairness is not being able to charge a player because the referee saw the incident at the time, fairness is rare. You just have to play the game as best you can.

There's no greater example of unfairness in the closing weeks of the season as the play offs play out before our eyes – for 30 years now this arbitrary system has decided the fate of teams and changed histories as a result. No one can really claim, can they, that a system is truly fair when finishing 3rd gives you no greater advantage than a team over 6th – still, the National League seem to have twigged this, and there are plans for a new system that requires a harder journey for those that finish lower – for me, fairness would entail 3rd going straight to the final, 4th playing the winner of 5th v 6th, and thus rewarding position. The truly fair system would rid us of play offs altogether, but I appreciate what they add to the excitement of a season, and how they keep more teams involved until the very end. They are not without merit, and City certainly got quite a good story out of them.

And football will remain unfair too without help from technology, but that's probably a conversation for another time – at least there is talk of retrospective punishment next season for divers and feigning of injury, but I will believe it when I see it, and it's hard to prove an injury is being faked even if it is fairly obvious.

As for City, the fairness was not always apparent but in the end the levels of performances were not quite good enough too, though gaining over 2 points per game used to be something to cheer about – not any more. As this season saw our best away record ever, it is clear the problems lie closer to home, and the Etihad must become a fortress once more like it was in title winning seasons. There are signs in recent weeks however that packed defences are starting to be unpicked, but issues remain, and they're not all in our defence.

Still, as we are told, United, under the tutelage of Jose Mourinho, a man more adept at drawing than Tony Hart in his prime, will have had a more successful season than City if they are victorious in Stockholm next week. It will be a trophy City can't win of course and the League Cup was not a priority, and they should have been knocked out in the semi-final anyway – as I have said before, sometimes things are just out of a manager's hands. Criticism of Pep is understandable and permitted, naturally, it's been his worst season as a manager and we must compete for trophies next season, probably win something too, but I know who'd I's rather have as manager right now, I know who I'd rather watch for the next 5 years. It's not a team with Fellaini in it, a manager who whinges incessantly, hangs players out to dry and even admits he really doesn't want to be playing the remaining league games.

And when this City side has finished four consecutive seasons above United, it shows just how bad they've been spending money when you consider we'll probably have to give Mangala away in a raffle, take a big loss on Nolito and Nasri, and sell Hart for peanuts because it's what we do, and probably pay half their wages after they have all gone too.

Still, an exciting summer awaits, rumours will abound and there will be big signings, of that there can be little doubt, though as Pablo Zabaleta showed, it's the little ones that are often the best. With no major summer tournament, despite our moans and groans over the past 8 months, we'll be desperate for it all to start again come August. I'm glad of the break, but the excitement of a new season will never dwindle. Have a great summer, and until next season, goodbye.

Football Doesn't Matter

Apologies for not talking about football for a short while. I appreciate you reading this book, but the fact is that football doesn't matter.

Normally, like the bitter bertie I am, I'd be cheering on Ajax to beat Manchester United in the Europa League final. This time though, I barely cared. For anyone from Manchester, the match seemed to have lost some of its sparkle.

A couple of days earlier, a terrorist attack on the Manchester Arena, as an Ariana Grande concert finished, claimed the lives of 22 people. Young girls, parents, friends joyous after a wonderful night out. It's hard to comprehend. Impossible.

It hit a lot of us hard. I had walked through that exact spot days earlier for a gig. I will walk through it many times again in the future. I felt some guilt about how this hit me harder than terrible things happening far away, but it's a natural reaction I guess to terrible things happening in your home town, the town you have called your own for over 40 years, in a location that holds so many happy memories. That's what I struggled with most, apart from the appalling loss of life and the terrible impact on their families and those survivors struggling with what happened. I go to a lot of gigs. And it occurred to me that the moment when you leave the venue, after a show that you have enjoyed, is one of life's greatest moments. The joy at what you have witnessed, the adrenaline, perhaps the sweat too. It is a magical time. And that was the moment that another human being decided to wreak horror on so many people. Mostly young people who had been looking forward to this night for months and months. It's hard to accept, hard to put into context.

So with all that in mind, it was a stark reminder, in the worst way imaginable, that football is not that important at times like this. United might win, they might lose. I couldn't muster the effort for the result to matter that much to me. Though naturally I'd still have preferred if they had lost.

I'll be back next season of course, willing every curse on the team across the town, hoping my team is the best in the land, and refusing to acknowledge any of their players are any good. The life cycle continues on regardless, and football will take centre stage once more.

But occasionally it's good to step back and acknowledge that it's just a game, and your life should not be shaped by it. That's how I hope I live my life from now on, but I'm not hopeful.

A quick note on Lingaard's celebration after their Europa League victory, which attracted plenty of criticism. I have no problem with this cross-club rivalry, and we'd see plenty more of it in the coming season. It's natural, it is what defines rivalries. Let's not pretend that players are any different from us or should act in a different way. We're all football fans at heart.

However, there is a time and place for such acts, and days after a terrorist act is not one of them. If Lingaard had a shred of intelligence, he would have realised this, mere minutes after holding up a banner honouring those that had died in the attack. Sadly he is more interested in dabbing, stupid dances and what's more his social media input suggests a man lacking much maturity. We should have expected no better from the odious rat.

A Summer Of Change

Aleksandar Kolarov Leaves

Over the weekend, the day finally came. I thought that day would be during the summer of 2016. I previously thought that day would be during the summer of 2015. And prior to that – well, you get the idea. Aleksandar "jingle bells" Kolarov has left Manchester City to join Roma, and not even on loan, as is the tradition for those that depart for sunnier climes (by which I mean anywhere). For a man who professed a desire to return to Lazio one day, it seems he took a wrong-turn at the airport, but his departure was done on his terms, and he departs with many good wishes.

When I think of Kolarov, thoughts turn to May 19th, 2013. It was a miserable end to a miserable season. City had lost the FA Cup final to a soon-to-be-relegated Wigan Athletic, Roberto Mancini fell on his sword, and then Brian Kidd reluctantly guided City to a lacklustre 2-3 home defeat against Norwich City. Even the rare sight of a Jack Rodwell double couldn't save us. Cue one of those end-of-season laps of dishonour from the City players that no one really wanted.
Only this time Aleksandar Kolarov, not for the first time that season, managed to get embroiled in an argument with one of the few remaining fans as the walkabout occurred. It summed up quite well not only the season that saw United crowned Premier League champions but also his time at City, but with five trophies and seven seasons under his belt, he deserves to be remembered for more than that last game of the 2012/13 season or his other unflattering moments.

As we all know, many a City player has proved divisive during their time at the club, but few more than the Serbian left-back signed by City for £16m in July 2010. Hell, I changed my opinion of him hour by hour some days. Boy he infuriated me at times.
It wasn't that he was terrible, but he was a player who I felt could have been more. He **looked** like the real deal. Hard as nails, athletic, powerful, with a left foot like a traction engine – not quite fast enough,

but not a million miles off the archetypal modern full-back. However, in the end he was never quite consistently good enough, but when we've reached the stage where Championship players are valued at up to £20m, in seven years at the club Aleksandar Kolarov will be viewed by my good self as a good value purchase who contributed to City's success.

It was a bumpy ride though. An early injury that stalled his progress was symptomatic of a rollercoaster seven years at the club. With the signing of Gael Clichy on 2011, Kolarov spent the next five years battling with the Frenchman for the left-back slot, with varying degrees of success. Neither proved a calamity, but neither was good enough to help City compete with the world's best, but at a club allergic to spending money on full-backs they both got plenty of pitch-time.

His appearance record reflects the duel he had with Clichy. Twenty four league appearances in his debut season was followed by just twelve in the historic 2011/12 season, then twenty the season after. After the spat at the Norwich game, I scored him 4/10 for the season and his departure seemed inevitable. He stayed though, and was one of our better defenders as we won the league for a second time, even gaining a respectable 7.5/10 score from me – by the end of that season, he was widely regarded as our first-choice left-back, with thirty league appearances under his belt and a new three-year contract beckoned.

The problem with Kolarov though was that he could never keep it up, never sustain good form. He was capable of sumptuous free-kicks and killer crosses from the left that were almost impossible to defend. He was also capable of hitting balls into row Z, bad positioning and giving off an air of being uninterested. When eventually Pep Guardiola reinvented him as one of our more consistent central defenders of last season, it seems it was Kolarov who decided his time was at an end, and asked to leave. Obviously central defence was not for him. Pep makes no effort to persuade those not willing to stay to change their mind, and that was that, an unfortunate end at a time when his versatility could have been more useful than ever after the summer cull of ageing full-backs that has left some City fans nervously counting down the days until the season starts and tracking private jet flights from the south of France.

I digress. For all his faults, Kolarov had his moments. The aforementioned form of the 2013/14 season helped keep Champions-elect Liverpool at bay and despite a lesser contribution to the first title win, a late equaliser against Sunderland proved crucial in the end. When he was in the mood, few hit a free kick better, and when he sneaked in a curling free-kick at the Santiago Bernabeu, I thought he had inspired the biggest of all away wins – but it wasn't to be.
Never mind. Few could put in a better cross, and few were so readily available to play without injury, suspension or the need to stir up trouble through agents or manager fall-outs. He was professional throughout even if some felt he didn't seem overly committed to the cause week-in, week-out. One hundred and sixty five appearances, eleven goals and five trophies suggest he played his part, but in the end, a club managed by Pep Guardiola and a club coming off the back of three underwhelming seasons needs more, it needs to be the best.

At the age of 31, Kolarov gets his final payday and City get a modest fee for a fullback before the inevitable happens, and the legs begin to flag. Another of the old guard has departed, as the team goes through one of its greatest revolutions. Kolarov will never be regarded as a City legend, never appear on the pantheon of greats, but he did his bit, representing the club for seven seasons and helping shape some wonderful memories for us blues. I wish him all the best in the future, and say thank you Aleksandar. City TV will never be the same again.

STAN COLLYMORE – PEP GUARDIOLA MIGHT NOT KNOW WHO I AM, BUT MARADONA DID, AND HIS PENIS IS BIGGER THAN PEP'S (I IMAGINE)

Goodbye My Friend

Sometimes, goodbye is the hardest thing to say. City's final home game of the season was over, and the tradition for a club that has not reached expected heights is familiar around the country – a reluctant squad troops out to give their thanks to the 2000 or so strays that have remained in the stadium. Not this time though – people still left, got to get home after all, early starts and all that, but the majority remained because there was unfinished business. It was the first of what will be a series of painful goodbyes over the coming years.

We watched as Pablo Zabaleta opened up and welled up, as I pretended not to, he gave his thanks and we gave ours. As Pablo said, it was the right time to move on, but he loves the club so much. The feeling is mutual. It was a perfect send off for a player that embraced everything to do with Manchester City football club.

Days like this have been creeping up on us City fans for a while now – the golden spine of our team that gave us more success than we could have once imagined have grown old together, as not even David Silva can defeat time itself, though he's giving it a good go. Kompany, Toure, Silva, Zabaleta, players all into their 30s, their futures often questioned, their position at the club perilous in recent times. In the end it was Zabaleta that cut ties first, his legs finally giving in to the demands of a 60-game season, and the day we knew was coming but still hoped never would, had finally arrived.

Zabaleta said in his farewell speech that he did not know if he would stay for long when he arrived, and as few of us knew much about him, we probably felt the same. The day before the takeover of 2008, the day before everything changed forever, he arrived for a modest £6.5m fee from Espanyol. Neither he nor the fans could have envisaged what would follow.

There was little focus on his debut, as all eyes followed Robinho round the pitch as City fell to Chelsea, a certain Frank Lampard running the show. And it must not be forgotten that he was never initially one of the first names on the team sheet either. Signed in 2008, in those heady days when he still had hair, he has thus become one of the longest-serving players at the club, Vincent Kompany arriving just before him, Joe Hart before that.

Despite his long tenure at the club, there is still a slight over-egging of his dominance of that right-back position. He may have joined in 2008, but it was a good four years until Pablo really came into his own, developing along with the team. In that crazy 2011/12 title-winning season, Micah Richards was often preferred for the right-back slot, Zabaleta only starting in just over half of the league games. He still contributed of course, but it was after that season, as Richards' performances tailed off, that Zabaleta truly shone. Very quickly he was our clear 1st choice at right back, and more than that, one of the best right backs in the Premier League, maybe in Europe too. It wouldn't last forever, but for a couple of years he was the sort of full back we'd sell family members to have in the team right now.

So consistently good were his performances in the 2012/13 season that he even made the PFA team of the Year, an accomplishment by a Manchester City player akin to me being bombarded with racy texts from a love-struck Natalie Imbruglia. That was the peak for him as a player, though the following season was far greater for the club and him in general. Sadly, in recent times, the legs have gone, the hair too, and the body cannot keep up with the brain. Having almost left last summer, it is no surprise he did not last until next season. At 32, he still has football in him, so it was the right decision for all.

But why was Zabaleta different, why was he special? He wasn't our greatest player, though his peaks were up in the clouds. He wasn't our longest-serving player, though his time at the club was substantial. Nor will he be our most decorated, the feeling being, whilst he has accumulated a good few trophies, he and others such as Kompany, Silva and Toure have somewhat wasted the last two or three years, trophy-wise.

It was something else. Something he and our club captain share.

You see, the thing that defines a legend can be for numerous reasons, such as a special goal at a crucial time that saves the club from ignominy or wins a club a trophy.

Nope. That wasn't Zabaleta's legacy – he scored a few goals, slowly creeping into double figures, scoring a big goal in Rome and an even bigger one on THAT day. Maybe he should have scored more, but that's by the by.

No, it is for another reason Pablo became a club legend – because he absorbed himself into the club, he cherished being here, he adapted to his new country, his new city, his new club. He became, quite simply, one of us, but with the added responsibility of shaping our history. He was the antithesis of the stereotype of the modern footballer – living in (relatively) modest accommodation, living a normal life, eating normal things, by which I of course mean fish and chips. No back or front-page headlines, no lurid rumours, no forgetting where he had come from and what his responsibilities were at the club. I've no idea what he earns, I've no idea who his agent is, if he has one. He said the right things to endear himself to City fans, but unlike others he meant what he said. From the day he arrived, he has been a model professional, even when he no longer became one of the first names on the team sheet. An exception to the rule, to the feeling, even if it is exaggerated, that most players are just passing through, doing their job and earning the big bucks before moving on to pastures new. The antithesis to the (false) perception of City's players as mercenaries, he came to play football, not for the money. He connected with the fans when so few do, and he's the player we dream we'd be if we ever got the chance to pull on that shirt for real – as a certain banner once commented, god chose him to play on our behalf. I paraphrase and I'm an atheist, but I stand by the sentiment.

When a player kisses the club badge, the shirt, it can seem an empty gesture, almost an embarrassment in the heat of the moment. When Pablo did it, it was real, it was true, it came from the heart.

But there's more to him than that. A warrior on the pitch, but never dirty with it, he was committed, respected, hard-working and professional throughout, the sort of footballer who perfectly suited the bloodied head bandage and torn-shirt image popularised by Terry

Butcher. Heart on sleeve, unquestioned commitment, a player who would never ease up, never back off, never fail to admit to failure, would play until he dropped.

333 appearances for the man with little of the devil in him. His style fit the league perfectly too - everything you want from a full-back in one handy package.

At his peak, the best right-back I have seen in a blue shirt, and forever my favourite.

He has, quite simply, been a hero at a time when we were desperate for them. Living in the shadows for so long, we all had our favourites, but were they heroes, were they legends? Was their ability enough to earn these titles? A couple were, yes, but we needed more, we needed players that took us to new levels that changed the image of the Club. And Pablo Zabaleta helped do that.

I hope he stays in the Premier League as I'd like to see him continue to play football, as long as it is not for a direct rival – West Ham would make sense, though he'll struggle to find a decent chippy near the Olympic Stadium. I also hope we see him again, I hope he can return and play some part in the club's future history and help shape more magical memories. If not, keep using that life-long season ticket at least. And the West Brom game was special because it is rare that we not only have witnessed such a long-standing servant of the game leave us, but that we got the chance to say goodbye.

I would find it hard to truly cry for a departing footballer – it is sad but life moves on, new heroes emerge, the world keeps revolving. I'll save the tears for soppy films and the day I learn Line of Duty is gone forever. But this is one of those few departures that leaves an indelible mark on me.

Just remember this. Always be yourself. But if you can't, well - you know the rest.

He is, quite simply, **the** fucking man.

All the best, Pablo. In a cold, cynical world, I will truly miss you.

Season Ticket Prices

Tuesday morning, 10am. The moment of truth.
I opened the email, knowing what to expect, and I was not surprised.

The rumours, for once, were true, kind of. City has released season
ticket prices for the 207/18 season, and prices had risen by an average
of 2.5% it seemed, though 5% was the initial rumour. A few freezes, a
few rises more than 2.5%. Prices decided by a random number
generator it seems.

I don't need to read a single line of the club blurb to know the
justification that the club will present to fans for the rise – competitive
prices, especially compared to rival clubs, monthly payments, cheap
seats available, help the club compete blah blah blah.

My ticket is well-priced, the rise manageable, just £10 spread out over a
year, but for me that misses the point. And whilst 2.5% on £380 is
peanuts, it's obviously more the greater the cost of the season ticket. It
will be £40+ for some.

For the outlay on the team, the last three years have been rather
underwhelming. Hey, that's football, I for one don't demand success,
but coming off 36 months that has largely flattered to deceive, the club
could have made a gesture. The country is on its arse, many long-
standing fans have already been priced out of attending, times are hard
for so many, and a club owned by billionaires that has raised revenue to
one of the largest in Europe away from match-day revenue and will only
raise it further in the coming years could have helped the fans and taken
the smallest of hits. Or by freezing prices, no hit whatsoever. With Pep
Guardiola reportedly complaining about the atmosphere and demanding
Txiki sort the problems, he then goes and raises prices, a move that will
dull the "match day experience" even more.
So with expanding corporate areas, tunnel clubs and tyre sponsors, no
rise was needed. Piss off the fans and drive them away, and the
atmosphere gets even worse. Reduce prices and they get the full crowd
every match, they make more money on the day, the atmosphere

increases, some deserters may return and the home form might even improve.

Let's cut to the chase. What the f**k were they thinking when they decided to do this? All those club surveys all the feedback gratefully received, the supposed monitoring of online forums. To hell with it all, eh?

The key point for me is this: the money gained from each rise is irrelevant – meaningless. A loss of support from the fans for such meagre gains. With each passing year at City, with each rise in commercial revenue and with each TV deal, ticket sales comprise a smaller wedge of City's total revenue – I have heard that it currently accounts for 15%.

All of City's match day revenue could have been covered for a year just by the rise in the last TV deal – not all the revenue from the TV deal, just the increase compared to the previous one. With that in mind, consider how much difference a 2.5% rise makes to City's ability to compete. It's a televised game (or part of one), it's helping pay one of our 70 loaned out players' wages for a few months, it's putting revenue up by a fraction of one percent. Worth it, City?

Paying for Messi? It would barely cover the private jet over here, let alone his digs at the Lowry as he acclimatises to horizontal rain and four seasons in a day.

Let's not forget that the difference between finishing 3rd and 4th in the Premier League is £2m for starters, more than double what these rises will bring in. Fall to fifth and City could have taken a chunk off ticket prices and it would lose them no more than the drop in league positions. And still that stupid Platinum scheme persists, allowing loyalty to be bought, and still prices for single purchases are the most exorbitant of all.

Football fans like to make gestures, most of them empty threats. Never getting Sky again because it's all United fans on the panels. Nor BT, biased arses. Not buying a Sharp product, never having a red car.

As I said, mostly futile nonsense. But for those that were already disillusioned with modern football, even a small price rise could be the final straw, the tipping point that makes a minority of fans decide not to renew, to commit their weekends to B & Q, garden centres and Football Focus. Others will drop out of cup schemes instead, so any money gained will be lost elsewhere, attendances for the smaller games will dwindle and the empty seat counters' heads will explode with glee.

We must stop the idea that fans are there to be fleeced – that if a price is affordable, it is acceptable. Of course my season ticket, at £390, to watch the best set of players I have witnessed, is good value. Of course a £10 price increase, spread over 10 months is affordable, whatever my wage. But I'm sorry, that's not good enough. Fans have spent 30 years being fleeced by their clubs, who knew they had a monopoly and a near-captive audience. Ticket prices have increased by almost 1000% since the 1980's and we all accepted it. Thankfully in recent years, once we ignore the pitiful bedroom-dwelling banter boys counting empty seats, many have said enough is enough, and have given up or fought back.

So yeah, this small rise means nothing in the scheme of things. It's the price of one takeaway, a padded cinema seat (only the best for me), or a medium coke in the foyer. But I'm not going to shrug my shoulders this time and move on.

The rise makes no commercial sense. You wonder how City's decision makers sat down and came to this decision. The need to get that revenue creeping up, come what may? Cos this will make a huge difference! Small increases are a classic tactic to creep the prices up, but I'm not sure City has read the situation very well on this occasion. Not everyone has had a rise either – it seems from early indications, as I type furiously without the full facts to hand, that the £299 seats have remained at the same price. Nice move by City says the cynic in me (that's basically all of me), as they can still claim to have the cheapest seats in the Premier League. Expect this price to continue to figure prominently on all promotional material.

And that's what frustrates me when it boils down to it. This was a missed opportunity. Other teams are announcing price freezes – they understand the economic situation, they see where the game is heading if they keep making football more and more expensive to attend. Even the kings of leeches over at Old Trafford have frozen season ticket prices for many years now. So did City look at the situation and come to the same conclusion? No, they managed to somehow antagonise fans with little gain for themselves – rises too small to make any noticeable difference to the business model, but rises nevertheless that will piss off sections of our fan base.

I'm aware this comes across as whiny, ungracious snowflake behaviour. Don't get me wrong, I love what our owners have done for this club – it's changed everything, my experiences have been transformed, probably forever. The club have done many wonderful things, and priced many tickets well, especially in cup competitions – and the prices for the 3rd tier of the south stand could not be disagreed with – they were spot on. Monthly payments was a life-saver for me, an excellent change from the powers that be, and new age price bands for next season seem to have helped a few too. Credit where credit is due.

In the early days after the takeover, I felt the owners' wealth gave them a wonderful opportunity to do some different, unique, for City fans, to lower prices to ridiculous levels – Financial Fair Play probably stopped any notion of that dead in its tracks anyway, but now, with record revenue and further riches guaranteed, a small gesture would not only have been welcomed, placating the fan base, but would not have damaged the team on the pitch. Levante are giving regular attenders free season tickets next season, but it seems City can't even freeze their prices.

I just don't get it. It seems you can't even personalise your card anymore either, so sourcing that picture of the 1981 team photo was a complete waste of time too. Still, frees room for a new sponsor on the back of the cards.

Damn you City.

That was a long whine for a £1 monthly rise on something I commit so much of my spare time too. If you're happy with prices I would not wish to persuade you otherwise, I neither expect nor demand universal outrage over a 2.5% price rise that precedes another £150m summer spending spree. But it is so frustrating to me. This club could be different, it could be better than the rest. And it could be that with little or no sacrifice. It chose not to for the price of a scoreboard.

Still, can't wait for the first game in August.

Transfer Swoops

It was a day like any other. City were bring linked with every player on the planet, and some I was sure did not even exist. Nothing seemed imminent though. Then a journalist informed me City had taken out an advertising slot at his newspaper for 6pm that day. He said this probably meant one thing – City were announcing a signing.

This was quite the surprise, even more so when we discovered who it was. Bernardo Silva, a player that had only fleetingly crossed City's transfer radar. City had kept this one very quiet, especially as he had been long-linked with United, and a move there seemed almost inevitable, much to my disgust when recalling his performances against City last season. A player with David Silva levels of ball control was just what United needed.

But no, it seemed that City had nabbed him, and at 6:50pm, slightly later than anticipated, City announced his capture. I was buzzing.

This to me was a coup. An exciting player with sublime ball skills, young, not yet at his prime. Exactly the sort of transfer that excites. I can't wait to see him in a City shirt, though as always he may well need time to get used to the league and style of play.

Ederson Moraes

I'll be calling him Ederson from now on. He is Brazilian after all.

The signing of Bernardo Silva was exciting. This was necessary.

The problem with City's goal keeping situation was obvious. City needed a new one. Claudio Bravo is undoubtedly a good keeper – he must be. You don't fluke your way into top clubs and captain your country and much more. But the bottom line is that it has not worked out for him at Manchester City. It turns out he has had to deal with a significant illness to his daughter during his first season at City, a horrible situation for any parent to go through, as we would discover again later in the season, but you don't really have the confidence that this alone was the problem. Bravo seemed to shrink in goal – he stayed rooted to his line, and far too many shots flew past him.

Bravo looked like he would remain, especially with the exit of Caballero, but he surely could only be back-up of City wanted to be a major force. And thankfully Pep agreed.

Few of us can claim to be experts on the Benfica player, captured for £35m. He is deemed to be good with his feet, and a rising world star in his position. Let's wait and see – either way, City had to get someone, and naturally the fee has caused plenty of mock outrage in the media, this being a world-record fee for a goal-keeper.

Strange really that you can act shocked at such a fee. Why should goal keepers cost less? There's simply no logic to it in my opinion. Expect not a word of criticism when Liverpool sign Butland or Pickford for north of £40m It was ever thus.

The Dani Alves Saga

The rumours were clear- City were on the verge of signing Dani Alves on a 2 year deal. Quite an exciting rumour, if truth be told. He was getting on, so was a short-term option, but still he has been one of the best, most explosive full-backs of the past decade or more, had performed well for Juventus, and was free. He ticked all the boxes.

Well that is until he was spotted in Paris, and I decided he wasn't all that. City had received plenty of assurances that Alves only had eyes for City, so as he honeymooned, City were relaxed. That proved to be a fatal mistake, but I don't really blame City at all. If a player changes his mind in this matter, it's probably best he doesn't come. City can't gate-crash a honeymoon, nor should they rush things when they have been told he will sign once back from his holiday. Alves changed his mind, for reasons we can probably guess at, and that is that. He was a short-term option, so it was hardly the end of the world, especially as he's always come across as a tit, but it did mess up City's transfer strategy. A free transfer for a full-back would have made other acquisitions much easier, but now funds would have to be diverted as City sought to replace the entire full-back roster. Things were about to get even more expensive.

Kyle Walker Signs

The day the game "had gone" proclaimed Ollie Holt as City spent the most money ever on an Englishman, or a fullback. Imagine how much he would cost asked Gary Lineker, if he could cross. As the season showed, exactly the same amount Gary.

So what was the fee? It seems to range between £45m and £52m probably because it includes add-ons. He'll probably activate those add-ons, so it's most likely just over £50m.

City had been haggling with Daniel Levy so were never going to get a bargain, but once the Alves deal fell through City moved quickly and got the deal over the line, despite their intention not to be taken as mugs in transfer talks. I don't think they were though – this was the price that needed to be paid to get Walker, so City got him, and filled a huge gap in the squad.

In the January transfer window, Liverpool would spend £75m on Virgil Van Dijk, but naturally the Liverpool-infested media all agreed it was good value for money as it was a position Liverpool desperately needed to strengthen in. That's OK then.

As for how Walker will do, considering Trippier is far better (and remember. Ibe>Sterling), time will tell. But his pace and energy alone will add an extra dimension to the team.

Danilo Signs

You wait ages for a bus…..

A left-field signing this, that aroused little excitement, but then signings don't have to be exciting, they just have to be good.

This was City reacting to the Alves fall-out, and plugging the gap his defection caused. I'm no expert on Danilo, so it's another wait-and-see transfer. However at least City are getting the players in to fill gaps. Some fans were panicking by the start of May that we hadn't addressed such issues. Danilo was great at Porto but bombed at Real Madrid which doesn't necessarily tell us much. He seems to be versatile too, which is a big plus. £27m is peanuts too nowadays. What a crazy world we live in.

Benjamin Mendy Signs

Hell yeah!!!
The final piece of the full-back puzzle is put into place. And what a piece! Another exciting signing, Mendy is the all-action rampaging full-back that any fan would like to see in their team. His attacking intent will hopefully help transform the team. Another member of last season's electric Monaco team, though I am rather saddened to see the vultures circling as soon as they have any success.
£52m is the reported fee, another player arriving with a big price hanging over him, but I doubt Mendy will worry too much about that. City have retired an entire full-back compliment, and the replacements are younger, faster, more energetic, and should help implement the blueprint of Guardiola, who probably realised quickly this was business that should have been done a year ago. You live and learn.

He seems quite a character too. Always important when considering team morale and all that.

City's Director of Football, Txiki Begiristain, said: *"Benjamin has all the qualities we are looking for in a full-back. For such a young player, he has a wealth of top-level experience.*
"He is undoubtedly one of the world's best full-backs, our number one target in this position. We are all delighted to have him here at Manchester City.
"I'm sure he will prove a fantastic addition to the squad."

The Other Departures

I've mentioned Kolarov and Zabaleta, but the summer saw quite the cull of City players. Here's the main bunch of those who departed. There's a lot so I'll try to be brief.

Willy Caballero – out of contract, and soon off to Chelsea as their back up instead. Never got the love at City, but gained redemption as our Carabao Cup winning keeper. Extra points for that win coming via penalties against Liverpool. I was the only person who thought he was quite good, but with the odd game here and there, he could not put together a case to be 1st choice keeper, and couldn't put in consistently good performances.

Gael Clichy – part of the great full back cull of 2017, which saw a number of ageing former international full backs callously thrown onto the scrap heap. Clichy was a regular 7/10 performer, who never scaled any heights, and have a few low periods, but played his part in the most successful period in the club's history. At £7m he was a steal too. Another model professional who never moaned and never gave up, he should be recognised for what he gave the club, even if he was not one of our greatest performers.

Bacary Sagna – also part of the full back cull, Sagna arrived on a free, with his best years behind him, did a job as part of the squad, then left. Worthwhile acquisition, but his time at City was too brief to make too much of a recognition. That's actually harsh for a player that spent 3 years at the club, and made 54 appearances for City. To me though he never felt more than a back-up player in the twilight of his career, though he got plenty of game time during the 2015-16 season. Nevertheless, he never let us down, and he departs with my best wishes.

Fernando – like Sagna, was at City from 2104-17, made 64 appearances, scoring four goals. And yet I can remember little that he did if consequence. He was a defensive midfielder of course, so that may not be surprising, but the fact is he never really shone at City, doing a job and nothing more. From the Javi Garcia school of "did alright, I suppose", he left in the summer to Galatasaray for £4m. Few noticed him leaving, but again he was a model professional who got on with it but he never really scaled any heights.

Kelechi Iheanacho – one of the greatest pieces of business City have ever done, which probably isn't saying much. Iheanacho moved to Leicester in the summer for £25m. You can quote the states to me as much as you want, with Iheanacho having one of the best minutes-per-goal ratio of all Premier League strikers, but I never really rated him. He knew where the goal was, but that was not enough for where City want to be. He is young too of course, but for a player seemingly plucked out of nowhere, this felt like great business for City, and allowed Iheanacho to get greater game time, which he needs. Or so I thought, but he has struggled at Leicester City, making my doubts seem all the more valid. City are thought to have inserted a buy-back clause in his contract – it will never be activated though.

A thoroughly nice bloke, I hope he makes me eat my words, just not at City's expense.

Nolito – a strange one this. A squad acquisition, Nolito was pretty good in the early months at City. Nothing amazing, but a good team player that put in a shift and was a good outlet in wide positions. He had a bit of fire in him too, and you wonder if this was what did for him. He also had a habit of trying to head-butt opposition players, which can be something of a problem when trying to win football matches. Anyway, he did something wrong, because he soon fell out of favour with Pep and was rarely seen, and off he went in the summer, moaning about the Mancunian weather. You should try living here for 44 years and stop moaning, what weather was he expecting? Anyway, no great loss to City, just another player passing through.

Jesus Navas – what more is there to be said about the man with the dreamy eyes? Whatever you think, he was another good acquisition for the club, that gave more than enough back and another model professional to boot. But you have to wonder what he could have been. He had pace to burn and the work ethic to go with it, but he just fell short on key aspects that could have elevated him to elite company. We all know that he scored far too few goals for a man in his position, but most of all we all know that his crossing would have you tearing your hair out. I'll remember him for the lightening quick goal at home to Spurs, his Wembley goal and his Wembley penalty, and as a good squad player who was never quite good enough.

Wilfried Bony – no offence, but utter relief that he has gone, back to Swansea. I always try and be positive about signings, as we are a well-run club now and there must be logic behind any acquisition. Thus I thought that Bony would be a good Plan B for City, a physical, robust forward player with a hammer of a shot. A player to give us options when the pretty passing failed. Sadly it could not have gone worse for Bony and City and all we got was a succession of Instagram poses. Quite good Instagram poses, but still. There were a few injuries to hamper him further, but it seemed the move to City was a leap too far. He did not fit, and he could not perform to the level he had achieved at Swansea. You wonder if he ever will again. The failure was made worse by jettisoning Dzeko soon before, making Bony effectively a replacement for the Bosnian. Now as is often the case, history has been re-written about Dzeko, a player who was poor in his final season at City, and not particularly in demand when Roma snapped him up. However, obviously he was an upgrade on Bony, and his Indian summer at Roma has only made Bony's signing look even worse, if that is possible.

Jason Sancho – an annoying exit, one of England's future stars, who felt that his progress would be blocked at City. You've got to admire a 17 year old moving to Germany, and he is already getting appearances and goals for Borussia Dortmund, so it's hard to criticise his move, but I have little doubt he would have got some playing time at City soon – he is only 17 after all. We'll never know, and you get the horrible feeling that a Pogba situation is brewing, whereby we try and buy him back for loads of money in a few years' time. Anyway, you have to be pragmatic about it all – we nicked him off Watford, Dortmund nicked him off us, so it's swings and roundabouts I guess.

Pre-Season

City participated in the usual pre-season tournament far, far away, for purely financial reasons. This time around it was named the International Champions Cup, featuring three English clubs that were not champions and Real Madrid. City lost 2-0 to United, and I couldn't have cared less. I then proceeded to care even less about a 4-1 win over Real Madrid and a 3-0 win over Tottenham Hotspur.

City will be back as actual champions for the 2018 version, with an even weaker squad than last time. Players worked on their fitness and our American fan base got a level of access to players that Mancunian City fans have never had, and City's profile was raised further, so it's all good.

Ins, outs, generic new kits, season ticket rises, unimportant pre-season friendlies and boredom. Lots of boredom. It was time for some proper football.

The 2017/18 Season

Brighton & Hove Albion 0 Manchester City 2

It's back! A new season, new hope, new expectations, new teams to play. The sun is out, fans in shirts and no coats savouring the beginning of another 9 month rollercoaster ride. Buckle up.
Thank god, after a summer devoid of much meaningful football.

"The first game is always complicated, in my experience, even with Barcelona - especially against a promoted side when they have the passion and are under no pressure at all," said Pep, and it certainly was, but City prevailed in the end, and it's hard to make too many conclusions from an opening day game. Three points will do nicely though.

It's always good to get back into the swing of things though. Nine more months of ecstasy, frustration, hair-tearing and more. Pep's under pressure to deliver this season, it will be fascinating and no doubt stressful to see what lies ahead.
Short-sleeved weather, blue skies, perfect conditions for a football match, and another season began.

Walker and Danilo operated down the flanks as full-backs, Aguero and Jesus started together, and the debate will no doubt continue as to whether they can operate together effectively in the same team, though as mentioned, today was not the day to decide. Aguero did gift-wrap one chance to Jesus in the first half, but his header, whilst back across goal, was too tame and the keeper saved before the ball was scrambled away.

There was not a lot else to talk about. Brighton kept their shape well, were organised, and restricted a team with 78% of the ball. Ederson flapped at a couple of crosses that caused City problems in the 2nd half, but that was Brighton's only real outlet for chances – a couple of shots fizzed past the post - eventually class told, helped by bringing the likes of Leroy Sane off the bench, with a great De Bruyne interception leading quickly to a Silva precision pass and a delightful Aguero finish and no little relief.

One own goal later from Dunk from a Fernandinho cross, and we could all relax, and enjoy Mendy's social media revolution. Crying emojis at the ready everyone.

Still, seven consecutive opening day victories for City with this result. Nice. And as always, with teams at the start of a season, a lot of City's stellar squad are yet to make their mark. Until then, winning is all that matters. The season is up and running – onwards and upwards, hopefully.

Into the autumn months, the hectic December schedule, a New Year with new hopes, the crucial spring schedule, the nervy run in. Who knows what lies ahead?

What lay immediately ahead, bizarrely, was a trip to Girona. Perfectly normal to have a pre-season friendly after a season has started, after all.

Of course the official reasoning behind such a trip was at odds with the ACTUAL reason. City painted the trip as an intensive training session, a chance for Pep to get his players together after the summer and work on stuff.

This reasoning rather overlooked the fact that Manchester is capable of hosting training sessions, both intensive and relaxed. Anyway, we all know this was an agreement no doubt linked to the tie-up between the two teams, and there was little harm done by flying south and back.

City lost the friendly 1-0, and I couldn't care less (see earlier friendlies for more details). Some players played, some didn't. Then they all came home.

And I went to Turkey for a holiday.

Manchester City 1 Everton 1

<u>Man City</u>: Ederson, Walker, Danilo, Kompany, Stones, Aguero, De Bruyne, D. Silva, Fernandinho, Otamendi, Jesus. Subs: Bravo, Sterling, Mangala, Sane, Bernardo, Toure, Foden.

Ah that's better, the stress and frustration of bygone times, and a few more grey hairs when I assumed I had reached my limit.

But first, a spoiler alert – you're going to hear about this referee later on in the book too.

Let's cut to the chase though – you could watch football for 100 years, on a continual loop, you could put a three year old in charge of every match and have Neil Custis running the line and you won't see a worse refereeing decision than Bobby Madley's 2nd yellow card for Kyle Walker for daring to move close to Calvert-Lewin. It was an abomination, so bad a decision I'm almost coming round to the idea of match-fixing, and it left City with the proverbial mountain to climb.

Let's be honest though, City weren't playing well anyway. If anything, the red card angered them into a stirring second half where it appeared as if the visitors were a man down, not City. Eventually they lost a man too, but far too late to have an effect on the game.

Perhaps the three at the back formation was part of the problem. It was not a formation that would see much light for the remainder of the season. Especially troublesome was having Sane as one of the wingbacks. It required defensive responsibilities, and that is not really Sane's thing. Aguero and Jesus also paired up in attack, and struggled along with everyone else.

Having said that, there was plenty of intent, but not much incisiveness – City were threatening most just before sloppy play cost them a goal. It had to be Rooney, naturally. Ederson could not quite sort his feet out, so the ball hit his foot, the post then the back of the net.

Yet bizarrely, City were better with ten, and dominated the 2nd half. The introduction of Sterling was vital, and despite missing a good chance he eventually equalised with a sweet volley. Seven minutes was not enough time to find a winner, but time enough for Schneiderlin to get a 2nd yellow card. Too late to make a difference though.

A frustrating night, but not the end of the world at this stage. Tactically Pep might have overthought things, but certainly atoned for any errors in the 2nd half.

That Tunnel Club looks nice though. How the other half lives, eh?

And the good thing about watching City on holiday is that you can order a beer and forget about it all in minutes. Which is what I did.

The Window Slams Shut

Well it's over. The dreary, rat-infested battlefield that is the transfer window is thankfully a thing of the past, for a few months anyway, a snarling mosh pit of PR, lies, agents, numbers I cannot comprehend and as always, top banter and the lexicon of the window where players push for moves, stall on deals, Clubs smash records, deals collapse fall through go to the wire, aces move, flops stay, bids are lodged, clubs prepare offers, rumours are quashed, United repeatedly cool interest whilst City are snubbed and personal terms just need to be agreed before the £3m two hour presentation video can be filmed . All over, and now we may even be able to concentrate on football for a bit, until something else distracts us of course.

Previous transfer deadline days, and the days preceding them, have been fairly quiet for City in recent years – no need to endure Jim White's screeching or Sky's shiny toys to see what's happening, though the internet has ensured we don't need them anyway, the internet being Sky Sport's sources after all. This year was different however, as City tried desperately to sign Alexis Sanchez, in vain as it turned out. Little did we know however at the beginning of the week that Raheem Sterling, the player who saved a point against Everton and won 2 against Bournemouth was going to feature so prominently in the week's narrative. And what a perfect example it was of the odious faecal-smeared industry that a minority operate in under the guise of sports journalism.

It's jealousy from me really, bitterness. Earlier this week I "ummed and arred" for 2 days about what to write for a piece I needed to do, wanting to ensure it was up to the right standard, that I was happy to put it out there for the 200 people who would actually read it, if I was lucky – I changed my mind 5 times at least on the subject matter. Meanwhile, paid journalists are being handsomely rewarded for writing long fact-free missives on nothing more than fabricated transfer rumours that spread round the internet faster than a bush fire. The truth is little more than a leaky garden hose trying to save a single property – utterly irrelevant.

Why care will ask many? Because it bloody matters that's why. Because these narratives ensure a young English player is booed at every ground for 2 years, which may well affect his form and thus City's results, and because lies should not be left to fester, bad journalism not excused and because I just care, whether you do or not. I don't care about any reality TV, but you can if you want.

So how did Raheem Sterling become involved in the transfer window? You probably know the story by now. John Cross, a man who is to arsenal what Duncan Castles is to Jose Mourinho, Wenger's Comical Ali, a PR rep who was happy to fiddle as Rome burned, as the deadline loomed, decided that City had offered Sterling in part exchange or maybe a full exchange for Sanchez. City denied this, there was never any proof, it is a spurious rumour at best, and Cross was back-tracking faster than a Liverpool parade bus by early evening, so, a rumour to be taken with a pinch of salt by anyone with the minimum of brain capacity.

Sadly that is not how some of the modern journalism industry works nowadays. No need to collaborate, the rumour spread and eager lickspittles sat down and filed copy as if it were fact, an easy, easy copy to submit and to hell with the accuracy. And the easiest way to use a rumour to denigrate is with the classic strawman argument, something by the way that Martin Samuel is king of.

And so it came to pass. Adam Crafton over at the delightful Daily Mail started the ball rolling, questioning Pep, asking – isn't Guardiola meant to be the super-coach that turns Sterling into the next Sanchez??
This was the ultimate strawman argument, based on a false premise that City were looking to get rid of Sterling, using an argument that probably has never been uttered by anyone ever until now, and also assuming that Pep is more than a mere human, and could even turn me into a Premier League footballer. There will of course always be footballers Pep cannot mould and will not want to, but that's by the by. Whether Pep converts Sterling into a world-class player will be down to Sterling as much as it will be down to Pep. But of course the backlash to the hype that surround the arrival of Guardiola was the inevitable questioning of him every time City failed, and questioning why he allowed failure to

happen considering he is such a god amongst mere mortals, denigrating by hyping his supposed brilliance to levels few ever considered him to be at.

But anyway, John Cross's story had legs now, and when a story on the internet has legs, it can't be stopped, like Phil Jones trying to keep a straight face whilst eating a packet of Haribo extra sour tangfastics. It ain't happening.

So naturally the anti-Pep articles were merely a matter of time, and we were not to be disappointed. Ian Herbert followed, also in the Mail naturally, wondering why Sterling's stock was so low with Guardiola? That's a player remember who has just scored two vital goals for City, which suggests he has some stock. I'm sure Herbert joined the throngs slagging off Sterling as per usual for his England performance a couple of days later, many a journalists happy to slag Sterling for his inadequacies, but then happy to point to potential and stats when looking to defend him against his evil manager.

According to Herbert, City have shown themselves ready to respond to Arsenal's attempt to structure a deal including Raheem Sterling as a makeweight for 28-year-old Alexis Sanchez.

Apparently, the statistics demonstrate that Guardiola has not developed him in the slightest as a player, even though anyone with eyes and the intelligence to understand the difference between red and blue could see he improved last season. But hey, Opta statistics to back up his blinkered view instead, so who am I to argue? Naturally Neil Ashton over at the S*n was parroting a similar line, stating clearly that City were willing to let Sterling go, stating Sterling was surplus to requirements, facing an uncertain future, fearful he will be squeezed out – who knew that Neil Ashton had the inside track to the mind of Raheem Sterling. The one comment on this pitiful excuse to fill internet space started with the words absolute tosh, and there's little I can add to that.

Why bother getting worked up indeed? As alluded to already, it bothers me if it affects the team, if it affects the relationship between manager and players, and we know that lies have seeped into the football fans consciousness a million times before. Dare I mention attendances? It's probably best that I don't. We should after all be thankful that at least these lies divert from reporting on his car's cleanliness, his house, his new watch or any other snide, creepy insinuations made whilst stalking a young black man. Also be thankful that there's always a granny-bothering drink-driver with the morals of a republican senator to divert us further.

And I care because I care about the industry, and admire the many superb people that work within it nowadays, away from the likes of Custis, Ashton and his ilk. The good stuff has moved, and is accessible to all. The best source of City news is from a reporter who supports United, but is a professional who works without prejudice and reports things as he sees it, using excellent contacts and a keen eye. It is possible.
I dallied after university with journalism, but another year unpaid would have destroyed me, and in a rare case of prescience from my good self, I saw how the industry may go – 10 years reporting on village fetes and angry residents pointing at potholes in roads without ever getting where I wanted to be. And now it's worse than I could have imagined, hits meaning everything, reporters rarely reporting but nothing more than mouthpieces and PR fronts for football clubs. Journalists creating their own news cycles as John Cross did this week, a whole industry stirred into action by an unsourced rumour. And so I think it's right to highlight the inaccuracies and bullshit that flows forth every day – journalists are and should be accountable, they are free to air opinions of course, but preferably with some sort of evidence and reasoning, not an argument thinner than Wayne's to Colleen the other day. No need for insults, that gets you nowhere, though with Neil Custis and Ollie Holt, reasoned arguments didn't either, just a twitter blocking instead, but it's the only chance to hold people with influence to account. So I'll keep doing it myself, in the same way that when I write crap, and I've written plenty of it, I too get held to account. The only real problem is that Ashton and Custis and others don't care what we think – they get hits, they've done their job – that's all that matters for some football journalists nowadays. What a sorry state of affairs.

How Manchester United Made Money Signing Lukaku – WITHIN A DAY!!!!

Sale of 3 million United shirts within 6 hours globally. £70 x 3,000,000 = £210,000,000, Minus some small costs for production, fabric, transport etc = **£157m** profit

(extra letter K's and U's have been shipped in from Belgium due to the demand)

6 million social media likes on Instagram, Twitter, Facebook and Tinder = **£12m** in advertising revenue

Image rights - **£18m.** Per week

Sale of Lukaku bed covers and hot water bottles in Megastore - **£8m**

Proposed opening of 6 new "Dab Universities" with Paul Pogba over next 3 years - **£24m**

Savings on Rooney's canteen bill over 2 seasons - **£2.4m**

Losing Rooney's image rights - **£64m**

Allowing Rooney to leave United for free meant Everton could sell Lukaku for more – saving United approximately **£16m**

As United still owe Everton £15m for Schneiderlin, and United inserted Keane sell-on clause, Lukaku only really cost £30m. Convert that fee into euros, then convert into Turkish lira, convert back to sterling and take off the first number you thought off, and the true value of the transfer fee is - **£14.2m**

Bournemouth 1 Manchester City 2

Cometh the hour, then another half hour, then another 7 minutes, cometh the man that is Raheem Sterling.
Needs a bit of work, that intro.

Phew. That's all that needs to be said. Phew.

The 2nd and final game whilst on holiday meant sharing hotel facilities with a number of crowing cockneys. They weren't crowing by the end.

Pep made four changes from the Everton game, with Sergio surprisingly dropped to the bench. Danilo was in, and Mendy made his debut, which greatly excited me. City reverted to a back four, but the performance did not improve as a result.

So what to make of this match? One of those where you take the points and run. Enjoy the joy that a late, late winner like Sterling's gives you and try not to analyse a game this early in the season too much. Bournemouth are generally quite compliant to City, as Eddie Howe refuses to compromise his principles, which can rather play into our hands. But not on this occasion, where City struggled to find any rhythm or tempo, and Jesus's goal was a rare highlight.

Not every goal conceded has to be uber-analysed, not every goal needs to apportion blame on someone – sometimes an opposition team will score a goal and you just have to hold your hands up and acknowledge a great strike or a nice move. This was one hell of a strike that gave Ederson no chance whatsoever. Take a bow Charlie Daniels, and his foot like a traction engine.

And this was not a Bournemouth side that played like one that has lost its opening two games. They showed plenty of promise for the coming season.

It was a close game – Ake could have been sent off for a trip on Jesus, King was a threat and hit the woodwork, as did Otamendi, and King also shot straight at Ederson when he probably should have done better. A team with four changes from the one that drew with Everton struggled to gel. We got to see Mendy, and whilst we can't take too much from his debut, he showed flashes of what a dangerous player he should be.

Again, it's hard to predict the season ahead from the opening few games, so I won't attempt to. After oodles of stress, City emerged with seven points from the opening three games, which is just fine. Liverpool up next though, and City could do with going through the gears, because it will not be easy, and we won't get the leeway we got at Bournemouth or Brighton.

It will make for a good quiz question one day asking in which match was Raheem Sterling sent off? I understand rules need to be followed, but really... Mike Dean though was just being Mike Dean, failing to comprehend the joy of a 97th minute winner, failing to notice that the City fans came to Sterling, not the other way round, so he never technically left the pitch, and because refereeing standards are just generally poor, however hard the job may be. The BBC claimed this was the first dismissal for excessive celebration in the Premier League in 6 years. Hmm.

Extra point for Aguero too for wading in to help City fans suffering from the ridiculous over-zealous stewarding.

What a shame that a post goal celebration in the pool was cut short when the manager informed us it was closed due to a child depositing a poo in the shallow end. Ruined the day for me.

Manchester City 5 Liverpool 0

Well, whatever the circumstances, I never thought I'd type out that score line.

A big game early in the season always leaves me uncertain as to what to expect. Even four games in, players are still getting used to new systems, the season as a whole, and summer signings are being drip-fed into line-ups.

Aguero was back in the team, paired with Jesus up front. Otamendi and Stones partnered in defence, and Danilo completed a back three with Walker and Mendy up the flanks.

The first half-hour was scintillating stuff, with attackers on top. Salah was dangerous, and Otamendi struggled to cope with his trickery. He lacked a cutting edge though. Nevertheless, it was City that scored first, Aguero rounding Mignolet to coolly slot home. Stones missed another good chance to increase the lead, so what followed can hardly be called as definitely deciding the victors.

Of course it was still a big moment and Liverpool fans will call it key, despite the fact they were trailing at the time. Naturally this incident has overshadowed the actual match, to the point that it's easy to forget City won 5-0. The score line is quite important after all - City netted 5+ goals in a game versus Liverpool for the first time since March 1937 (5-1).

To be honest, and I am being honest, there's little controversy if you're not so blinkered that you fear a conspiracy against your side. Mane clearly endangered the safety of an opponent, to the extent I thought Ederson was in serious danger as he lay on the floor.
It clearly fits the criteria of a red card (read the rules if this confuses you), the actual extent of the injury is irrelevant, that's down to pure chance, and intent to injure is also irrelevant, as few players go out to maim opposition players – if intent was the criteria we'd hardly have any red cards, but it isn't.
Mane made a bad error of judgement by attempting to go for a ball at-

head-height whilst running at speed and when he must surely have been able to see an onrushing keeper.

Anyway, Ederson required eight minutes of treatment. The clues are there as to what the punishment should have been.
"Serious foul play - a tackle or challenge that endangers the safety of an opponent or uses excessive force of brutality must be sanctioned as serious foul play."

Liverpool fans should focus not just on the red card in determining why this result happened, but also the attitude and approach of the team and manager with ten men, which essentially ended the game as a contest.
They were pitiful in the second half, and City gleefully ran riot, after Jesus headed in a second prior to half-time.

Aguero teed him up for another in the second half, before Sane slotted home then curled home a beauty from outside the area to seal the rout.

I'm a bitter, cynical old man, but hey, if I can't take joy from the Liverpool players, slumped heads, trudging back to the half-way line after yet another City goal in that 2nd half, then there's no point going on.
One of the highlights of the season, whatever happens during the next eight months or so.

Just the 66% possession for City – tough game!

And for Claudio Bravo, his sole appearance in the league for the rest of the season, until the point when the title was wrapped up.

- This was Jurgen Klopp's heaviest defeat in all competitions as Liverpool manager and his joint-heaviest ever managerial loss (lost 6-1 with Mainz v Werder Bremen in October 2006).
- Sergio Aguero has scored in all six of his Premier League appearances against Liverpool at the Etihad Stadium, netting once in each game.

- Gabriel Jesus has been directly involved in 14 goals in his 12 Premier League starts for Man City (10 goals, four assists).

City go top then, ahead of United on goal difference.
Early days, but a promising enough start to the season even if top gear has not yet been reached on a regular basis.

Thoughts now turned to the Champions League. City had been given Feyenoord, who were up first, and an exciting Napoli side. The top seed allocation was quite kind to City – Shakhtar Donetsk.

The Rise And Fall Of Gary Neville

Poor Gary Neville. He used to have it all – the best looker in the family, a glittering career, and a revelation in the punditry business. He was going to fill Manchester with cutting edge buildings and himself live in his own teletubbies style pad in the countryside. He was given his first managerial job too, in Spain, and the world was his oyster. He was in demand, and then some.

So where did it all go wrong, how were we left with the wind up merchant we had to endure this past few days? Well Valencia I guess. Turns out that commenting on matches is easier than actually organising the teams playing in them, and with his tail between his legs he was soon back in England, chastened, damaged, and it seems, changed.

Now we all hated Neville as a player of course, because he hated us, and the scousers too. I don't really see a problem with that, as if it was a City player hating United, you'd revere him as a god. He acted like a fan, an obnoxious one, but still. He probably did take it too far, to be fair, all those "in the zone" faces in the tunnels and blanking of opposition players as he got fired up for a match, but that's Gary for you.

As a pundit though, he split City fans because some dared praise him – he was the proverbial breath of fresh air – he looked at things rationally, actually analysed, and seemed impartial. There are probably 2 points that spring up immediately from this. Firstly he was fresh only because the air around existing pundits was so unremittingly stale, occasionally putrid, a Paul Merson diatribe or Danny Mills acerbic put down the equivalent of the toilets after the finals of the vindaloo and prune tasting World Cup final – there was a gap in the market for sure to actually rationalise play and decisions, and it was all the more frustrating that this gap existed when you consider the excellent analysis afforded to other sports, whilst the biggest sport of them all has to put up with your Owens your Savages and your Mersons. It seemed to suggest that football fans were thick and couldn't cope with anything more than generalised platitudes from proper football men trapped in the 1980s, and the success of such people may show such a view to have some foundation. Secondly though, Neville knew that to succeed he had to throw off the red cape he had worn so proudly for all his life. He had to be seen to be impartial to succeed, and for a while he gave it a good shot. Occasionally the mask would slip, but on the whole, he said it as he saw it and his reputation blossomed further.

But then he went to Spain and he came back from Spain. There are brits who have holidayed for longer in Spain and there seems to have been a change in his approach. It's hard to say his Mane comments were anti-City because we were playing Liverpool, but to blame Ederson's injury on City's poor offside trap is one of the most absurd tragi-comic things I've heard for quite a while. At least whilst commenting he is diverted from destroying the landscape of Manchester city centre, but still, he seems angrier now, and with good reason. His mask has not only slipped, it's lying in a flooded gutter somewhere near his latest grand architectural plan in Bolton.

But he has certainly blended in to the punditry arena in one aspect – you see if there's one thing a co-commentator cannot bring himself to do, and it's always a "him", is admit they are wrong. You've all seen and heard it – an Owen or a Savage makes a bold claim on a contentious moment during a match – replays show them to be completely wrong – we've all been there a million times - a decent man would accept they saw it wrong at real speed – but no, your Savage or your Owen will either enforce a lengthy radio silence, or concoct some horrendous straw man argument as to why their original view still holds some merit. And with Gary Neville and Sadio Mane's red card, we saw this carried out in glorious technicolour post-match. Perhaps I am being harsh – perhaps, having been confronted with the clarity of the laws of the game that made it quite clear that a red card was a perfectly acceptable decision, perhaps having listened to the overwhelming evidence that backed up such a decision, perhaps Gary still truly believed in his view of events. But to be honest, was he ever going to back down? Has Gary ever been knowingly wrong? It's hard for me to say, as I've never played the game at a high level and all that.

Gary dug in though – and it was inevitable that on "Not-So-Super Sunday" there would be an incident that would have Gary wetting himself and hurrying back to the twittersphere to make some laboured point or other. And so it continued. And so it still does due to Liverpool laughably contesting the severity of the ban. Will we ever hear the end? I guess I'm not helping, come to think of it.

Yep, we've got a season of this, because poor Gary can't comprehend the difference in endangering an opponent when you karate kick an opponent at head height whilst running at full pelt compared to clipping someone as you fall or brushing an arm from a slow or standing start. This is somehow a mystery to a sizeable slice of the population. I mean what if Mane had got there first? Well he didn't did he? What if my aunty had balls, what if Jennifer Lawrence had a thing for grey haired beer bellied middle aged pessimistic dour bloggers and podcasters? The world would be a very different place, and better for it I think we can all agree.

On the plus side though, Gary's had a better time of it than John Cross over at Arsenal HQ, a Sunday Supplement staple, which tells you all you need to know -funny how his widely discredited Sterling offered to Arsenal story, and all the scathing anti-Pep articles that followed, have been consigned to history. Move along, nothing to see here, and as always no accountability for any of the spurious stories that pop up in the media on an almost daily basis. Still, john's had a better week than Tony Gale, who thinks a man karate-kicked in the face and receiving oxygen should man up and walk of the field waving nonchalantly to fans just like Tom Heaton did with a dislocated shoulder, because of course the two injuries are exactly the same. Proper man is Tom, you'd want him besides you in the trenches, along with Tony, a man who would walk of the field with a ruptured cruciate ligament to prove that the modern game's gone soft.

But before Gary plans his next architectural masterpiece, perhaps a bright orange apartment block that will sadly require the destruction of the rarely-used cathedral, he could turn his hand to the written word. After all Gary sees things we never see, so his input could be priceless. If he turns to podcasts, then us podcast regulars are done for – let's hope Sky keep paying the big bucks. And if they do, perhaps the next time a goalkeeper is lying on the ground, barely conscious, requiring 8 minutes of medical treatment before being stretchered off, perhaps just perhaps Gary could show just a one iota of concern for his wellbeing. Just a thought.

Champions League: Feyenoord 0 Manchester City 4

So here we go – another Champions League campaign, and perhaps the first where City will truly be expecting rather than hoping to compete with the very best.

History will probably judge this as a fairly kind group, compared to previous groups anyway, and Feyenoord were as compliant as you could have hoped for. Struggling domestically, they stood out as a team playing with nerves, and lacking confidence. But still, City MADE this game look easy, and after scoring early, it was as pain-free as you could probably have hoped for.

So pain-free that the hosts even allowed John Stones to score twice, the first in less than two minutes, and City were three up within half-an hour before easing up, Aguero and Jesus adding to the tally.

The opening goal summed up the home side quite well, with a quite comical attempt by Vilhena to clear Stones rather tame header. He failed.

Aguero's goal was more typical of City's crisp passing style, but the home side did themselves no favours for the third, freezing in the false belief that Jesus was offside. It was easier than we could have hoped for, but City could never keep scoring at this rate, and it was not that surprising that they eased off the gas somewhat.

As for Feyenoord, they caused virtually no panic, with just 28% possession and one shot on target throughout the whole match. It was just the start City needed to the group stages, their first away win in the competition in seven attempts.

- Stones is also the first Man City defender to net a brace in the Champions League.
- Gabriel Jesus is the fourth player to score on his Champions League debut for Man City (also Balotelli, Kolarov & Nolito).
- Sergio Aguero has scored 18 goals in his last 22 appearances in all competitions for Manchester City.

So City top the group early doors, with top seeds Shakhtar Donetsk beating Napoli 2-1 in the other game, something of a small surprise to me despite the seedings.

You always have a guide, points-wise, in a Champions League group, as to what is needed to progress – the figure I usually abide by is 12 points. Eight can be enough though, so it's hard to judge, as it depends if there is a whipping boy team in the group. If there is, and Feyenoord may prove to be such a team, then the required figure rises. Whichever way you look at it, this was a mighty fine start.

Watford 0 Manchester City 6

A tough test for City against form team Watford, undefeated in the Premier League, this would provide a clear sign as to whether City were title winning material, against a side that would make life very hard for the visitors......actually scrap that, it was a complete and utter annihilation.

It was a strange match in a way. Six goals, but two were probably offside, but then there were numerous other missed chances, and torrential rain, and they could have had a couple too and Sterling even got a penalty rather than being booked for a dive because he's Sterling. All in all, a crazy day.

That's nine in five for hat-trick hero Sergio Aguero. Not bad. The crazy thing is that a hat-trick for Aguero barely raises the eyebrows nowadays. He just keeps doing what he does. His tenth treble for City, and sixth in the league.

You could argue that the Liverpool result was the first time City had gone through the gears this season in the league, but the red card will always leave an asterix next to the result. There can be no doubts about this performance. Watford may turn out to be a mid-table unspectacular side, but to win 6-0 away is a statement whoever you play. And despite the controversies over offside goals, it could have been much, much more. City had 28 shots in total, with 10 on target. Aguero's last goal was him back to his absolute best, a dribbling run and cute finish that spun inside the post. Beautiful stuff.

Watford were not bad either, to be fair. They could have scored a couple themselves, and should have had a penalty, when Walker clumsily clattered into Nathaniel Chalobah. It wouldn't have made much difference in the scheme of things.

- Man City (11) have scored more goals in their last two Premier League games at Vicarage Road than Watford (10) have in their last nine at the ground.

- Gabriel Jesus has been directly involved in 15 goals in his 15 Premier League appearances (11 goals, 4 assists).
- Sergio Aguero scored his sixth Premier League hat-trick; only Alan Shearer (11), Robbie Fowler (9), Michael Owen and Thierry Henry (8) have scored more.
- Aguero has been involved in 11 goals in five appearances against Watford in all competitions (nine goals, two assists).
- David Silva provided two assists in a Premier League game for the first time since March 2016 versus Aston Villa.

Carabao Cup – West Bromwich Albion 1 Manchester City 2

City's debut in their 4th most important competition, but victory attained. It was nervy stuff at times though, and did not dispel any doubts over how seriously the club will take this tournament.

Having said, this was not *that* weak a team. Bravo in net not surprisingly, and plenty of talent elsewhere – Stones, Bernardo Silva, Stones, Gundogan, Sterling, Sane, Delph. Mangala and Yaya too.

City started brightly, and were ahead after only 3 minutes. A cross found Gundogan, his shot was parried, but Sane rammed home the rebound. He didn't seem particularly overjoyed with his goal, mind you. Gundogan then found space in the area and had a shot blocked. From the resulting corner Mangala had a header well saved by Foster, Sterling put a dangerous cross in that no one could reach and Danilo had a shot blocked too. Jesus then fired over when he probably should have scored after a neat turn in the box.

I may have missed something rather important about that first goal. Not only did the home side not touch the ball until Foster parried Gundogan's shot, from kick-off, but there were 51 passes between every single player. Astonishing. Now *that* is how to start a game.

There were other chances too, but I haven't got the space to mention them all – special mention to a Sterling effort that was curling into the corner until Foster tipped it round the post.

The second half was somewhat different however. And an injury to Gundogan overshadowed anything else, after a crude tackle by Yacob, as the German advanced towards the West Brom penalty area. Thankfully, Guardiola seems to think the resulting injury is not that serious. Let's hope so after his wretched luck in the past.

Sterling then had a shot saved by the feet of Foster, his surges into the penalty area the dominant theme of the match. Finally the hosts fashioned a good chance, but Morrison prodded wide when he should have scored from just yards out.

City paid for their profligacy, Yacob equalising with a shot from a corner. Never mind, Sane saved any blushes with a beautiful curled finish to put City back in front after West Brom had spurned a further chance.

The end of the match was utterly chaotic for City though. Robson-Kanu could, and probably should have taken the game to an extra 30 minutes, but after pulling one shot wide he struck the outside of the upright with just the keeper to beat in added time. The visitors survived though, and Wolves await in the next round.

Manchester City 5 Crystal Palace 0

An ultimately comfortable win for City, who made hard work of it for a while.

More important though was the loss of a key signing for at least six months.

A line up that would be quite familiar through the season – the Sane/Sterling/Aguero axis, the Fernandinho/De Bruyne/Silva axis, and Otamendi and Stones in defence.

City probed, but the visitors were resolute, and dangerous on the counter-attack, Ruben Loftus-Cheek hitting the post with a deflected shot. Chances came and were missed, but they weren't that commonplace. Of more concern though was Mendy, who mis-controlled a ball, stretched to foul a Palace player, and did his cruciate ligament in the process. A devastating blow for player and team, though as is traditional in such circumstances he played on for a short while just to make matters worse.

As for the football itself, Sane finally broke the deadlock close to the interval with a lovely flick then low shot that is worth many a repeat viewing. Relief for the impatient hordes. Scott Dann tried in vain to head the ball away, but was helpless as Sane fired home.

Thankfully the second half was a different game altogether. Sterling doubled City's lead, prodding home Sane's precise low cross. City never looked back. He should have had more goals than he did, firing into the side netting when he probably should have done better, but soon did do better and prodded home an Aguero pull back, and it was game over.

Sane had a great chance smothered by Hennessey, but the keeper will have been disappointed to let Aguero's header from a Sane pass in, and Delph finished the rout with a lovely finish near the end. A professional job done in the end.

And it should be noted that 31 passes preceded the final goal – the most in the league this season, a record that remained until season-end. It may well become a theme with City. It also involved nine different Man City players. .

But we must return to Benjamin Mendy. The news is not good, and it is looking like the team will be without his talents for the majority of the season, if not longer. For all the work that was done to deal with the full-back problem in the summer, the problem has now returned with no obvious candidate ready to step in and deputise for him. Pep will have to get his thinking cap on, and whatever he decides, may have to change City's style as a result.

For the visitors, they still have not scored a single goal this season, and tough times may lie ahead.

- This is Manchester City's best ever goal return after six league games (21).
- Manchester City are the first side to score 5+ goals in three consecutive top-flight games in the same season since Blackburn did so in 1958-59.
- David Silva has been directly involved in seven goals in his last six Premier League appearances against Crystal Palace (four goals, three assists).
- Leroy Sane has scored five goals from just seven shots on target in all competitions for Man City this season.

RAHEEM STERLING BUYS LOOFER FROM POUNDLAND DESPITE OBSCENE WEALTH

Champions League – Manchester City 2 Shakhtar Donetsk 0

An interesting tie, against the group's top seeds, who had already put Napoli to the sword. There was a danger of complacency if City were to expect to win this comfortably.

As it turned out, the visitors were mightily impressive, even if City prevailed in the end.

A rare corporate jolly for me for this match, in the box of one of City's betting sponsors. I wasn't sure if food was included, so ate beforehand. When I got there, a member of staff was wheeling in a beef joint bigger than my head.

Naturally I forced a few morsels down pre-match. It would have been rude not to.

The line-up was once more fairly predictable, but of interest was Delph at left back. It would be a big test for him, but succeed and he could find himself featuring a lot during the season. Oh, and Jesus was in the side, Sterling dropping to the bench.

Let's cut to the chase. It was a great game, full of talented players doing great things. Yep, that's the sort of technical analysis you normally have to pay big bucks for. Shakhtar were bright and inventive with a Brazilian core, and posed City problems throughout. Poor top seeds? Absolutely not.

Class told in the end though, but it was never comfortable. Nevertheless, the home side probably should have been ahead early on, with Jesus slipping De Bruyne through, but he shot wide when through on goal, and thus still awaited his first goal of the season. Thankfully he didn't have to wait that long.

Marlos forced a save from Ederson, and Ferreyra headed wise after indecision from Ederson and his defence. He should have done better from close in. Sane too should have opened the scoring after a jinking run, but he too shot wide. So it was goalless at half-time.

Never mind, because De Bruyne's wait for a goal ended in the second half. And what a beauty. Laid off to him outside the area, he curled it into the top corner as the goalkeeper watched it go in helplessly, a strike reminiscent to me of his strike v PSG that took us into the semi-finals under Pellegrini.

The visitors continued to threaten, and Delph was being fully tested, but rising to the test. Shakhtar broke with speed and precision, and the City midfield and defence had to be on full alert at all times. Having said that, the hosts should have increased their lead. A sumptuous reverse chip from Silva reached Aguero six yards out but his volley was saved, and Sterling had one of his archetypal misses in front of goal from another great low cross from none other than Kevin De Bruyne as City fully exploited those legendary "half-spaces".

And then a missed penalty for good measure. You could call the miss karma, because it was undoubtedly a dive from Sane that conned the referee.

Or so I thought. Because watch it again and concentrate on upper bodies only, and Sane is nudged/barged in the shoulder. Soft perhaps, but at the speed he runs, it probably was a penalty after all.
Anyway, it mattered not, as Aguero saw his penalty saved. Frustration aplenty, as City could not put this tie to bed. Aguero then shot wide and Sane too.

But thankfully the 2nd goal did come eventually. Bernardo Silva, fresh on the pitch, beat the offside trap, and laid it back for Sterling to thump into the goal off the underside of the bar as Sane dragged two defenders away from him. Job done, eventually, and well-earned after a more dominant 2nd half display.

And the group table looks good – two wins out of two, City are well on their way to qualification.

Atmosphere & Pep – Bluemoon Podcast Audio Script

Against Shakhtar Donetsk on Tuesday evening, I was treated like a king. Yes, I was in a box at City (did I mention this?) – a strange experience for sure, not one I'd like to repeat on a weekly basis, as I was shepherded to the correct box by a new, female greeter every 5 yards. Sitting as I normally do in the 3rd tier of the south stand, I could view the game and the ground too from a different perspective, from new angles – could see the empty seats around the #Emptihad and mull over why we refuse to love this competition, whilst chuckling at Shaktar's hardy bunch of 100 supporters bouncing up and down.

I thought about this as once more Pep has been trying to gee up the troops for the Champions League, trying to boost sales and get everyone fired up for the competition our owners cherish more than any other. Naturally we didn't really respond, and the reasons have been well documented – and Pep needs to get his head round why rather than looking puzzled at the lack of atmosphere –he's an intelligent man after all, I'm sure he can work it out.

So Pep, if it's so important to you that the place is packed out and passionate, what you must do is clear, from a position of great authority. You do not speak to the fans and ask for more, as that will fall on deaf ears. People have made their decisions, and without change will not waiver, especially due to a few words.
No, you speak to the club, not the fans, you go to Soriano, Txiki, whoever, and you tell them that tickets are £10 for group games in the Champions League, because we don't need that extra fiver and we'll sell more tickets anyway. You tell your bosses that instead of scrimping on costs, you open up every possible turnstile in the ground, and insert more if need be, so no crowds snake for 100 yards pre-kick off, you hire more staff to serve refreshments, you tell them to get fully behind safe standing sections, the biggest factor of all after money, and rather than just say stuff, the club needs to actually do something.
There's been enough fan surveys, they should have got the message by now. And if you're that bothered about Champions League atmosphere,

lobby for the competition to become a straight knockout format. But that will never happen, because it's all about money, not the fans.

Safe standing must be implemented, and soon, if we value atmospheres at games, if we want our children to keep watching when they become adults. The government naturally have no interest in opening up such a possibility, so they should be lobbied, hard. The safe is not even needed in the title, because we don't call it safe sitting after all.

Naturally, safe standing is nothing like what some of us once experienced – merely standing in a designated spot with a seat behind you, as most of us do at some point in a match anyway. Spend more time on fighting for this cause rather than trying to get more TV money for the big six when the next deal comes along, and you might get more fans on your side.

All very ungrateful this I imagine some are thinking, especially with what has been served up in the past few weeks, but like Pep I yearn for that superior match day "experience", a ground that is rocking, a pie for under five pounds, getting close to the bar at half time if need be and not having to consider the ramifications of every City-related financial transaction because everything is so goddam expensive. At the very least buy a new tram or 2 for City fans, it would be nice to get home from a midweek match before midnight.

The corporate experience was weird though. Eating a meal 15 minutes before kick-off makes it feel like you are viewing everything from home, not in the actual ground. It is more an experience for non-City fans to network at, or for non-important games where you can relax without the pressure of the team desperately needing victory. Boxes themselves exist at all grounds, so don't dilute an atmosphere, but whilst I don't get wound up as much as some at people having to move seats, as I don't think we as fans have a divine right to any seat in a ground, to see an mostly-empty tunnel club section during a Champions League game makes you wonder where the priorities lie. Like we don't know.

Yep, the clamour by City and others for a bigger slice of the foreign TV money pie tells us all we need to know – from the moment of the Champions League's inception, with threats of a super league breakaway, through to financial fair play, AND the desire to reward success so that no one can break the cartel, football has been run for 25 years now with money and power as the end game.

There is a logical argument once you strip it down that big clubs should get more TV money as they are the clubs that make the league attractive and bring in a big slice of the revenue, but the even split is there for good reason, to retain some level of competitiveness throughout this league and not turn it into a closed shop, if it isn't already one.

Pay-outs based on league positions will simply increase the odds on the gaps widening, and creating leagues within leagues – and a less competitive league is surely less attractive anyway, so could lead to the bubble bursting at some point.

I dreamt the other week that I had taken over City, not sure quite how that feasibly happened, but then most of my dreams are beyond explanation of any kind. It sounds like a great job to have, owning the club you support, especially in its current state, but it's probably a poisoned chalice if you have a strong emotional bond to that club – the criticism of any decision would always be widespread.

But if you were in charge, what would you change? I've pretty much mentioned a lot of what I would do – before the sheik handed over control, I'd get him to build that 3rd tier in the north stand, plan long term say I. The family stand can go, it doesn't work for me. Season ticket prices would be halved for all, match day staff increased by at least 20%, food and drink prices reduced by a third, minimum, all season tickets would include free domestic cup match tickets up to the quarter final stage, Champions League group stage matches would be consistently priced whoever the opposition, at five pounds a pop.

Make the shop bigger, increase the range of merchandise, add at least 30 extra turnstiles around the ground over a summer break, and of all I have said so far sounds like a financial drain, I doubt it would dent our profits by more than a miniscule amount.

One youth player would have to be in every match day squad, in all competitions, free public transport would be standard for match days for all, and in the background, the new sponsorship deals would continue to be signed and sealed, deals that bring in the cash and are of no concern to us.

There would be a freeze on any more corporate expansion, as it is simply not needed – the demand is not there now, there is little reason to expect it to be there in 5 years' time. Disabled seating and facilities has thankfully improved greatly in recent years, and would under my ownership improve further.

See, it's easy. And we'd still be able to bid for Mbappe or whoever at the end of it all. We have the chance to be better than the rest, to make a stand for the common fan. It needed the sheikhs to get to this point, and god am I grateful for it all, but now it could change, with little detriment to the club's goals. Hey, I'll even throw in a couple of video screens in the south stand.

People, including myself, whinge too much sometimes about the modern game, and the match day experience, about little things like the tannoy or half-time entertainment, when the experience they always had is there if they want it – turn up, watch the match, go home. In that respect, nothing has changed, but the feeling has, and there are so many little easy things that could be done to un-sanitise the modern game. And when that call comes from Sheikh Mansour, pleading with me to sort things out, I'll be ready and waiting. It's the sort of thing dreams are made of.

Taxi For Aguero

Thoughts turned to the big match against the reigning champions Chelsea, but there was worrying news that rather overshadowed preparations. News emerged that Sergio Aguero had been involved in a car accident, in Amsterdam of all places. Thankfully, there was no serious injury, and that was the most important thing. Vitally, Aguero seems to have put his seatbelt on prior to the crash, worried by the driving of the taxi driver. He should have had it on anyway, but we should be thankful for small mercies.

Aguero suffered rib injuries, so would be out for a couple of weeks or so, but it could have been a lot worse. As to why he was in Amsterdam? Well, he had been given time off, and attended a gig there. It may seem weird to be travelling abroad prior to a big game, but Amsterdam is hardly that far away, and a car can of course crash anywhere. Let's just be thankful that the outcome was not worse. There were rumours though that Pep was less than impressed by Sergio's travel plans.

I guess your views on this ultimately come down to how players should be treated. Firstly, giving players off is certainly a good idea, for player happiness, and for player morale. After all, players come from around the world, and will have left behind family and friends when they embarked on this career. They should not be treated like caged animals. The other pertinent point though is how much freedom you allow a player when given time off. Do you demand strict itineraries, or do you trust the player to be sensible? I guess that differs from player to player. Aguero is a player you can generally trust. Pep might be changing that view in the future though.

Chelsea 0 Manchester City 1

Due to a wedding, this would be the only game I missed all season. Typical. Still it was the wedding of a United fan, so as usher I considered it my duty to relay the score to every single table at full-time. For all my faults, I take my usher duties seriously.

I add this next sentence at the end of the season. After clinching the league, I went on the Second Captains podcast with the highly regarded Ken Early to discuss City, including an unexpected grilling on human rights. Anyway, he asked at what point did I know the league was won. My answer was Stoke away, only weeks before it was actually won. But I added that Chelsea away, back in September, was the night I thought that this might be City's title to win.

Anyway, like one other game this season (more on that later), this was not a game where match highlights tell the story. Why? Well, because ask any City fan about City's domination in this match, and they would no doubt point out that highlights do not do that domination justice.

So with Jesus in for the injured Aguero, the rest of the side was as you would expect. The usual suspects.

And as alluded to already, this was a statement of intent. Only 1 goal, and an early missed header from Morata, and you could be forgiven for thinking this was a tight match won by one moment of genius. But it was not. City were dominant for the clear majority of the match, controlled the pace, and had the majority of the chances. The only surprise was that there was only one goal.

Still, it was fitting that De Bruyne scored it, his influence over this team growing week-by-week. And what a beauty it was too, giving Courtois no chance. Is there a more satisfying sound than that ball hitting the back of the net?

No. There isn't.

Anyway, City coped with Aguero's absence superbly, and threatened to score long before De Bruyne finally broke the deadlock, with Courtois making a brilliant reflex save from Fernandinho's header before the break. City never looked in danger once De Bruyne scored and almost added a second when Jesus' volley was headed off the line by Rudiger.

City had scored 16 goals without reply in their previous three league games, and despite the score line the domination was no less impressive. So City stay top ahead of United on goal difference.

And City dominating the possession does not surprise – but 62% at Stamford Bridge is remarkable – that is Chelsea's lowest possession stats since the 2003/04 season in a home league game.

And for De Bruyne, who I am compelled to award the Man Of The Match award, 9 of his last 11 goals have come from outside the box.

After that performance, as a fan the games can't come quick enough. So it is no surprise that instead we were all faced with another tedious international break.

Bluemoon Podcast Audio Script

The feeling of elation followed by despondency is one all too familiar to a football fan, and it was a feeling I felt the other day. England had dispatched Lithuania, Latvia, Macedonia or some similar country, I forget who, to end the qualifying campaign, a campaign characterised by fluent attacking football that left most opponents simply overwhelmed by Gareth Southgate's tactical masterclasses. It must be pretty gutting for the players to have to return to the mundane life of training sessions under the likes of Pep Guardiola, Jose Mourinho and Mauricio Pocchetino.

But the feeling wasn't really caused by anything on the field – I was taking in the euphoria felt at the imminent return of club football, when I saw online that England had a couple of high profile friendlies lined up for next month – I re-read that, then it dawned on me slowly, like that time the United fans at Sunderland realised that Aguero had scored v QPR, it dawned on me that this could only mean one thing – there's another international break next month. It was at that point I did wonder what I and all other fans had done in a past life to endure England and Glenn Hoddle's co-commentary on another 2 occasions in just a few weeks. It can't be anything short of serial killing or high-level corporate fraud. Maybe I ran one of those Ponzi schemes.

Anyway, John Cross was back on Twitter this morning as I wrote this, in classic John Cross mode – namely missing numerous points simultaneously in whatever cosy bubble he resides in. Crossy was lamenting people ignorantly tweeting about international football being a turn off – sorry, he said, in the ultimate example of irony, adding – but these journos and pundits are out of touch with the fans.

Meanwhile, in the real world, as was repeatedly pointed out to him in replies, international football is clearly the biggest turn off since I saw Ed Balls in sequins on strictly Come Dancing, and the reasons are plenty, some of which sadly mean I must agree with United fans of old.

You see United fans used to have a widespread distrust and apathy for the national side, even chanting Argentina at matches at one point. How we all mocked these arrogant fools, but they were right, and I feel that's where we are as City fans now – without the Argentina chants maybe, though we have a couple of heroes in blue from that neck of the woods.

Once I felt joy and pride to see Shaun Wright Phillips appear on a football pitch in an England shirt. Now I pray Raheem Sterling isn't picked, because, well what's the point? He doesn't need the shit, and more importantly, I certainly don't. Let's not forget that Sterling was once booed in an England shirt by Ireland fans.

Like supporting Celtic in the league, international football is on the whole boring and it's boring because it is designed to ensure the top sides qualify, and qualify they almost always do – Holland have mastered the art of messing up, Portugal have struggled at times despite flourishing at the last finals, and Argentina are permanently in crisis, but these are the outliers, and as soon as England won their opening group game, their qualification was pretty much assured – they don't even have to play well to qualify, as we have seen, and this team, which has won under a handful of knockout games in 20 years, is undefeated in qualifiers since a dead rubber defeat in Ukraine 8 years and about 40 games ago. This level of football is actually a step down from the club football many of us watch week in week out, which explains why a lot of supporters of lower league teams attach themselves to England, as at least for them they are seeing some improvement, maybe. A manager who played expansive attacking football would bring in more interest but no, the FA replaced Sam Allardyce with Gareth Southgate. Even moving games around the country would be a huge boon, as it was when Wembley was being rebuilt, but instead we have the world's most expensive stadium to pay off, a by-product of which has been to devalue the FA Cup too.

But the other key reason is simply that most football fans are morons, plain and simple. United players got the flak when they were the wealthy school ground bullies, and now City players do as they play under a club of inherited wealth in a world dominated by grouchy, blinkered ex-United players and the helium-fuelled scouse media cabal. Thus a succession of bad performances by Dele Alli, including a

European ban, an international ban for a one-fingered salute and enough dives to bring Ashley Young to orgasm is met with a shrug of the shoulders, whilst one misplaced Raheem Sterling pass merits a 10 minute Glenn Hoddle missive, and the half-time removal of the out of position City player. Not paranoia, just the way the world works.

The actual finals tournament is a different matter altogether, always an enjoyable experience, an excuse to watch 5 hours of football a day, if an excuse is needed, and since I gave up on expecting anything from England around the turn of the century, it's a stress-free version of the beautiful game. You get to see some of the best players in the world (and Fellaini) strut their stuff, and it beats the chronic boredom of a summer without football. England will stagger through the group stage before losing to Egypt on penalties, and then we can all enjoy the skill of the real contenders, the drama of a closely-fought semi -final or final, with everything on the line.

And whilst the life of an England fan during a qualifying campaign is something akin to watching dressage on an eternal loop, for other fans in the world, it has offered excitement, drama and pride, from Saudi Arabia to Egypt to Iceland and beyond.

And whilst I joke about the England experience, it's a shame really that this is my prevailing feeling about international football – when you look back to Euro 96, in a tournament in which England only played well sporadically, the atmosphere was amazing – it was a cracking summer, where club loyalties were put to one side and we celebrated as one a great tournament on home turf, great games, great weather great memories, similar to the experience Wales fans would have felt last summer. I now wonder if I'll ever experience that again as an England fan. Probably not, but with the younger England teams showing tremendous potential, let's hope that one day that golden generation actually comes along with the right manager to exploit their potential. International football should still have much to offer any passionate football fan.

Manchester City 7 (SEVEN) Stoke City 2

Always nice when you have to put the score in letters as well as numbers.

City's attacking strength and domination of the ball was always going to hand out a right thumping before long. Stoke were the unlucky recipients of said thumping.

An unchanged team for Pep, for only the third time. Had Pep realised that a stable team is beneficial? Maybe, but the team hasn't needed change recently, and Sergio was still unavailable after his taxi woes.

(he was on the bench, but still, it was never likely he would start).

There's little point drilling down into analysis. It was men against boys. Let's run through the goals instead. And then reminisce on one of the great performances of this or any season.

17 minutes – 1-0 –Gabriel Jesus fires in from close range after a Kyle Walker cutback (Sane had already missed a sitter).
19 minutes – 2-0 – The day's first example of utter genius. Sane squares for an easy tap in for Sterling, but that is not the real talking point. No, the seemingly blind reverse pass to Sane from Kevin De Bruyne was the definition of football porn. Utterly sublime, and normally I'd argue that it was one of the passes of the season. As it turned out, it might not have even been the best pass of the day.
And it's not even the complete story for that goal – 10 players touched the ball in the lead up to the goal, in a flowing passing move that lasted over a minute.
27 minutes – 3-0 – an almost embarrassingly average goal. Sane crosses for Sterling, he lays it back for Silva, he half-controls then prods the ball into the goal.
44 minutes -3-1 – uh-oh. The comeback is on. Diouf gets one back for Stoke. Not a bad move, but the goal owed much to the deflection off the sprawling Fernandinho.

83.5% possession in the first half. Madness.

47 minutes – 3-2 – wait up, what on earth is going on? Diouf's header is quite simply awful (hashtag Sibierski), but it deflects off Walker and into the net. Game on?

No.

55 minutes – 4-2 – Another De Bruyne cross, and Jesus is free in the middle to thump the ball into the roof of the net. Relief around the Etihad.

60 minutes – 5-2 –Foot like a traction engine! Fernandinho 30 yards out, thwack, top corner, game over! City's TV section would later include this in their "4 goals of the season" short video, but in such a season I'm not even sure whether it makes the top 10.

62 minutes – 6-2 – THE pass of the day? De Bruyne sees a pass to Sane that no one else in the ground does, Sane runs onto it and slots home. Utterly sublime from De Bruyne. Extra point for nutmegging the keeper. Might actually be pass of the season, to be honest.

79 minutes – 7-2 – a first goal for sub Bernardo Silva – he is fed by Sterling at the 2nd attempt and prods home expertly.

Thankfully for Stoke, the other City decided to ease off for the final 10 minutes, though David Silva did curl a shot just past the post. A sumptuous team display, and even after taking into account the standard of the opposition, one of the great performances from Kevin De Bruyne. Stoke City will be glad he was substituted after 66 minutes. Also, City scored seven goals in a Premier League game for only the second time – the first being 7-0 v Norwich in November 2013.

Earlier Jose Mourinho had bored both Liverpool and the nation as a whole to death, with a 0-0 at Anfield, so City go two points clear at the top. And next up, a biggie.

STAN COLLYMORE – IF PEP IS SO GOOD, WHY WON'T HE MANAGE A TEAM LIKE ROCHDALE FOR A CHALLENGE. EH?

Why Have So Many City Fans Fallen Out Of Love with Football?

Do you remember your first football game? Was it like mine?

The thrill of the floodlights looming over rows of terraced houses (it was of course a night game). The smell of Bovril and burgers and pies. The excited chatter. The clip clop of the police horses, the shrill of the fanzine sellers.

Game number 9 in your season ticket book. #random.

Through the rickety turnstile and into another world. The buzz, the claustrophobia, anticipation hanging in the air. And then up the steps and there it was, the lush green pitch lit up like a beacon, and the sweeping terraces. What a sight. I imagine I was crowd-surfed down the stand so that I was afforded a better view. The terrace was full, and it swayed as one. The songs were funny, risqué, always loud, the football electric as City tore the visitors to shreds. I was in love.

OK, maybe not. My memory of such things is appalling, but I imagine my first game was during the day. I accidentally stood in some horse shit outside the ground. Paid on the gate, or at least my dad did. Place was half empty, you could smell the piss from the outside toilets. City were crap, as was my meat pie, City probably lost to Coventry, the ball deflecting in off Andy May's arse. City were on their way down, and David Pleat would later hurtle across the Maine Road pitch as if evading the police, throwing himself into the loving embrace of a certain Brian Horton. A more immediate concern was the fighting outside immediately after the game, and the relief to get back to our car which, unlike the previous game, still had all its windows intact. £1 well spent.

Why this fictional rant, you may ask? Well it's do with modern football, and nostalgia. To do with the sanitised version of football we now observe, and why so many fans are falling out of love with the game. It's to do with the Taylor Report, Premier League football and football saturation, and how the game is losing a generation.

It seems there's a dichotomy at City that's been there for a good few years now. As the club regularly fields the best set of players it may have ever had, fans drift away from the game they once loved, the feeling persisting that things ain't what they were, and that the modern game leaves them feeling colder than a Boundary Park terrace in mid-February. It's hard to explain why so many fed Findus crispy pancakes for 30 years turn their nose up at a constant supply of steak dinners, but the disillusion is real and wide scale. But I'll try.

From the barely-disguised sarcasm earlier, you have probably figured out that I don't totally get on board the nostalgia trip that says football used to be so much better than it is now. Football in the '80s was grim, played in front of record low crowds, besieged by tragedy and under the gaze of a Prime Minister that regarded the fans as scum. Racism was rife, though women weren't, which may explain why a small few hate what football's become, football an escape from the drudgery of domestic life!

But the game had its charms that made most of us fall in love with going to a football match. Football hooliganism is of course a terrible thing, but going to a match felt like a real experience in those days. It was dangerous, it was electric, it was (sometimes) fun. It was affordable too, and you could stand, and not in a set place either. As a teenager it was an adventure, and it was something to do with your mates, a rite of passage in those mid-teen years without parental guidance, something I think that has faded in recent times. It was never nice to run through Stanley Park as golf balls whistled past your head, but your heart pumped faster than listening to Bournemouth fans sing "where were you when you were shit" or reading YNFA on Facebook mock empty seats or City's 8 year history, a world away from a sad Everton fan in his box room making memes for hits.

In the old days if you attended a game, every match seemed to matter, because before Sky and streaming and vines and social media, it was pretty much the only way to get your football fix, apart from the odd televised match, and the "wireless", newspapers and the Football Pink. Not forgetting of course premium rate phone lines to discover if we had signed Neil McNab.

After the Hillsborough tragedy, it was (correctly) deemed essential that the game needed reforming. The resulting Taylor Report called for all-seater stadiums in the top division, though Taylor wrongly thought that prices would stay competitive. They didn't, and the fuse was lit, destroying the support of some of its long-standing fans. Ticket prices have rocketed far beyond the rate of inflation since the report was released, and when Rupert Murdoch gambled his satellite company on English football, the glitz and glamour of the Premier League sowed the seeds further. The big clubs by now realised the potential to earn money, a European Super League was threatened, the cash-rich Champions League the trade-off from UEFA, and money truly ruled the roost long before Sheikh Mansour turned up at St James' Park looking for an English football club to invest in.

Rising ticket prices have excluded a generation of fans and gentrified the match day "experience", strangling the atmosphere as a result. It never fails to annoy when corporate areas are still deserted as a 2nd half begins, because most of that section of the crowd are still in the glitzy bar enjoying the bespoke hospitality.

Now I don't mind Guardiola, Klopp et al trying to gee up the crowd, asking for more support, but they haven't been sat where we have for the past 30 years, they don't understand, they can't understand how we got to this point. How could they?

City's owners too must wonder how apathy can be so rife when they have delivered so much. Understandable, but live our lives and they'd know. Not sure chippy teas and pale ales are their thing though, to be honest.

Fans are customers, the league is a brand. The Deloitte rich list is almost the alternative league table, and commercial sponsors are sucked in from around the world. Official Peruvian tyre sponsors, Eurasia rice providers, club-crested scooters in Singapore. Glass tunnels, corporate areas creeping round grounds, traditional fans kicked out of their seats, rising prices, don't stand up or you'll get thrown out, get to the ground seven hours before kick-off, follow the rules, sell your ticket via our agreed partner, behave. Crap tannoy, expensive food, players don't care, no youth players, all about money. Heineken are proud sponsors of the Champions League, but no drinking in the ground now! And never drink in your seat, or within view of it, you cannot be trusted.

All excuses for falling out of love with the game. But not the crux, I'd argue. Pick any specific moment in time in the history of football and you could list 100 things that were wrong with the game. You might not have realised it at the time, but still.

There's always been pros and cons to the game, it has never been perfect, run just how we want it to be, but we have always loved it. In the "old days" we knew no better, now we do, now we know how the rest of the world operates.

We're so well-informed. We know when other teams freeze ticket prices and we don't. About Bundesliga football, where every games cost two euros, and you get free transport, a half-time massage and a slap-up meal at Mrs Miggins' Pie Shop. We know about Champions League riches, every single thing our owners do, and what they used to do.

The owners' profile may have changed too but little else. It's a fallacy that in the old days owners cared about me. Peter Swales was a true City fan, for all his faults, but he didn't care about me. Francis Lee didn't care about me – he didn't even want to be in charge. Thaksin Shinawatra provided a free curry in Albert Square, for which I am eternally grateful, but he didn't care about me, avoiding the law his primary concern. And throughout the history of English football, there will be good and bad owners, and right now owners leeching funds out of the club they run.

So for me it must be something else that makes people drift away.

Maybe people have always drifted away. Maybe I live in an echo chamber, and am simply expressing the views of those I surround myself with, those that started following football at about the same time.

People don't stay young forever, they gain a family, commitments, jobs, they travel, they have other things that require their time. Football just isn't the priority anymore, especially when they can still see the game on the TV, or via more nefarious means. Where's the incentive to go if you can see the game without moving? The modern game, especially the Premier League ™ has been globalised and whored itself to every corner of the earth, been marketed until there's no marketing left to do, and is at least partially arranged for a TV audience, not a match-going one. Cup competitions too.

FA Cup rounds spread over four days, the final kicking off in the late afternoon, a draw during the sodding One Show, other crazy kick off times, Super Sundays, Friday games, morning games! London games that finish 20 minutes before the last train back up north. No one at the FA gives a fuck, after all.

It pains me to say it, but there's simply too much football to watch in the world – it's lost its sparkle. Saturation coverage has dulled the excitement for a big match, even if the hype has increased. After a million steaks, you crave for just one Findus crispy pancake.

And with money comes pressure, and the overriding desire to win. Money declares that finishing in the Top 4 is somehow a necessity for further success. And the cheating. God, the cheating.

Anything to gain an advantage over the opposition. Players rolling around on the ground when an opposition player's thumb brushes their shoulder. Diving. Faking injuries. Waving imaginary cards. Such a turn-off.

Don't get me wrong, I don't want Graeme Souness leg-breakers, violence, decrepit grounds, swathes of empty seats, uncovered stands, boggy pitches, tragedies and European bans. It was all crap. Now we just have a different type of crap.

I still love it though, always will. It matters to me as much as ever, it's just others disagree.

It's hard to nail down why different people have lost their love for the beautiful game, as the reasons will vary from person to person. But in my opinion, the main reason is thus: other commitments partnered with increasing costs and a dislike of the sanitised, "customer-focused" match day experience have meant a stay-at-home attitude when football is readily available in our living rooms. It wasn't really better in the old days, but as we age it's natural to pine for what went before, and to long for when everything seemed more "real". What we have right now is here to stay, so for those feeling cold, put on a thick jumper and try and enjoy the ride.

Champions League: Manchester City 2 Napoli 1

A nervy, thrilling end-to-end match that sees City pretty much qualify for the knockout stages of the Champions League with half the games to go.

This was supposedly the crunch part of the group stage – that weird bit in the middle when you play the same side twice. This all assumed that Napoli were the true threat, and it still felt like it, but Shakhtar had muddied the water, and had been greatly underestimated. Still, this was an exciting, vibrant Napoli side that were serious title contenders back in Italy, and the two matches would be a huge test of City's credentials. Napoli have won all their 8 opening league games, and in Mertens, Callejon and Insigne, have a front line that could terrify any opposition. Ghoulam at left back also stands out, having been linked with City like most players on the planet. He is some player though.

And in Maurizio Sarri, Napoli have a manager who is gaining a lot of attention around Europe. You feel this game involves two managers with a lot of mutual respect.

No surprises with the line up once again. Aguero remained on the bench. Hopefully the stability of selections would be a plus. Another big test for Delph at left back, who has passed previous tests with flying colours so far. No surprises too with Stones partnering Otamendi once more – a partnership that was truly blossoming, which is handy considering Kompany is injured once more.

Any nerves about this fixture were soon relieved however by a scintillating start from City. They were full of energy, movement and poise, and it was no surprise when they took the lead after 9 minutes. David Silva found space down the left of the area, his cross found Walker, his shot was blocked but Sterling was in the right place as always to hit the rebound home. Just the start City needed.

Four minutes later, after Ederson had expertly headed clear a dangerous through ball, City doubled their lead. Sloppy defending from the visitors saw De Bruyne gain possession, and the rest was textbook City – a burst forward, a precise low cross, Jesus finding space and slotting the ball home. City in dream land.

Sadly, if there was talk of a rout, it was to be ill-founded. Napoli re-grouped, and found their way into the match. That took some time though, but City could not kill off the match whilst still dominant. Silva mis-controlled a cross to him in the area, before a long range howitzer from De Bruyne hit the underside of the bar and bounced back into play.

There was more. Stones should have done better with a cross but his control also let him down, Jesus seized the loose ball, but his shot was blocked on the line. That third goal would just not go in. At this stage, City had had ten shots to nil, but only three were on target.

City's domination did not last. Ederson scooped up one dangerous cross, but then Napoli seemed to made their breakthrough, awarded a penalty for a Walker pull on Albiol. Never mind, because City's superb record at penalties continues. Mertens went for power, Ederson saved brilliantly, but just as importantly, Fernandinho reacted quickest to scoop the ball behind from almost under the bar. An escape for City after such total domination.

And that was how it stayed until half-time. Jesus missed a fair chance, and we saw the feisty side of Kevin De Bruyne, who David Silva had to drag away from the referee as the teams left the pitch. A scintillating half of football that did not disappoint.

Not surprisingly City could not maintain the domination of the first half, and had to keep their concentration. It was a case of missed opportunities though, as they still found plenty of opportunity to attack, most notably when Silva failed to release Sane on the left of the penalty area and was tackled instead.

And City almost paid for the profligacy. Napoli should have got one back when Hamsik had a near open goal, but Stones blocked superbly with his chest. However, there was fortune involved for City too. Sloppy play from Fernandinho saw him squander possession to Loureiro, and he then fouled the player in the area whilst trying to redeem himself. City were fortunate the referee played play on, then ignored the earlier offence.

And it was little surprise that a goal did come. Fernandinho was having a shaky period, to say the least, and when the exciting Ghoulam dribbled into the area, Fernandinho clearly brought him down. It was needless and put City on the back foot for the rest of the match.

Diawara took over penalty duty, and made no mistake. Game on with 18 minutes remaining.

Thankfully City held on. Jesus put the ball in the net, but it was disallowed for offside. The bloodied David Silva was replaced by Gundogan, and City got the vital three points even though the game remained dangerously stretched until the final whistle.

That's 10 successive wins in all competitions for City now. The key to success, as seen by Chelsea last season, can often be to go on a good run during a season, and City are doing that right now. Long may it continue.

Manchester City 3 Burnley 0

You can't beat a hard-earned victory with a sprinkling of faux outrage and fabricated controversy on top. And that's what we got against Burnley. Marvellous.

Oh, and all-time goal-scoring record too. I should probably mention that.

Twenty three days after his car crash, and Sergio Aguero was back in the team. In too was Bernardo Silva, as Sterling dropped to the bench.

The visitors were everything I expected – well-organised, drilled, and compact. They made life difficult, and really did nothing wrong. This was a case of City simply wearing down an opposition team with 77% possession. Bernardo Silva had a good chance saved minutes in, but good chances were few and far between.

And so talk was whether Sergio Aguero would equal the 177 goals of Eric Brook in this match, or even surpass it. In the end he had to settle for equalling it, with a well-taken penalty that finally broke Burnley's resistance after 27 minutes.

Ah yes, the penalty. It gave Sean Dyche something to whinge about post-match, and allowed the anti-City brigade to wield their sticks and moan about cheating and match-turning decisions. All nonsense, not surprisingly. I'll admit that live, I thought the decision extremely soft, from the other end of the ground. The replays showed Bernardo Silva's foot trapped under Pope's leg though. It's a fair penalty, however soft you may think it.

Anyway, City had further chances to score in the 1st half, but Burnley stood firm. What's more, they stifled City for much of the 2nd half too, without creating much themselves. Eventually though City put the game to bed with two quick goals.

Firstly that rarest of beasts, a goal from a corner, as Otamendi leapt like a salmon and headed home between the legs of the defender on the line. Then Sane raced clear and slotted home to put the game to bed. A tough game, but another three points, the run continues, the lead at the top now a healthy five points. United lost at Huddersfield, as the title race swung City's way at this early stage.

Next up…the wonders of the Carabao Cup

Could Dyche do as good a job elsewhere, say Arsenal for example? Hard to say until you give him the opportunity and Dyche clearly feels he is overlooked for such roles. Sometimes managers are perfectly suited to a specific role, to a particular club, and my gut feeling is that Dyche fits such criteria at Burnley. It would certainly be interesting to see how he performed with greater resources though. I doubt there's much clamour from Arsenal fans for his services, even in their current state.
In fact, if he was appointed, buy shares in Arsenal Fan TV immediately

Bluemoon Podcast Audio Script

Something changed last week. Something seismic. A bigger shift than that time Tony Pulis turned up at Wembley in a suit, bigger than the time Jose Mourinho ordered two of his midfielders to venture into the opposition half for a few minutes, and a bigger shift than Neil Custis complimenting Pep or that time Duncan Castles named Jose as only the 2nd most influential human in history. Yes, some sections of the football media seem to have climbed on board the Pep train. After Stoke, and after Napoli too, some of the praise was gushing, a dormant volcano erupting and spewing out hot praise to the masses, or something. I'm not good at analogies.

They'd held fire for a while – our promising start to the season was after all no better than all the other promising starts that had preceded it, and the underwhelming memories of last season were still fresh to many. Then a few thrashings were handed out, one abroad, one to Liverpool, a couple elsewhere, and some began to wonder if this was different – one victory later at Stamford Bridge, and it seems they had their answer. We were passing our first big tests, the wins were bigger, Kevin was barely human it seems and this felt different. Then Stoke came to town and the rest is history, backed up by an opening half hour against Napoli that I may not have witnessed the likes of before.

Of course it's early days, and with six months of a gruelling season to go, we can only talk of what is happening now – a couple of poor results, and Pep will be questioned once more, doubts will surface again as to whether the Premier League is too tough for him, not suited to his methods. And if City never lose another game under Pep, breaking all records known to man, and woman, he will still have his haters. None more so than Stan Collymore, holding a grudge because he misinterpreted pep not understanding a question 6 months ago and thus has acted like the POTUS ever since. I may have mentioned this a few pages ago. I'm not obsessed, honest.

There are remote tribes in the Amazon rainforest (them again!), cut off from outside civilizations for centuries, that if they came across a football would worship it as a god, and they have a better understanding of football and its context in the world far better than Stan Collymore will ever do. But people like Collymore are irrelevant now, little more than white noise being lost in the breeze. Your Keys, your Parry, your Castles, little more use than for me to retweet after a few pints too many. It's a full-time job, but someone's got to do it. They're not so much urinating into the wind, more trying to construct a 10 foot tower with a pack of cards as storm Brian passes through.

And with the praise, the talk of money has died down, in some areas at least, the talk just of scintillating football and nothing else – talk of what City have and not how they got there. Even Match Of The Day has been gushing. Even they couldn't drum up the energy to stoke a controversy from the Bernardo Silva penalty. The FA couldn't even be arsed charging him. What's going on? Before you know it, they'll be talk of Kevin De Bruyne making the reserve list of the PFA team of the year, and it is then that we will know that we have finally arrived.

Jose Mourinho has helped; the dull pragmatic fayre on offer just across the city borders has made it harder to simply point to money buying success. United's football has simply elevated City's football to new heights. Jose may well succeed with this pragmatism, this determination never to lose, but visually it is like comparing a rich, juicy freshly baked steak and ale pie with an omelette that has been flipped from its pan and has been stuck to the ceiling for 3 days solid.

Ronald Koeman's shambolic tenure with lesser but still very significant investment has proven further, and this may astonish you, that money alone is not a guarantee of success or even improvement. Arsene Wenger's rollercoaster ride from good to abject to average and back to good also keeps the hacks occupied, and Arsenal Fan TV too, and Jurgen Klopp's failing empire has been manna from heaven, the press dogs homing in for now on the weak spots of managers away from the Etihad. Jurgen's halo has slipped right off, Shankly no longer even sending him messages of support from heaven, the toothy smile and energetic touchline shtick wearing thinner than a polar ice cap or the hair on Wayne Rooney's head. Conte's nightmare fortnight, after the triumph in Madrid, shows that a fortnight is a long time in football, and Pep must beware. The vultures are circling, Pip Neville expressing an interest in the Everton job, and if there is a god he must show himself immediately and make this happen, whilst the usual calls to give it, whichever job it is, to Giggsy until the end of the season keeps us all chuckling for a few days longer.

Over at Wembley, Pocchetino is rightly praised, but it must be tempered until they actually win something – the Liverpool match was after all their first league home win of the season.

Even the most old school style hack can't ignore the evidence for ever. Even the guy who wants every top job filled by an Englishman, who is aroused by the idea that the Premier League sucks in foreign managers and spits them out, their careers ruined, bald frauds queuing round the corner at the jobcentre, their sophisticated continental methods undone by a Rory Delap long throw or Peter Crouch at the far post. It wasn't supposed to be like this.

And for City, for now, it isn't. 14 shots conceded on target in 9 games. Touching 70% possession in matches. 39 goals, more than anyone at this stage, at this level, since the days of Queen Victoria. 11 successive victories. That damned dodgy defence keeps keeping clean sheets too, damn 'em. Top of the goal charts, top of the assists charts, top of everything. Hard not to praise really.

And of course the praise is forthcoming because you can see Pep's ideas come to fruition, you can see what he was trying to do last season make more sense now, and you can see players improving, sometimes dramatically, in front of your eyes, not just improvement from huge investment.

Praise may be forthcoming too with the knowledge of what may come, with the knowledge that this is still not a complete squad. A midfielder at left-back, the main left back out for the season, Gundogan yet to feature heavily along with Bernardo Silva, nor Danilo, with Sanchez possibly on the way on the cheap plus 2 more defenders and the eventual introduction of the likes of Foden and Brahim and well, that's what you call a serious squad, playing right now strictly to instructions, suffocating the opposition and allowing little respite.

You don't get trophies for praise, and ultimately we shouldn't care what a Daily Mirror journalist thinks of our team, only what we ourselves think, but it is still warming to see the appreciation of this team almost globally right now. It's something we couldn't have imagined in those dark days when we yearned for just one Singapore taxi driver to know our name. Maybe. The rise of the internet and social media means that there is nowhere to hide any more for a supporter of a poor football team. It's a good time to be good. With Pep, we should be in safe hands for many years to come, and it seems that finally others have realised this too.

Still need to sort the turnstiles out though.

Carabao Cup: Manchester City 0 Wolves 0 – City win on penalties

Well it's fair to say that that didn't go quite as I expected.

Multiple changes, and a downturn in performance levels. It was ever thus. But cometh the hour (and the 90th minute…and the 121st minute…and…) cometh the man – Claudio Bravo the hero of the night, saving City and somehow the home team progress to the next round.

It was tepid stuff, in a competition that City players clearly could not rouse themselves to match their normal intensity. Tepid for me too, sat at home nice and dry. The cost of modern football has meant sacrifices must be made, and this was an obvious choice. I chose well, despite the happy ending.

The side felt like a random squad selection thrown together, but was still pretty strong. Disappointing then that they failed to score for the first time this season. Mangala and Adarabioyo did not work, especially for Mangala, muscled off the ball multiple times, though some were on the edge of being acceptable challenges.

So thanks to Bravo, making three great saves, and two in the penalty shoot-out. Aguero could not grab that goal-scoring record, but scored the winning penalty with a panenka, as City scored all 4 penalties.

Did I care about the victory? Well yes, but it is hard to quantify how much we as fans should care for the competition. It is clearly 4th priority for Pep and the players, the intensity during the match showed that, in a game where Jesus, Sterling, Aguero and Bernardo Silva started. However, past finals have given me two of the most enjoyable days out of recent years, so onwards and upwards!

As for Yaya Toure, the less said the better? He was not terrible, but the old Yaya is no more. I applauded the decision to give him a one year contract, as his desire and all-round performances at the end of last season merited it. However, he has not brought that form forward into this season. He has not had much chance to, to be honest, but clearly he is not impressing enough in training to be given greater responsibilities. What's more, when he does get a chance, he needs to take it. He did not do that against Wolves, and his City career once more looks like it will peter out.

Still, Aguero was no better, peppering shots at goal all night, with little success. I guess anyone can have an off-night. Pep blamed the ball, which he argued was not good enough in this competition. Ever the perfectionist is our Pep (demanding for example that the grass be cut to a length of 19mm at all times).

Still, let's look at the positives – City are through, our penalty record continues unblemished, and I always enjoy seeing Zinchenko get a run out, a young man with a bright future I reckon – he looked spent long before the end though, and Gundogan too left the pitch looking like his next injury had already arrived.

An interesting tie in the quarter-finals – Leicester City away.

STAN COLLYMORE – DUNCAN CASTLES WAS RIGHT – CITY'S TACTICAL FOULING IS A STAIN ON THE PROUD HISTORY OF ENGLISH FOOTBALL

Vincent Kompany & Divided Loyalties

As City edged past Wolves this week as the Etihad witnessed its 1st penalty shoot-out, after a nervy defensive display, one thing was clear – this is not a City squad that still does not require improvements if it is to become truly elite and compete for the top honours. Mangala was, well, Mangala whilst Tosin is not ready yet, if he ever will be, and of course the true back up to the in-form John Stones and Nicolas Otamendi is in Barcelona at the moment seeing the king of doctors, after yet another small injury morphed into a lengthy lay off.

I have debated online this week with City fans I respect the rather curious theory that surrounds our club captain, namely the assertion, or to describe it more accurately, accusation, that Vincent Kompany thinks more of his country than his Club, to the detriment of his paymasters, and to the detriment of his fitness.

I'm sorry, but I simply cannot agree (and I'm not sorry really either). It's funny though how some players are judged differently from others a certain Mario Balotelli was often a waste of space for Manchester City football club, yet he seems to have received less stick than our club captain. I like Mario immensely as a human being, a complicated young man with little malice, but on the pitch he hindered the side many a game, yet criticism of him was rarer than a forward De Jong pass. Kompany, who has brought so much to this Club over 9 years, is still distrusted by many for how he has handled his fitness – but could it really have played out any other way?

After all Kompany was known as the glass man even before he joined city, at Hamburg. Injuries were surely inevitable whichever path he took.

I don't blame clubs for protecting their assets, they will always look after their own and they are businesses with extremely expensive assets, but they know when they sign players that they have international duties too, that's part of the deal – to argue a player should automatically devote his time to club matters over country is simplistic, as they are perfectly capable of doing both. It's not a case of one or the other, and being paid a wage by a club is not an excuse to feel pressured to dismiss opportunities at national level. A club in 2015 would not sign an African player then have a hissy fit when he couldn't play for his club every other January.

United of course always used to have players pick up handy injuries over international breaks, especially when there were friendlies to play, but I don't know the rules then, or whether Ferguson bullied subservience from international managers. I can only state what the rules are now, and if a player has not retired from international duty, he cannot turn down a call up – it matters not one iota what the club wants, or what the player wants if he is called up, he must go, on crutches or in a wheelchair if need be. Hence on a recent international break, Kompany was called up, looked over by the Belgian squad doctor and sent back home. Utterly needless, utterly pointless, the world and his dog knew he was not fit, but the blame lay with the Belgian manager Roberto Martinez for this charade, not Kompany, who by law has little say in the matter – after all, UEFA can apparently even ban a player from domestic matches if a call up is refused.

My argument with Kompany is that he is going to get injured come what may – international football may not help as it heaps extra games onto a fragile body, but to expect Kompany to retire from international football with a World Cup looming, his swansong with the strongest national side in decades, maybe ever, is naïve in the extreme. Are we now criticising players for having pride in their country, is that now a crime? If Kompany had retired from international duty would we really expect him to be fit as a fiddle right now? I doubt it would have made the slightest of difference.

Of course Kompany may still have made mistakes – he can be called up and state he does not feel fit, he can request not to play, that his body needs care and to be handled delicately – maybe he has pushed himself too far too soon in the past, but none of us know really what has gone on. He has to play at some time, and if his body is not up to regular football - he will get injured sooner or later be it for Belgium or City. And what if he has made mistakes? He is desperate to play, and must have been through hell physically and mentally over the past few years with more false dawns than an arctic winter, so maybe we should cut him some slack.

I just feel that expecting Kompany to jack in playing for his country is ridiculous – it takes the emotion out of the game – we all feel that much of international football is boring and our English contingent would be better off not playing for all the stick they get, but that is the fan's view from the side lines, and you can't tell me most English players still won't get a feeling of deep pride every time they pull an England shirt over their head – it is an honour after all to represent your country – be it football, any other sport, even maybe a Eurovision song contest, at a push.

The real regret with Kompany is that his body prevented him from achieving more than he did. That we didn't get a full career out of him, didn't quite get enough moments like those in our title winning seasons, like that winning goal against United in the run-in, not enough times did we see him lift a cup having climbed up the Wembley steps. And with his latest injury, just as we began to believe again that there might be life in the old dog yet, we now know with some certainty that the end is near, at City at least, that the future City team will be one without our inspirational leader – in the past few weeks, John Stones and Nicolas Otamendi have shown us a different City, as another era comes close to an end.

I hope though that there is one last swansong, for club and for country. I hope his body gives him one more crack of the whip – gets him involved in what I hope is a title winning side, maybe a cup winning one too, and that at least once he can lead out his side in Belgium and that the side reached its full potential for once under his tutelage, though not at England's expense of course, though it matters little. I think he's earned that right after all, and I wouldn't begrudge him putting his country level in importance with his club as he reaches the twilight of his career.

West Bromwich Albion 2 Manchester City 3

Oxygen masks at the ready as City travelled east to England's highest ground. Always a good day out, and this was no different. Drinks in Birmingham then a short train ride to the ground – what's not to like?

A line up with a couple of mini-surprises in it. Aguero was back on the bench, Jesus preferred. Cue rumours of a fall-out. Sterling benched too, with Bernardo Silva given a start. Whilst I'd liked to have seen Sterling, as he clearly deserves plenty of playing time, it is good to see Bernardo being eased into the team. There has been no rush to implement him considering the form of the team and the strength of the squad, but for a signing that excited me so much, I can't wait to see him fly. Let's hope he does.

A strange game though in many respects. Up and down. City dominated in every respect apart from goals. Profligacy, sloppiness, three points. The last bit's the most important bit.

Sane's bullet put City ahead, a nothing through ball from Barry was suddenly in City's net, Fernandinho scored from far out once more, but it almost trickled its way in via a defender. The third was great, but Silva missed chances, De Bruyne hit wide when he should have scored, and a mistake from Otamendi late on meant a couple of minutes of nerves when the game should have been long won. Still, they did win, and that's what matters.

City still 5 points clear of United, but 8 points clear of 3rd place Spurs. 12 points clear of Liverpool in 6th. It's beginning to stretch out. Keep it going City, keep it going.

That's already eight goals for Sane this season, and he is flying. You wonder come the end of the season just how crazy some of the player stats may be.

On a minus note, Jesus flattered to deceive. You do wonder if we are getting ahead of ourselves with him. He is still very young, and it shows. Far from the finished product, but still with a huge future ahead of him.

Let's not panic just yet, and we all know that Pep loves the energy and movement he brings to that front line.

- Manchester City have made the best start to a Premier League season after 10 games, collecting 28 points (won nine, drawn one) with a goal difference of+29.
- The Citizens are now unbeaten in 21 games in all competitions (won 17, drawn four) - the longest run without defeat in their history.
- Guardiola's side have now won their last eight Premier League games by an aggregate score of 32-5.
- City completed 844 passes in this game; the most by a team in the Premier League since the start of the 2003-04 campaign.
- West Brom, meanwhile, have lost 15 of their last 16 Premier League games against Manchester City (drawn one), conceding 43 goals in this run.

Elsewhere, there was great news for Phil Foden, his stellar rise continuing as England came back from behind to defeat Spain 5-2 in the U17 World Cup Final – and Foden scored twice. What a prospect he looks, and thankfully a true blue too, so his future at City looks assured, unlike Sancho.

There has been criticism (as always) of City for not giving the likes of Foden and Diaz game time, but he is 17, how many other 17 year olds are regulars in a top side? None, that's how many. And the experience of a World Cup victory means much more for now. Pep will hopefully use him sparingly, and ease him into the first team squad. There is no rush – after all, in 5 years' time, he'll be younger than Sterling is now.

Champions League: Napoli 2 Manchester City 4

Wow. Just wow.

City qualify for the knockout stages of the Champions League with two games to spare, and will probably do so as group winners after one of their greatest European nights. A scintillating display of football from two wonderful football sides, and a game where City showed mettle and mental toughness in abundance to storm to victory against one of Europe's most exciting football sides.

It was not a team sheet that filled me with confidence either. Danilo stepped in for Walker at right-back, whilst Gundogan was in for a rare start and David Silva was demoted to the bench. Pep was clearly making rare concessions to the opposition, with their electric front line in mind.

And for a while, it seemed to have backfired. Napoli started the game at full throttle, and City were pinned back. It was no surprise therefore that Napoli opened the scoring, Insigne placing the ball past Ederson after a wonderful 1-2 and a sublime return pass from Mertens that split the defence. The Italian league leaders were on fire and were causing huge problems down Danilo's right side, with overload after overload. City found themselves behind for the first time since Bournemouth away, on 26th August.

Luckily for City it was just the single goal though, because you wondered how long Napoli could keep up such intensity. And the answer was not for that long, as City slowly but surely came back into the game. The tide was turning, you could feel it, and Aguero had a shot deflected narrowly wide.

Gundogan too had a shot deflected over, but when the equaliser came, it was from an unlikely source, Otamendi leaping like a salmon at the far post to power a header home. Game on.

Further chances followed. City were now breaking with real intent. Otamendi again found himself at the far post but seemed to hit the ball backwards, before Stones headed onto the crossbar seconds later from the unintentional Otamendi pass.

The second half continued in a similar vein. Only a tremendous defensive block denied Sterling after he had wriggled free in the area, but once again when a goal did come, it was from an unlikely source. Stones met a cross and his header bounced a yard over the line and back out. City had turned it around, and got the reward that their domination had deserved.

I say an unlikely source, but this was Stones' 3rd goal of the Champions League campaign.

The goal saw the tides change once more. Napoli woke up and showed more attacking intent. Insigne rattled the bar, and then the equaliser arrived, out of nothing really. A loose ball in the area, Sane swung at the ball, and was adjudged to have fouled Albiol. Jorginho sent Ederson the wrong way and it was all square again. What a game.

City were not done though, but had to weather further pressure. They almost led when Jose Callejon was picked out by Mertens and was only denied by an excellent Ederson save.

The biggest moment was to come though. Seventy minutes approached on the clock, the game hanging in the balance. City broke at speed via Sane but he was tackled, and it broke to Aguero and for a split second the Napoli defence opened up. Aguero did not need any more encouragement than that, broke into the area and slotted the ball home,

So that is it. Sergio Aguero, Manchester City's all-time record goal scorer. An amazing achievement by an amazing player. And what a time to break the record. Legend status was assured many years ago, and it is astonishing to think that all this time later he is still here knocking in 30 goals a season for fun.

Both Silvas came on, for Aguero and Gundogan, and City sealed the victory late on with Sterling, having dominated possession and the chances after going ahead. De Bruyne fed Sterling on the right of the area, he advanced and slotted the ball home. Game over, and the greatest of results.

For Napoli, a campaign full of hope is threatening to fizzle away. With them 6 points off Shakhtar in 2nd place, they will need to beat them in their next game, and then hope City don't wave the white flag in their last game having already qualified. It's looking like the Europa League at best for them.

And this was the first time an English team has won in Naples.

A great result that puts a marker down in Europe. No rest for the wicked though, and next up would be a rather interesting game against Arsenal at the weekend.

Manchester City 3 Arsenal 1

On and on and on and on. City just keep winning.

A familiar side. Walker back in, Silva back in, Aguero Sterling and Sane up front. A familiar 11, basically.

As always with a match against Arsene Wenger, Arsenal were of course cheated out of a result and the referee was a disgrace. Back in the real world, City were far and away the better side, but only profligacy made this game tighter than it should have been.

City were dominant before De Bruyne opened the scoring on 19 minutes, but couldn't make the domination count. As for the goal, it was almost too simple. A one-two with Fernandinho, De Bruyne advanced and slotted the ball into the far corner from the edge of the area.

That's the truly wonderful thing about De Bruyne, one of the key assets that lifts him above just about everyone else. This goal was scored with his left foot, supposedly his weaker foot. But you would not know from watching him which is his weaker foot. You might expect all professional players to be adept with both feet, but it is not that common, and certainly rare that they are as adept with both feet as De Bruyne. As a defender you cannot shift him onto his weaker foot or shepherd him a certain way because it will not work.

As for Arsenal, one snap shot from Ramsey was saved well by Ederson down low to his right. But that was it, though you could argue that for all City's domination, clear-cut chances were thin on the ground.

Five minutes into the second half however, and City doubled their lead. It was the rarest of beasts – a Sterling foul that the referee actually penalised. Outrage at the decision was laughable; Sterling was through on goal and was nudged or barged even in the back by Monreal. It was a clear penalty, but as alluded to, gave Arsene Wenger his get out of jail card, gave him something to shout at the 4th official about and embarrass himself over in the post-match interview.

Aguero did the rest, chipping in off the post.

The introduction of Lacazette seemed to unsettle the home side, Ederson almost fumbling an Iwobi shot into his own net, and it was little surprise when he took a Ramsey pass and slotted home into the far corner. Suddenly City were not so comfortable as we assumed.

Still, it did not matter for long. Jesus had a shot saved that should have ended in the back of the net, before Silva found acres of space in the area and squared for a simple goal for Jesus. And for once, Wenger did have a cause for complaint. Silva's foot and lower leg was definitely offside when the pass to him was made. Hard to argue that Arsenal lost the game on this mistake though, as they were losing anyway with 15 minutes to go.

Anyway, tough. City get so few decisions, it just made it sweeter. I've got a lot more to say about Arsene shortly.

United lost 1-0 at Chelsea, so City have now opened a significant 8 point gap. So far, so very, very good. Another tough fixture to follow though – they are coming thick and fast.

STAN COLLYMORE – PEP'S PRETTY TIKA TAKA FOOTBALL MIGHT DELIGHT THE GULLIBLE, BUT A 0-0 DRAW AT ANFIELD WILL ALWAYS BE MORE IMPRESSIVE

A Case Study Of Arsene Wenger

I've not got the best of memories. I'd struggle to tell you what I had for my tea last night, but little random memories through time stay in the mind, and it is as I contemplate the life and times of a certain Arsene Wenger one particular memory sticks out.

I once had a chat with a United fan – don't worry I was fully inoculated - some 10-15 years ago and he wasn't happy despite his team hoovering up all trophies available, and some Charity Shields too. He wasn't happy because we were discussing Arsene Wenger. His point was simple – that everyone went on about how Alex Ferguson was the biggest arse in football, which was a theory hard to dispel, when Arsene, a man every bit as odious, if not more so, got a free ride, feted by the media, fawned over as some erudite professor, when he was, to put it bluntly, not very nice, an edited version admittedly of his words.

At the time I faked a smile and took his argument with a pinch of salt. All that success and he's moaning about the rough ride Ferguson gets! Unbelievable, and yet, with each passing year, I've slowly come to realise that everything he said was essentially true.
Ok, maybe Arsene Wenger is not more odious than Alex Ferguson (I was using a bit of hyperbole there) in the same way diarrhoea is not as bad as malaria, but he could certainly give the champagne socialist from Govan a run for his money.

And so on Sunday we saw peak Wenger, the whiniest odious toad you will find pacing a touchline in this country. And I can say that safe in the knowledge no FA charge will be forthcoming, as it seems Wenger can call Raheem Sterling a diver and question the integrity of referees with no comeback, so I should be fine.

All managers are myopic to some degree of course, but Arsene "I didn't see it" Wenger is the pick of the bunch and always has been. The fact he doesn't see incidents that favour his team may perhaps be linked to his 90 minutes of haranguing 4th officials, for which he also receives no comeback. No wonder he didn't see fit to comment on City's disallowed goal in the FA Cup semi- final or the handball at the end of last season's Emirates league game.

The reason is probably simple – Wenger's shtick, like some others in his profession, is to deflect and divert from his own failings, and creating a separate narrative is the best way to do this.
Who this is for nowadays is anyone's guess, but he is fooling no one. Most arsenal fans are fed up with him. He has outstayed his welcome more than the drunk uncle at Christmas. His methods have repeatedly failed, his stubbornness held the club he claims to love back for many years and his outbursts are increasingly as irrelevant as his team.
A specialist in failure said Jose Mourinho, but failure is never Arsene's fault, it is always someone else's, his team the subject of more bad luck than the man who won the lottery the day Donald Trump finally nuked North Korea.

Much like Jose Mourinho's mind games, the world has moved on and left such masters of deceit behind in its wake. Wenger's unique brand of myopia simply opens him up to derision time after time after time- it would carry more weight if he was still competing for the top trophies, though still be odious, but in his current situation it does him few favours.
It's obvious to all that Wenger shouldn't still be on the touchline fiddling with his ridiculous oversized coat, but remains because he seems to have nothing better to do, because he seems to think he is responsible for the financial situation at the club, because he is one of those managers who always pulls out a result or two or an FA Cup when seemingly doomed, and because the board haven't got the balls to sack him, happy to count the dollars whether winning trophies or not.

Amidst all the hilarious "bants" about empty seats, it should not be ridiculed to see them appearing at the Emirates – after all, would you pay over a grand a season to see the same story played out year after year, groundhog year ad infinitum, as the manager picks up a £9m basic wage to repeat the same mistakes, to dole out the same false hope after briefly topping the table sometimes in September or November before the inevitable decline.

True greats of the game , and Wenger was definitely one once, move with the times, they revolutionise, they adapt, reform, they rebuild – and more importantly right now, they know when it's time to go, rather than hanging around like a post-Xmas dinner fart.

What Wenger said at the weekend though, after another defeat to a top four side, was a low even for him. His call that referees should work harder, though of course only for incidents that go against his side, was pitiful , especially as the actual offside goal was marginal when you consider the two players involved were moving in opposite directions and you stop the replay when the ball is first touched for the pass, not after it has left the foot, as most media outlets unsurprisingly seemed to do. His hatchet job on the non-diving Sterling, a player he would love at Arsenal and who has had enough shit thrown his way in the last few years to last five lifetimes was an utter disgrace, and I hope that the reports that City are furious are true and this matter is not dropped even if the FA are happy to turn a blind eye. Wenger and his acolytes need to know in the strongest terms that such talk is not acceptable. A man with a shred of decency would have apologised by now, or at least attempted to clarify his comments, but we all know Wenger would never do anything so gracious, so do not hold your breath.

Because of all this, there only remains one option. A concerted campaign by City to wind up Arsene Wenger. The easiest way to do this would be to concentrate on soon to be freed Alexis Sanchez and Mesut Ozil. Pep needs to start praising them in press conferences. The website should run compilation videos of their greatest moments for no reason whatsoever. They should have 20 foot Xmas cards delivered to them at Arsenal's training ground, signed by all the City squad.
Wenger can't complain, he started it.

Arsenal fans are keen to proclaim that you can't buy class, though unwittingly their manager has pretty much proved that, and it seems it can't buy a title-winning team either. I hope he stays there for decades. I hope every game against Arsenal we score 2 offside goals, get away with four blatant pulls in the penalty area, and my ultimate dream is to one day be given a goal where we barge their keeper into the net, like they tried in the game on Sunday.

Just imagine his post-match interview then, I'd probably buy it on DVD.

I remember when Arsenal were a force to be reckoned with, a giant of the game. I remember when the manager's words and mind games had an effect and mattered in North London and beyond. I remembered when we clapped their side off the pitch they were so, so good. Sometimes you see my memory is quite good.

And I just remembered one more thing too. It was risotto; last night I had risotto for my tea, fizzy Vimto and a Mueller corner.

Leicester City 0 Manchester City 2

The bogey sides are falling one by one. But for once, or perhaps for the second game on the row, City got a helping hand from the match officials.

That apart though, City were excellent again. Whatever seems to be thrown their way they seem to overcome right now, and they are suffocating teams into submission.

Kompany was in the side, always good to see, though it would prove to be a decision with consequences. Jesus started, with Aguero on the bench. The rest of the team is what you would expect.

And the controversy that would be referred to after the match occurred early, and thus is the first thing to deal with. Let's be frank – Vincent could have been red-carded for fouling Vardy, and if he had, we'd have little cause for complaint. The question is whether John Stones would have got round to cover if the foul had not occurred – it's touch and go for me. File this under "quite fortunate".

Still, and I say this without blinkers, and am writing this having revisited the match at the season-end. If this possibly fortunate decision is the biggest break City got this season, we can hardly consider ourselves to have been lucky over the 9 months. As we all know by now, these things most certainly did not even themselves out.

Anyway, what followed was a tough, hard-fought victory. We restricted Leicester superbly on the whole, Maguire striking the post with a deflected shot in the 2nd half, but City controlled the vast majority of the match. Chances were not flowing, but the pressure told late in the 1st half when Silva controlled a through-ball superbly and crossed for Jesus to tap in. Then De Bruyne did what he does best early in the 2nd half, with another thunderbolt from outside the area with his supposedly weaker foot. City were comfortable thereafter, and dominated, Leicester without a shot on target for the whole match.

This sort of result is the true mark of champions. Leicester may not be of the same standard as two years ago (naturally), but it's still a tough ground to visit, and City just keep taking the points in potentially tricky matches. On and on they go.

Of greater concern was an injury to John Stones, who appeared to go off with a hamstring injury after half an hour. Mangala proved to be an able deputy, but the last thing City need is Stones out for at least a month when in the form of his career.

City remain 8 points clear. Happy days.

STAN COLLYMORE – WHY PEP GUARDIOLA'S PITCH-SIDE ATTIRE DISGRACES THE MEMORY OF BRIAN CLOUGH

Champions League – Manchester City 1 Feyenoord 0

A strange night, in many respects. Raheem Sterling's late goal maintained City's 100% record in the group. Pep made seven changes, and it showed.

It was a gamble that paid off – City are guaranteed top spot in the group, and a draw would have been enough for that. This was a game where complacency almost cost them any points, which would have put a very different perspective on the final game, even though Napoli beat Shakhtar Donetsk 3-0. With the United match looming after the final group game, the victory allows a weakened team to be used pre-derby.

City however have been looking at a first defeat of the season had Sam Larsson and Steven Berghuis shown greater composure in front of goal, the latter striking the bar with a rising shot from close range in the second half.

Of course City had their own chances, and scraped home after a lovely 1-2 between Sterling and Gundogan, Sterling chipping the ball over the keeper to seal victory. Gundogan's pass will be forgotten quickly when this season is over, but it should not be. It was the true moment of class in a subdued game.

Aguero was off the boil, missing good chances, and Bernardo Silva shot tamely when he probably should have scored.

And kudos to Kevin De Bruyne for getting himself booked, so that he conveniently is suspended for the dead rubber game.

Mangala did quite well. You can't ask for more than that.

The win preserves City's 100% record after five matches of this season's Champions League, extends their unbeaten start to the overall campaign to 19 games and gives Guardiola his 50th win as City boss, in just his 75th game.

Huddersfield 1 Manchester City 2

If you believe in the narrative of champions being made by hard-fought victories when the team doesn't play that well, then you're in luck. This was surely a classic example of just that.

More to the point, does this show the resilience and mental strength of potential champions? This was the first time City have come from behind at half-time to win a Premier League away match since April 1995.

But all in all, this was an unexpected struggle. The home team did well to restrict City from creating opportunities, even if they rarely ventured forwards themselves. 80% possession for City sounds good, with 14 shots on goal, but clear chances were few and far between.

Huddersfield had zero shots on target, so it's good to know typical city, whereby we lose without the opposition having a shot, was not a factor on this occasion. The home team made 94 successful passes all game.

Aguero had a goal correctly disallowed for offside, Otamendi fired narrowly over, Aguero spurned a couple of half-chances in good positions due to his poor control, and Sterling had a rebound deflected behind too. Fernandinho then fired over too. So there were chances of sorts, but City were far from slick.

So naturally Huddersfield took the lead from a rare foray into City's half. Kompany had already almost headed into his own net, and from the resulting corner, a flick on hit Otamendi on his shoulder, with no time for him to react, and went in. Own goal, and a half-time deficit that few would have predicted.

But in the second half, City gradually wore Huddersfield down, making 336 passes to their 37. The winning goal may have had an element of luck, but it mirrored how the game was going.

First though came a quick equaliser from the penalty spot to calm nerves. It was a penalty, and there were claims for one on Sterling minutes before – basically, despite all the desperate attempts to make out Sterling cheated to get City back in the game, there was at least one penalty amongst those two incidents. Aguero did the rest, and City were back in the game.

Aguero had a shot saved, Fernandinho clearly dived, and then at last the breakthrough, another shot saved it rebounded off Sterling's knee and City were ahead. A complete turnaround from the side that has only been behind for 57 minutes so far this season. City held on, for a hard-fought three points.

Eleven straight wins in the Premier League, eighteen straight wins in all competitions. This is a team going places.

And for Raheem Sterling, his 12 goals already make this his most prolific season.

There was still time for a red card, Rajiv van La Parra sent off probably after the final whistle after pushing Sane, as it all kicked off as the game ended. Handbags at worst.

Three points, relief, we move on.

STAN COLLYMORE – WHY I AND OTHER JOURNALISTES WILL NOT TRULY EMBRACE GUARDIOLA UNTIL HE HAS WON THE CHAMPIONS LEAGUE EIGHT TIMES WITH PLAYERS BORN ONLY IN STOCKPORT

Manchester City 2 Southampton 1

Who knew before this game that it would give City fans one of its best moments of the season? If this is a mid-season slump from City. I'll take it.

As the commentator said on the YouTube video I've just watched, as Sterling's shot hit the back of the net – "THAT WINS TITLES!"

Like at Huddersfield, City were not at their fluent best. A side without Sane or Silva and with Jesus on the left only threatened in patches. Like at Huddersfield, and Feyenoord as well, Sterling came to the rescue late on. Only this time, it was really late on.

Credit to the visitors. They were well organised and very dangerous from set pieces, and should have scored twice in such situations. Having said that, Aguero should have scored two headers also, though the first chance was hit towards him at such speed he could only act off impulse alone.

Still, in the end, the misses did not matter. De Bruyne's wicked free kick was deflected in by Otamendi early in the second half, Romeu rifled in an equaliser with just 15 minutes to go, and it looked like City were going to let their healthy lead at the top slip. Little did I know what was to come.

What made Sterling's 13th goal of the season even better was not just the time of the goal, with virtually the last kick of the game, but the drama that had immediately proceeded it. Only a minute before he had put the ball in the net, but it was inexplicably disallowed for a non-existent foul. That just made it all the sweeter when he did it again. From utter joy to despondency and back to utter joy in 60 seconds. It was astonishing, and one of the biggest celebrations of a goal in a long time. I had plenty of space to celebrate in too, considering the early leavers had buggered off.

Special mention too to Benjamin Mendy for trying to catch Sterling as he went on his goal celebration run, even though he has the small matter of a cruciate ligament injury. Probably not the best idea when you think about it.

And then there was the curious case of Nathan Redmond. Yep, Pep was on the naughty step again, for showing his rather unique passion on the touchline as the teams left the pitch. It was a bit weird, but Redmond didn't seem to mind – if it had been anyone else, the manager probably would have been shoved away. Anyway, Pep decided to pass on some thoughts on Redmond, football and the wider world, and got pelters not surprisingly. He probably shouldn't be doing things like that, but it's no big deal.

STAN COLLYMORE – WHY MANCHESTER CITY WILL NEVER BE AS BIG AS MY BELOVED ASTON VILLA, WHERE CLASS IS NOT BOUGHT

Manchester City 2 West Ham United 1

How considerate of City, to make this title race interesting. To get fans of rival teams' hopes up, before cruelly dashing them, week after week. Yep, for the third league game on a row, City win it late on - though this time with a good seven minutes to spare.

Recent slogs had clearly persuaded Pep to change things around and rest a couple of players. This is what caused many of the problems though. Whilst City remained threatening throughout, especially after half-time changes, City always looked vulnerable at the back against an average side.

So no Fernandinho, so Danilo was left-back and Delph had a stab at defensive midfield duties. More worryingly, Mangala partnered Otamendi at the back. At half-time Danilo was hauled off, Delph returned to left-back, and on came Jesus, with Pep complaining later that the hosts had been too slow. Eventually these changes paid off, David Silva stretching to prod home a cross. Relief, as it makes the next league game slightly less pressured. Slightly.

Adrian had plenty to do, it must be said. Save after save came along, and on another day perhaps this would have been a comfortable win for City. It's sad to see him in nets though, the decline of Joe Hart continuing at pace. Pep was right to get rid of him, we can see that now, but I still wished him all the best, and hoped he could recover his form. That seems unlikely in the near future.

City come from behind at half-time to win again. Nice. And another goal for Otamendi, who is becoming quite prolific. Marcus Rashford, England's great hope, can only dream of such a strike rate.

Another day, another record. City have equalled the longest winning run within a top-flight season, matching Sunderland and Preston (1891-92), Arsenal (2001-02) and Chelsea (2016-17). Taking last season into account, it is actually 28 straight wins on the bounce – truly astounding.

Next up in the league? The small matter of a Manchester derby. My stomach is churning already. Hopefully City's style will have returned by then.

RAHEEM STERLING'S GIRLFRIEND CAUGHT SHOPPING IN PRIMARK DESPITE WEALTH OF £49M SIGNING

Champions League: Shakhtar Donetsk 2 Manchester City 1

So there we are. After 29 games, City lose, at long last. Their first defeat since that FA Cup semi-final defeat to Arsenal.

Let's be honest, no one really cares.

City could have become the first English side to win all 6 group games, but it's hardly worth putting out your strongest side and pushing players to the limit to achieve the most obscure of records, especially with a derby on the horizon.

For the home team, there was much more at stake, though with Napoli eventually losing at Feyenoord, they didn't have to stretch themselves in the end either. Both City and Shakhtar qualify for the knock-out stages.

The team reflected the nature of the match. Adarabioyo in defence, Yaya in midfield, and most pleasing, Foden too.

And not surprisingly in a game where one team needed a result, City faltered, and we shrugged our shoulders and moved on. Yaya was predictably passed around, whilst Foden put in a solid if unspectacular display. None of us can expect him to be running the game at the age of 17.

Diaz got half an hour on the pitch too, so all in all what we take from the game is the experience gained by three youngsters.

And if Ederson is going to make the occasional mistake, as he did in this match, his timing is impeccable.

Anyway, there's little point discussing the game further, and City win the group. Now to find out who they will get in the draw.

And it is Basel – we'll take that! A team that have already beaten United this season, but that's not saying much.

Manchester United 1 Manchester City 2

Quick question United– can we play you every week?

Was this a huge match? Ask me afterwards! But essentially, no.

But then yes it was in a way too, because if City won, it would not only stretch the lead at the top of the table, it would be a statement of intent.

Having said that, after City won 6-1 at Old Trafford, United went on a long unbeaten run. So who knows?

I'm rambling. As I hate derby day so much, I convinced myself the game was not important as an insurance policy should we lose. Turns out I wasted my time.

Like Chelsea away, this was the "other" game where watching highlights does not tell you the full story. City's two goals came from United mistakes, Ederson made a great double save and on another day this could easily have ended up a draw.

The desperation of United fans to point out they almost got a point exists because they know it masks the real story – this was men against boys, sophisticated, exhilarating, possession football against dour, must-not-lose hoof-ball. Football was the winner. And City, obvs.

We need to look at the big picture. The game, as I mention above, told us everything about the direction of both clubs and their style of play. There was only one team you'd want to watch on a weekly basis, after all. Thankfully I support that team.

So City go eleven points clear. That's a tasty lead at the top at this stage of the season.

And how hilarious to see the screeching over the Herrera "penalty" incident. It was of course never a penalty, and should have been a yellow card for a dive. You could well imagine a referee giving a penalty though. Instead, the referee actually did his job and booked Herrera. Miracles do happen!

As the players approached each other, a foul was certainly looking possible, but Otamendi, after his mis-control, had the sense to withdraw from attempting to make a tackle just short of Herrera, who put his foot down to Otamendi's and then proceeded to throw himself into the air as if he had stood on a mine. Amazingly he then spent much of the week bemoaning the decision. Are footballers really that stupid?! We can see replays you know!

Anyway, Mourinho calling City "lucky" just made the day even better. *Asked whether the title race was over, Mourinho replied: "Probably, yes. Manchester City are a very good team and they are protected by the luck, and the gods of football are behind them."*

Ha ha ha ha ha ha ha ha ha ha ha ha ha ha ha ha ha ha ha ha ha ha ha ha ha ha ha ha! The new "bitters" – as they have been for some time now. I'll say one thing for Mourinho – he's a manager perfectly suited to his current club.

City saw the game out easily – see my moments of the season for more details.

And amazingly this was a day that still had more to give. Well, the subsequent days did anyway. News emerged of a "fracas" in the City dressing room after the game, culminating in Jose Mourinho having milk thrown over him. Seriously City, you're spoiling us now. There was talk of an FA investigation, which obviously wasn't going to lead anywhere, and didn't.

More classic deflection from Mourinho, no doubt, a conflict constructed by him to deflect away from his derby home defeat. Job done, as always, but the league table stays the same so ultimately futile.

Duncan Forts Minute By Minute Match Report on Manchester Derby

3 minutes: Early sign of things to come. Otamendi out of position twice for a throw-in, fortunately for him United do not take advantage.

4 minutes: Jose tactics clear, using personnel available to him to best effect, considering transfer market restrictions and growing injury list. Guardiola already looks stressed and uncomfortable. Is this job getting to him?

14 minutes: Pep Guardiola steps two yards out of his technical area – naturally there is no punishment for this clear breach of the rules.

18 minutes: Fabian Delph bypassed by Martial for third time so far this match. Still think he's a top-class left-back? Well, do you??? Well??!!!!!!

27 minutes: Beautiful cross by Valencia not anticipated by any teammates. Astonishing his development under Jose.

32 minutes. **P**ogba **L**eaves **E**derson **A**drift, **S**triking **E**legantly **L**eft **O**nto **V**alencia. **E**xcellent **M**ourinho **E**mbarrassing **J**osep. **O**nward **S**urges **E**xpectedly.

33 minutes: Guardiola looking exasperated on the touchline. Is the pressure getting to him? Is the end near?

36 minutes: Mourinho the antithesis of Guardiola on the touchline. Calm, collected, and writing notes that will surely deliver results. Not many could carry off grey hair like he does.

43 minutes: City take an undeserved lead. David Silva, possibly offside, prods home after Lukaku was unsettled, possibly because he was expecting to be tactically fouled.

45 minutes: United's magnificent response brings almost instant dividends. City's defending is once more pathetic, as it usually is when they are actually tested, and Rashford coolly slots home. The youth player who cost United nothing (£0) has been the best player in this first half. No argument.

45 minutes: Half-time, and it's all-square. Mourinho will be the happier of the two managers however. His team's relentless team ethic forced a mistake from City's overpriced defenders, and City's goal was rather fortunate- Pep will surely accept that?

52 minutes: De Buyne commits a yellow card offence, but naturally avoids punishment. Can't be upsetting Pep's boys now, can we?

54 minutes: How much luck can one side have in a single match? Yet again a ball ricochets to a City player, and Otamendi's speculative stab at the ball hits the back of the net. Yet again City cunningly do not tactically foul Lukaku even though they usually would, and this once more unsettles the striker.

67 minutes: David Silva's tactical fouling once more highlighted as he gets away with a trip on Lingard. Referee Jon Moss giving Pep carte blanche to continue this tactic.

75 minutes: City's stellar expenditure on full backs has made all the difference to this match. Understandable that Mourinho feels he cannot compete with such wanton spending. All things considered, this can be seen as something of a moral victory for Jose.

79 minutes: Proof (if proof were needed) that the match officials do not want the home team to succeed today. Otamendi takes Herrera's legs away from him in the penalty area after another characteristic mis-control, and astonishingly the referee books Herrera for simulation.

84 minutes: The footballing gods are not dispensing any justice today, that is for sure. Ederson saves not once but twice with his face, and I very much doubt that he knew anything about either.

92 minutes: Shocking timewasting from the away team, as they desperately call for the full time whistle by holding the ball in the corner. Not the expressive, free-flowing football we were told Pep would bring to the Premier League.

FULL TIME: Manchester United 1 Manchester City 2: Somehow Manchester City take 3 points, in the biggest smash and grab of the season. Mourinho will be rightly incensed not only by the bad fortune suffered by his team, but one of the worst refereeing performances in living memory. A hollow, cheap victory for the visitors, who show the expected lack of grace in the changing rooms afterwards.

RAHEEM STERLING POPS OUT FOR BRUNCH DESPITE NOT CURING CANCER OVER THE WEEKEND

A TALE OF TWO CITIES (a relevant piece from last season now perhaps being proved redundant)

It seems like a lifetime ago. I was writing my dissertation on how the inspiration for the "Red Terror" favoured by the Russian Bolsheviks lay in the French Revolution. I had no grey hairs, the world had never heard of Facebook or Twitter, and knew little of Donald Trump's tiny, tiny hands. Sad.

Football was soon to "not-quite-come-home", the Tories were unravelling under the slate-grey John Major, and Blackburn Rovers were going for the Premier League title, up against Manchester United, no less. Manchester City were fighting relegation, so little surprise there. The problem was City now had to face Blackburn, at a muddy Ewood Park, and their own battles meant no leeway could be given to a team with the SAS up front, a team who would only lose one other game at home that season.

So the joy and relief was palpable when Nicky Summerbee's shot was palmed out by Tim Flowers and the onrushing Paul Walsh swept the ball home to put City 3-2 up, a lead they would hold on to, completing a fine 2nd half comeback after trailing at the break. It was 1995 and City would stay up with four points to spare, and Blackburn would win the title. I had to find a job, had no money but City were safe for another year, and only another year. It was the best of times, it was the worst of times.

City fans could not know the other relevance of that night, however - because it was the last time City would overturn a half-time deficit away from home in the Premier League, and turn it into a victory, for another – well, I don't know, as we have reached 2017, and the feat hasn't been repeated since.

Twenty two years. You'd get less for murder. During that period there were 94 games with a half-time deficit, of which 11 ended in draws and 83 in defeat.

And it's a statistic that has been on my mind again recently, as that non-penalty award against Everton the other week got me agitated. It's hard to argue that not getting a penalty could make much difference in a 4-0 defeat, though Gary Lineker was keen to suggest our penalty against West Ham before adding four more was a turning point the previous week. However, this is City, and there's the nagging feeling in my head that when we score first we are a joy to watch, but under adversity, we are most certainly not – and thus that non-penalty could have been crucial. The feeling may not be true, but it's there nonetheless, even if Spurs and Andre Marriner rather ruined our latest two goal lead.

Hence my mention of the stat about coming from behind. Is this a team that is mentally weak? And what does that even mean? Does a team need a leader, a Roy Keane, a shouter, or is good football more important than a never-say-die attitude? Influential footballers or commanding footballers? Do City now need both?

The problem with this stat is that it is such an arbitrary choice. The laws of the game dictate a break halfway through the game, so stats can be created around this break - but should mental strength be judged just by how a team reacts after a break, an orange segment and a stand-up routine from Eddie Large? There are surely other factors – coming from behind at any stage in the game, late winners, late equalizers, performances that stats cannot measure, such as City's recent victory over Burnley with 10 men - and what the stat clearly fails to address is cup games, home games, rallying to get a draw and the rather pertinent point that City weren't that good for much of the period in question. And as shown by the continental practice of rotating captains, often awarding the honour to the oldest or longest serving player, it is perhaps more of a British characteristic to seek a warrior on the pitch to aid performance.

With all this in mind, I had a look at results over the past few seasons, to get a general view of how City do when we go behind – and it's crucial this season when City are more prone than anyone to concede an early goal, more prone than any team to concede from the first shot on goal, the last six shots against City having ended up in the back of the net.

A delve through the past few seasons shows plenty of evidence for both sides of the argument. Let's take the 2015/16 season for example. A disappointing season, as we all waited for our saviour to turn up. In the league, City were behind at half-time in 9 league games – 4 at home, 5 away. They went on to lose all 9. However in cup competitions we see a rather different picture – we came from behind to defeat Borussia Monchengladbach, held our nerve in a cup final penalty shoot-out (having come from behind in fine style in the 2nd leg of the semi-final) and in the season as a whole scored 6 late winners and came from behind in the second half at Watford. There was a fair bit of resilience in Paris too that proved crucial to reaching the semi-final of the Champions League.

The previous season? Well this wasn't the greatest of seasons either, but it's interesting (to me, if no one else) to note that City only trailed at half-time in four league games – we went on to lose three and draw one. Again, the cups show greater resilience. We came from behind against Bayern Munich to defeat them. Twice, if we also lump in a previous encounter. We did the same at home to Sheffield Wednesday in the FA Cup, throwing in a late winner for good measure.

2013/14 shows a similar theme – behind at half-time in the league in only four games, and we went on to lose all four. There was a stirring comeback in the League Cup final against Sunderland though, and we saw off Watford in the FA Cup after a disastrous first half. Was mental strength in abundance at Wembley, or did individual brilliance shine through?

And this season? A comeback against Arsenal has banished another unpalatable stat regarding home game comebacks, and then of course there was the Barcelona game. Plenty of resilience, as seen at Turf Moor, but not consistently.

But for me there are two clear examples of the team's resilience – namely both title winning season run-ins. Of course the narrative was painted that our rivals both choked at the last hurdle, handing us undeserved titles. There is after all always a caveat when City win any game (Bayern Munich weren't trying, penalty not given, kit clash, sun was in their eyes), but on both occasions the City team kept their nerve and won a succession of tough, nervy games. United at home, Newcastle away, THAT GAME, Everton away, and more.

But back to the present day. When Everton's second goal went in, I had zero faith in City staging a comeback – the game was pretty much up in my eyes. Putting my endless pessimism to one side, that lack of hope is not necessarily down to me sensing a soft underbelly in this Manchester City team, more just a comment on our current form, or level of performance. Or maybe it's just our inability to ever put in a good performance on Merseyside.

So for me, there's no perfect formula for resilience on a football pitch, for overcoming pitfalls. Even today there is an article in the Mirror suggesting City need Arsenal's mental strength to be more successful, an Arsenal side that annually bottle a title challenge. Yes they have scored plenty of late goals, but they have had fortune and they have had skill, and good teams tend to score late goals as they do more of the attacking and a "lesser" opposition often retreats to the edge of its box and relinquishes possession. Maybe City simply need a big man to lump it up to instead, but the City team is capable of fighting to the end, as they showed in Pep's first game. This season alone we have scored late goals against Sunderland, West Ham, Borussia Monchengladbach, Stoke City, Steaua Bucharest, West Brom, Leicester City, Watford, Crystal Palace, Hull City and West Ham – they just weren't all winners.
You put a fighter in the side and you lose a separate quality elsewhere. Teams often need guidance on the pitch, they need organisation and a kick up the backside. The nagging feeling persists that the City team of recent years can sometimes lack resilience and let its collective heads drop.
In the end though, good players, the roar of a crowd and moments of quality are just as important as a shouter and a captain with blood running down his shirt.

(the stat was thankfully put to bed away at Huddersfield, as you will already have seen)

Stan Collymore: The Man, The Legend

It started out as a small affair. A rented room above an inner-city boozer. A small buffet was put on, and only six people turned up to hear the keynote speaker.

Before long though, it had grown too big for its location. A village hall was hired, and for some it was standing room only. Then a small theatre. They queued round the block that night.

Two years later, and the Blocked By Stan Collymore On Twitter Society (BYSCOTS) has a three date run at Wembley Stadium. Tickets sold out in under 10 minutes, websites crashed when they went on general sale, and front row seats are said to be going for over £2,000 on Viagogo.

I jest of course. Wembley wouldn't be big enough, there are after all long-lost tribes in the Amazon rainforest that have been blocked by Stan after harmlessly tweeting about rural car parks, and if you haven't been blocked, you're probably wondering who I am talking about.

But considering some of the controversies in Stan's life, and social media users' eagerness to mention them whenever he has any opinion, I guess blocking billions of people seems the easy thing to do, even those that just want reasoned debate and to point out what drivel he spouts on an almost daily basis for hits, clicks and to feed his ego, an ego that truly believes he has the knowledge and experience to offer advice to the likes of Klopp, Mourinho and Pep Guardiola, amongst others.

Ah yes, Pep Guardiola. Here lies the greatest tragedy of Stan Collymore's writing career. A misunderstanding over a question asked at a press conference, that Stan, in his wisdom, took as a personal attack on him, and has spent a year avenging, via his risible Mirror columns.

His initial reply was the most tragic of them all. Having created his own feud, his column was entitled:

It's fine if Pep Guardiola doesn't know me - Brian Clough did, rated me highly, and he got his success from scratch.

In it, Stan spent much time explaining to Pep Guardiola, who I doubt has ever spent 10 seconds reading Daily Mirror clickbait, what he had achieved. Pep, an intelligent knowledgeable man, will have known all this anyway, not that he should care.

And here's the crux of it all - it was obvious that Pep was not mocking Collymore in the press conference. It is not his way, and if you watch the clip, you can see he is clearly confused by the question asked of him (in Spanish) as soon as the reporter in question starts speaking, and does not fully understand the reporter's point, or at least why it was being asked. That's it. End of story.

Except, for one person with a persecution complex, that was not it. It was just the beginning, especially as it involved a manager of a club he has shown plenty of hatred for in the past.

And so we have been treated to a year of Collymore gold-dust. First up, Pep's delusion:

"If Pep he thinks he's going to turn up and outplay everybody in the Premier League and think a team are going to let his side have the ball for 90% of the time and pass pretty patterns around them so they can get a result, then he is absolutely deluded."

But not as deluded as you, clearly.

Stanley's latest article may have been dressed up as an attack on the weakness of other clubs, but at its heart it was once more an excuse to dampen down the idea of praising Pep Guardiola's Manchester City team. As you'd expect, his argument was weaker than a Rio Ferdinand urine sample.

But if you were to ask fans who have watched the English top flight for a number of years how this season compares to those gone by, then I'm sure many would say that, overall, City are playing in the worst quality league they have seen for a long time.

Where City will be judged given their huge spend is in the Champions League, when they take on Barcelona in the Nou Camp, Bayern Munich in the Allianz Arena and Real Madrid in the Bernabeu.

It's classic Collymore. Shifting the goalposts, making up his own rules, then making a definitive statement of what constitutes success or brilliance according to his own self-imposed restrictions and sense of superiority. Still, the good results just kept coming, so he had to shift his emphasis so what, especially as 5 English teams reached the knock-out stage of the Champions League. Not bad for such a terrible league.

Pep Guardiola doesn't have to go all Tony Pulis by wearing the club shop but if he doesn't want to wear a suit on the touchline then he should at least don a tracksuit. There's a standard of dress at some of our great cathedrals of football and, while Stone Island is fine for the stands, it's not fit for Premier League dugouts.

Yep, the barrel truly has been scraped to well beyond an inch of its life. We're gonna need some new barrels. Stan duly obliged.

The post-match knocking of Manchester United following their goalless draw at Liverpool has been quite stunning. I even heard some Manchester City fans crowing, 'We want to win games and win them well'.

Which is rubbish — I don't remember it being about style over substance for them two decades ago when they were scraping through third-tier finals at Wembley.

City just wanted to get up the leagues back then and they didn't care how they did it.

Yet here they are, 20 years and a billionaire sheikh later, basking in the gloriousness of life in Pepville.

It may well be pretty nice at the moment there but I will tell them this.

If I was still a player I'd have been much happier with a 0-0 draw away from home against our biggest rivals than scoring seven but conceding two to a Stoke team who will finish in the bottom half of the table.

What did we actually learn about City at the weekend? Not a lot.

We know they'll score fives, sixes and sevens at times this season but we also know they'll concede goals that, really, they shouldn't.

It doesn't matter if you win 10-4 or 1-0 you still earn the same number of points, but ultimately it will be the number of clean sheets you keep that win you the title.

*Don't get me wrong, some of the football City have played this season —
not least on Saturday — has been amazing, absolutely superb.
But what will determine Pep Guardiola's success is not how they play, it's
whether or not they can get one more point than the team in second.
That isn't a given while they are conceding two goals in games against
teams such as Stoke.*

I'll keep the rebuttal to this drivel simple, in teams even Stan could
comprehend. In the last eight seasons, the team with the most points
has won the title in every season. The team that has kept the most clean
sheets has won the title in one of those eight seasons. Manchester
United kept the most clean sheets last season and finished sixth. As of
mid-March 2018, City had conceded fewer goals than any team in the
top four divisions anyway. Which is weird when they keep conceding
two goals to "the likes of Stoke".

*Tottenham are probably the only team in England, everything
considered, that I would pay money to watch,' Collymore now writes in
his Daily Mirror column.
'Not Manchester City – good to watch, but I just can't get excited about
them as a club. They are trying to build the best team with the biggest
budget. What does that mean?
'Is it a great team or do they simply have the biggest budget? Anyone
can do that.'*

The equivalent of United fans' regression since 2008 as City have grown
and grown – money doesn't guarantee you success, players are all
mercenaries, wait until the oil runs out, the sheikh will get bored, they'll
never be as big as us whatever they win, EMPTY SEATS, EMPTY SEATS!!!!

Anyway, shame on the Mirror for allowing Collymore to use a series of
articles to play out a personal vendetta against an individual. Though if
the paper that hires Robbie Savage for his opinion gets hits, they won't
lose any sleep over the matter.

Stay strong Stan. The next few years may not be to your liking.

Important Non-City Games

Many a time I have seen football fans comment on results of other teams, teams competing with their team, their goals for the season similar, and comment with disdain that the other team's results don't matter, as long as *"we do what we need to"*.

Rubbish of course, because that rather ignores how league tables work, and other teams' results are sometimes as important as your own – mainly because you cannot rely on your team however good they may be in your eyes, to win every game and not rely on results elsewhere. I admit to obsessing too much to how other teams do, calculating through fixture lists and probability about whether City are going to stay ahead of the pack, though at the start of a season I try my hardest to stop this stupid habit, because this early on it is ridiculous to ponder how games will affect a league table in 9 months' time and because football is far too unpredictable to project points tallies for teams.

However, I saw such comments yet again recently about other teams results not mattering, and it got me thinking about the key results in City's recent history that weren't actually City matches. Games not involving City that definitely mattered to us, that helped alter our (recent) history - so I'd thought I'd list them, because after all, if I spend any more time discussing transfer rumours or net spends I'll be taken away in a white coat, and so may you.

Millwall v Wigan – FA Cup Semi-final 2013.

The most obscure match on the list. City were up against Chelsea in the other semi-final, the general feeling being that whoever won that match won the cup, so I was not unduly worried when Wigan beat Championship side Millwall 2-0.

Well that backfired, and the rest is history, because even considering the shambles of City's pre-match preparations, the rumours and the sluggish performance, I doubt Millwall would have posed much of a threat, whereas Wigan of course put the icing on the cake of a bad season and on Mancini's stay at city.

Liverpool 0 Chelsea 2 - 2014

When talking of games that altered City's history, two stand out above all others in recent times. And 1st up, we must talk of one specific Liverpool game that will live long in my memory from the 2013/14 season – and it is of course their 2-0 home defeat to Chelsea, when Steven Gerrard and Liverpool's title hopes slipped away. It's about the only time too that an arrogant Jose Mourinho strutting down the touchline has made me grin ear to ear, rather than want to smash my television into a million tiny pieces.

That last 10 minutes was more stressful than the 2012 winner takes all derby against United (well, almost). The relief when Chelsea broke and scored that 2nd is one of my favourite non-City moments, especially as a Liverpool player had just air-kicked right in front of goal – right then, I knew the title should be ours again, and we didn't disappoint. Now many will also quote the manic 3-3 draw with Crystal Palace some days later, and boy was that last 10 minutes hilarious, but even if Liverpool had won (by under 9 goals), then the title was still in City's hands, in fact we may well have won once more on goal difference. Instead, that late collapse gave City breathing space, needing only 4 points from the last 2 games, making the final game at home to West Ham a bit easier to bear.

Manchester United 4 Everton 4 - 2012

There's one game that stands out above all others for me though. What else but the 4-4 draw between Manchester United and Everton in the spring of 2012. This was a game that changed everything.
Ever followed a match on teletext heart pounding praying for a final whistle? Well this was a modern version of that for me – with City due to play Wolves later in the day, my friends and I turned off the TV in disgust as United went 3-1 up. The feeling was clear, United just weren't letting this lead go, and City had cocked it all up. We went to the pub to drown some sorrows, and then by the time we got there it was 4-2, but then almost immediately 4-3, and then via some live scores updates, Everton had somehow equalized.

But damn, I recall there was still almost 10 minutes left, more if Ferguson had his way, and the joy was tempered by what I knew was coming......my friends went out for a smoke, the tension too much, even though some of them didn't actually smoke – I sat alone in the pub, refreshing a web page for 10 minutes, but that goal never came – suddenly the league was back in City's hands, kind of.

I'll be honest, at full time at Old Trafford, I almost wet myself – proof that other matches do matter – City beat wolves 2-0, relegating them, and never looked back – well apart from that last half hour of the season, but victory was never in doubt, I'm sure you'll agree.

RAHEEM STERLING JOKES AND LAUGHS JUST DAYS AFTER ENGLAND FLOPS DRAW WITH TUNISIA

Bluemoon Podcast Audio Script (from last season)

Every City fan in the world remembers those moments as if it all happened yesterday.
Ninety three minutes on the clock. Desperation has set in. The ball is brought forward and released to Sergio Aguero. He lays it off to Mario Balotelli, who lays it to his side as he falls to the ground. The ball spins free in the area, and Aguero, who has continued his run, takes the ball past a defender, and as the whole world stops on its axis.....

He smashes it over the bar.

City try again to get that elusive goal, but it's too late. United win the league, and Mancini is dismissed soon after losing the FA Cup final to Wigan the following season, City finishing 2nd once more.

Well of course, that's not quite how it all panned out. But what if Aguero, in that precise moment in time, had blazed the ball over the bar? Would Roberto Mancini be considered a failure, a deity for capturing us bitter blues our first trophy in 35 years, or just seen as quite good?

What that moment shows for me is the fine lines of football – in fact it's the greatest ever example of that. And proof for me that managers should not be judged on results alone – perhaps that's something to discuss another time so I'll try and wind this ramble round to video technology instead, eventually.

And then I thought of something else too.

You see, I remember a message board member I considered rather sensible opining a few months back that tactics aren't that important really in the scheme of things, something that made me spit my tea all over my laptop, especially as Chelsea were in the middle of their winning streak after Conte had changed the team's formation with spectacular results. A ridiculous comment, but it sparked some debate on what the factors are for winning not only games but silverware.
Now good players are the obvious first factor, the main one of course, and the manager is second, as he dictates everything, the conductor of

the orchestra, and as Jose Mourinho showed last season or even Claudio Ranieri this season, when they aren't in control, results can really fade away – unless you wish to argue that owners are more important, which I guess is valid for some clubs – I mean it's rather important in our recent history.

There are so many other factors too though, factors specific to some teams and not others. I'll briefly list some in no particular order. Location is one, as I do feel being situated in Madrid makes convincing a top player to join you rather easier than in a rainy city in north England, who in turn can persuade players easier than a manager stationed in Siberia. Location also decides the league you play in, and thus the riches that may be available, which leads back to affording better players. Good marketing can add to revenues, and good scouting and a good youth setup can all be influential.
Another factor is pure luck – teams have been relegated on the bad bounce of a ball or won trophies due to goals that crept over that white line. Seasons and form can turn on one unfortunate injury, and there's often little you can do to affect the fickle hand of fate.

And the reason I mention all this is one factor that is simply too large to ignore now, and is spoiling the game somewhat for me – because as I watched another night of Champions League football, of players picking up yellow cards and 2nd leg suspensions because opposition players threw themselves to the ground at the merest whiff of contact, and as I shook my head at the ridiculous penalty decisions, and thought back to how City had been robbed in so many of the big games this season, the factor that cannot be ignored is referees.

Now to mention City's decisions in big matches will naturally bring out the critics, and the old clichés of every club having decisions go against them, and how it all evens up blah blah. But the fact is that with even decisions in big matches this season, City would probably be in the top 2, and hanging on in the title race, despite all the many flaws we've all decided the team has.

The fact is, the game is too fast and players too happy to deceive for referees not to be assisted. Games are being decided by little moments not of sublime skill, but how a human being interprets two fast moving bodies coming together, or trying to decide if two fast moving athletes moving in opposite directions were in line when a ball from 30 yards away was passed – it's not acceptable for the biggest game on the planet – whether or not City have been unlucky or not this season, it is logical to suggest that a title or a cup will soon be decided on such fine lines, as has happened many times already – you only have to ask Southampton fans how they can have a legitimate goal disallowed in a cup final when the matter could have been resolved in 10 seconds.

Now of course the game's appeal is strengthened by the glorious moment when the ball hits the back of the net and the players wheel away and celebrate, and the crowd go mad, delirious at what has just happened. Imagine Aguero's goal celebrations and those of the crowd v QPR being curtailed for a minute whilst the referee asks the video ref to check for any infringements – the best 10 seconds of my life may have played out slightly different, but hey, the end result would have been the same, and there's too much at stake for us to ignore technology now. There must be a way to make it work, for crucial decisions at least, though not for every single foul.

I'm sick of football a bit right now – not because of the money, and the fact the players live in a bubble – not because of glass tunnels and £6 burgers, not because I am expected to arrive at the ground an hour before kick-off, or because of the horrible feeling City's board will not have the sense to freeze all season ticket prices for next season. No, I'm sick of it because I'm sick of moaning not at performances, which I could easily do quite a lot of the time, and of course have, but about decisions, and the effect they have had. Some will argue sport still needs controversy – that's fine, it's the stuff we talk about around water coolers now, that most people watch TV on streams, iplayers and on catch up – but clearly wrong decisions are not controversial, they're just wrong decisions – and football, in fact any sport in the world is better off when clearly wrong decisions are eradicated.
It's common sense to me, and when so many other sports have already

worked this out, it seems bizarre that the biggest sport of them all is left behind. Let's trial it, let's see how it works – I mean, just imagine the day you see a Raheem Sterling foul rewarded with an actual penalty – that's something to tell your grandkids about.

Article re-visit: I laughed at those that turned their noses up at video technology (VAR), laughed them off as dinosaurs who had to move with the times. I'm not laughing now.

I was a keen supporter of video technology, and do not dismiss it now, as trials are there to iron out problems, but the problems have been plentiful. In its early incarnation, it seems designed for a TV audience, like much of the sport nowadays. If this technology is going to work, those actually at the game need to be informed of what is going on.

But the main problem is one alluded to in the old article – it takes away the eruption of pure joy experienced when your team scores a goal. The solution is hard to ascertain – a system that looks at just clear offsides or blatant mistakes is where this will hopefully lead. But the naysayers will have a field day whilst we try and iron out this brave new world.

Duncan Forts Article – Daily Record
(possibly a spoof, but how could you tell?)

Have no doubt that Pep's current Manchester City side are at times a joy to watch, but when you dig deeper, you realise that the football is not as pure as some might have you believe, a view proliferated by the Pep acolytes (as many call them) that dominate the media. There are two areas that stand out when you look at their performances.

Firstly, City clearly like to apply the "dark arts" at certain sections of matches, and the statistics back this up.

City's left-sided players foul opposition players between the 45th and 60th minutes of midweek matches in October more than any other Premier League side, more in fact than any team since records began*. Their average fouls by left-sided players shortly after half-time in midweek matches in October (AFBLSMSAHTMMIO) is 2.4, well Clear of the next highest team, Burnley, who average 2.394. By comparison, Jose Mourinho's so-called "dour" tactics brought an average AFBLSMSAHTMMIO of a mere 2.04, despite Mourinho focusing a lot of play down that side of the pitch. This is a very revealing stat, and suggests that as the season entered a crucial stage, when challenges are made or wither away in the autumn mulch, Pep Guardiola was instructing his players to tactically foul opposition right-sided players early in 2nd halves to retain control of matches. Manchester City players received a single yellow card in this section of midweek matches in October, showing an unusual leniency from match officials, effectively allowing City "carte blanche" to continue with this policy unchecked.

(*yesterday)

Secondly, a look at City's purchases reveals an interesting anomaly when analysing signing on fees paid to the agents of players born in Yorkshire on a weekday. It shoes a skewed market that favours the oil money funds used to collect City's band of highly-paid players from the north of England.
This is interesting and important to City's success for two reasons: firstly, because Jose, I mean I, say so. And secondly, because by targeting

agents of players from Yorkshire, an area that has produced an abnormally large number of England players, City have gained an advantage over other clubs. Some might argue an unfair advantage. What's more, according to the Institute of Transfer Laboratories (ITL), City have paid more on Yorkshire-born footballers in the past two years than Manchester United have in their entire history. It is little surprise therefore that Jose Mourinho feels he cannot compete financially with his council house neighbours across town.

RAHEEM STERLING FLAUNTS WEALTH BY BUYING YET ANOTHER HOUSE

for sister

Human Rights – December 2017

How are you enjoying the latest phase of City bashing, the increasing desperation to find something, anything to have a go at City for? The sheikhs never got bored, the oil never ran out, the empty seats started appearing everywhere, the winning run never ended, the 1st big test they encountered was passed, as was the 2nd, 3rd and 4th. Even the lottery of penalties couldn't bring down the evil pep empire.

The big clubs, not that we are one to some, are there to be got at, that's the price you pay for being at the top table, having the money and the players and the coverage. Still, some attempts to get at a team playing this well have been rather amusing. There's the little things – like claiming that Ederson hasn't made a save yet, so let's not judge him until he has, or suggesting more seriously that the team must be doping, cos they keep running around and doing better than other teams. How dare they. It's almost as if we have excellent squad depth. The players that were overpriced mercenaries are now priced correctly but explain why we are doing well cos we spent so much on the best, thus corrupting the league, and if pep really wanted a challenge he should go manage Barnsley. I hear their chops are excellent.

All this started with a classic case of the media creating its own narrative, then arguing with itself until we were all bored to death. Questions began to be asked by certain members of the print and TV media, never by City fans, only by the media, if this City side, yet to win anything those season, not that it's possible to before New Year, was the greatest in Premier League history, because as we all know, football began in 1992. To repeat myself, whilst the odd City fan may wonder if it's the best City side ever, very few cared one jot, at this stage at least, in comparing it with great teams.
Anyway, some in the media thought it was the best, which is not that surprising when the current City side is breaking not only Premier League records on what feels like a weekly basis, but also top flight records too, and with a couple more wins, European records even. Anyway, this naturally created a huge backlash by outraged fans defending their own teams greatest sides, some tedious debates, and some seemed incredulous the side currently breaking all records known to men could somehow be considered one of the greats, especially with all the cash spent and all that, the great sides of the past of course constructed with peanuts from a bunch of plucky part timers brought

together on a hope and a prayer.
Don't forget to put that asterisk next to all City achievements.

The latest phase of City bashing could be considered the most serious -
the human rights records of our owners. This got a few City fans
confused, arguing that our own country has an appalling record on
human rights, but that's irrelevant, our government does not own a
football club.

This is not a topic that can be flippantly dismissed -well in reality it can –
some City fans don't care in the slightest, as my quick questionnaire this
week proved - we rather lose our moral compass when lording it over
other football fans is concerned, all football fans would to some degree,
or perhaps you could argue that if we didn't care before, and most
British people do not have sleepless nights over what is happening in
other countries, which rightly or wrongly is not surprising, they've got
enough to worry about, so they could argue why start caring when
ownership of a football club is concerned. City are after all an
investment for our owners, just like buying Barclays shares was, and I
doubt anyone has been boycotting that bank, I doubt few fans care
about the sweatshops where their kits are made, or with United's
sponsorship deals with the same country, their new tie up with Russian
state owned Aeroflot, the Qatari ownership of Paris Saint Germain, their
sponsorship of Barcelona, who remember are more than a club, or
voting for a government arming much of the middle east suffering, and
on and on and on. I'd mention Chelsea's owner, but I'm too scared to.
Do we question ownership, but allow sponsorship deals with such
countries? Where should the line be drawn?
I welcome concern over human rights, we all should, we should fight for
more equality across the globe, just be consistent, and also understand
that the way another country is run may seem alien to you, but it does
not make it wrong, which is a general point on my behalf, not a specific
point ABOUT my club's owners. Anyway, I look forward to everyone
refusing to watch the 2022 world cup on principle, and the boycotting of
the tournament by a raft of players.

Still it's great to see so many football fans who wouldn't have previously
even raised an eyebrow at the slaughter of thousands on a weekly basis

around the world suddenly take up such a keen interest in human rights in the Middle East,

And be such experts in such complicated matters too. And what convenient timing too for such a discussion to take place. Still, our owners, whatever good or bad they are up to, and I don't have the answers, are now more in the spotlight more than ever, so that's no bad thing. People with a greater understanding of geopolitics and morals will have to explain further whether we should be protesting in the streets at what out owners do in their home country, or whether we are all hypocrites. I wish I cared more, but I don't, I've always been a voyeur, watching my team through bad and good with no input in their fortunes, my pennies making little difference to things, so I'll leave the arguments to others. I just know they're damn fine businessmen, and football is of course now a business, a very lucrative one at that.

But we football fans are so desperate for success, we'd definitely lower our morals if it suited. When Thaksin Shinawatra took over City, we were really desperate as a fan base. I knew little about him, but as details emerged of his tough love ruling style, I sought evidence that it was not as bad as it seems – cognitive dissonance I think they call it, views that I found discomforting soon swept aside – thank god though he only stayed one season, because even I would have struggled with that man in charge for a long period, and a million free curries in Albert Square would not have changed that. Well a bit maybe, but my point stands. – if your team is in the doldrums and a rich benefactor comes along, questions are not asked – you are generally thankful, hell even an Italian dictator with a Hitler moustache named Mugabe would probably pass all fit and proper tests.

But as I have already alluded to, I am no expert in Middle Eastern politics, so perhaps I should move on, and contemplate what phase 12 of the "anyone but City" crowd will have lined up for us.

Phase 1 for Duncan Castles has been to suddenly lose his internet connection, but there will always be others ready to step in and take up the reins. With each victory comes new angles, new hot-takes, new opportunities for united fans convinced Mourinho took over a much worse squad than pep to tell themselves that this domination will not last. With all papers covering the unsurprising news that city want van dijk, sanchez and a Yaya Toure replacement too, they may have to get very creative in the coming months.

MANCHESTER CITY SPEND IS GREATER THAN THAT FOR HS2, TRIDENT AND US DEFENCE BUDGET (COMBINED) – AND IT CONTINUES TO GROW

Writing exclusively for the Trafford Advertiser, Duncan Forts explains in simple factual ways just how Manchester City have ruined football for everyone, forever, especially the magnificent, proud, noble, non-greying, erect tactician Jose Mourinho.

Premier League: Swansea City 0 Manchester City 4

Ederson, Danilo, Otamendi, Mangala, Delph, De Bruyne, Fernandinho, Silva, Bernardo Silva, Agüero, Sterling

Well that went as well as could be expected!

City maintain their 11 point lead at the top, and more records are broken, as we shall see shortly. Two goals too for David Silva, who Pep refers to as an "animal" – of the nice variety.

That didn't need clarification – all animals are nice.

Such was City's dominance, there wasn't even time to worry about old boy Bony coming back to haunt us. Not that it was that likely, let's be honest.

Swansea threatened briefly, but once David Silva had put City head, there was little doubt about the outcome of this match. Whilst Ayew had tested Ederson, Fernandinho had also had a good volley well-saved by Fabianski.

And what a great opening goal too – a lovely cross from Bernardo Silva, and a delightful flick into the net from David. The defending was appalling however.

If Swansea weren't already up against it already, then they certainly were when a free-kick from Kevin De Bruyne from the left went straight in. Game pretty much over.

For all of City's dominance this season so far, City took a half-time 2 goal lead for the 1st time in almost 2 months.

It could have been much worse for the home side. Aguero forced a good save in the first half, then Silva missed a sitter early in the 2nd half after some lovely passing sliced open the Swansea defence once more. A third goal seemed inevitable.

David Silva just missed out on poking in the ball after Fabianski saved from Aguero, again, but soon got his 2nd of the match as Sterling supplied him and he waltzed through a demoralised defence and lifted the ball over the keeper. It was a beautiful, delicate finish that history will forget in a season of so many outstanding moments.

All that was left was for Aguero to shoot wide, Ederson to superbly save a deflected shot and for Aguero to finally get the goal his all-round game has deserved after a scintillating run.

Victory brought more records – the longest winning run ever in the top flight of English football – Pep Guardiola teams hold the same record in Spain and Germany.

Arsenal , Spurs and Liverpool are now closer to the relegation zone than they are to City.

Arsenal are closer to the bottom team Swansea than they are to City.

City have a better goal difference than Liverpool, Spurs and Leicester combined.

City are averaging over 3 goals per game.

46 - Manchester City already have more points than they have managed in six of their previous 20 completed Premier League seasons - 93-94, 95-96, 00-01, 03-04, 05-06 & 06-07.

David Silva has been involved in 13 Premier League goals in 17 games this season (five goals, eight assists) - already more than in the whole of 2016-17 (11 goal involvements in 34 games)

Just the 79% possession for City this time around. Unacceptable.

STAN COLLYMORE – MY ROLE IN THE 4-3 WIN OVER NEWCASTLE – AND WHY PEP CAN ONLY DREAM OF MASTERMINDING SUCH A VICTORY!

Manchester City 4 Tottenham Hotspur 1

A joyous day as City dominated a team that has posed so many problems in the past. Of greater relief though was the fact City didn't have two key attacking players out for the rest of the season as match officials once more failed to protect City players on the pitch.

No David Silva, which is always a concern, but we couldn't complain with the available alternatives.

City started brightly, and you could tell that this was going to be a great match, for the neutral at least.

As for the first goal, what I imagine history will judge as a collector's item – a Gundogan header. The Spurs defending wasn't the best, but the goal, a precise contact that sent the ball into the bottom corner to the right of Lloris was a classic case of the theory that sometimes standing still is better than snaking around the area trying to find space. Gundogan had the tiniest of runs from the penalty spot and the corner duly found him in acres of space. 1-0.

And the confidence an early goal can give a team cannot be underestimated. City looked lively from the start, but were now looking super-confident, swarming all over the opposition defence. Sane was at his best, Aguero had a shot parried and Sterling thrashed the follow-up over the bar when he should have at least hit the target.

That dominance was not converted into further goals though, and a Kane shot that curled just past the far post was a stark reminder that the home side could not rest on their laurels, carrying a solitary goal lead into the break.

This was made even clearer at the start of the 2nd half, when the visitors had their strongest period, their only brief spell of domination during the 90 minutes. Ederson saved a long-range Kane shot, Spurs threatened around the box, but most importantly, Spurs should have been down to 10 men.

And later on, 9.

Two challenges by Spurs players that were so clearly red cards it's not even open to debate – a lunge from Kane on Sterling that left studs on lower leg could easily have broken bones, and Sterling is probably fortunate it did not. The referee had no idea, facing in the opposite direction. I don't know if he liaised with his linesman, but a yellow card was a cop out.

Perhaps the Alli challenge on De Bruyne wasn't quite as clear on first viewing but it certainly was on the replays – another disgraceful, dangerous tackle from someone who is certainly "that type of player", a petulant, nasty rat who gets away with it because he is English perhaps, like Kane before him.

Either way, City did not need the man or two-man advantage, and gradually took control. Before the goals though, another of those Sterling misses. Sane forced a save from Lloris with a stinging shot, and it fell just to the left of Sterling who reached and somehow, from a few yards out, poked the ball over the bar. The flag may have been raised, but he was not offside, and it was a bad miss.

Never mind, because with 20 minutes to go, Kevin De Bruyne came to the rescue, reminding us he can shoot better with his weaker foot (left), than most Premier League players can with either foot. A rocket of a shot that Lloris could only parry into the back of the net. Breathing space for City.

Four minutes later and it should have been three. Let's be honest, De Bruyne's fall under a challenge was soft, one of those I'd be apoplectic about if it happened against us, but is generally, for reasons that escape me, largely accepted in the game by pundits and professionals alike nowadays. It shouldn't be.

So perhaps some karma as Jesus hit the post, and for good measure we had another poor Sterling miss as he hit the rebound over the bar.

But soon Sterling, who had been electric, but finished atrociously made amends from a distance even he couldn't miss from, as Sane's beautiful low cross found him just yards out and he carefully guided the ball into the net. City rampant, and the game was now over as a contest, and this would be City's 16th consecutive Premier League victory. Astonishing.

And if Sterling couldn't miss the third goal, he could have scored the 4th goal blind-folded. A horrendous mix up between Lloris and Dier allowed Sterling the luxury of almost walking the ball into the net. Spurs' heads had gone as soon as the 2nd goal had gone in.

Such a shame then that City could not also take away a clean sheet from this game. Eriksen's late shot did not seem particularly powerful from outside the area but it was precise and evaded the hand of Ederson. Still, not much to complain about after yet another satisfying day as a City fan.

It would be unfair to single out players in such a complete performance, but it was good to see Sane back to his best, and he terrorised Trippier (who, lest we forget, is better than Walker) all afternoon.

And so City go 14 points clear, with United still to play West Brom the following day. Two points dropped in 18 games is hard to fathom.

And an important caveat for Raheem Sterling. It soon emerged that earlier that day Sterling had been the subject of racial abuse outside City's training ground. It takes "balls" to then dust yourself down and play an important football game later that day, so perhaps on this occasion we should excuse the odd miss. After what he has been through in recent years, it's sometimes a surprise he is even up to kicking a football at all.

It's natural for us to pour scorn on the ex-United pundits that are everywhere right now, especially when we consider the dour, slapped-arse faces of the likes of Paul Scholes and Ryan Giggs when discussing City victories in the past. But few pundits have been more complimentary than Rio Ferdinand, who was gushing about City's performance and especially Kevin De Bruyne (who covered more ground, 12km, than any player) after the match on BT's coverage. As he rightly pointed out, City's play tires out opposition teams both physically and mentally. And as he also said on another occasion – "Manchester

City is the best team in the world".
Even I wouldn't have claimed that.

Some Words On David

All we knew initially was that David Silva was absent for personal reasons. People probed, wanting to know why. Normally this would annoy me intently. Mind your own business. But then we're all emotionally involved with David Silva. Any problem for him is a problem for me.

What's more, I know nothing of his private life, and have never needed to. So knowing so little just made me, or others, rather more anxious. Anyway, eventually the truth emerged via Silva himself. He was a father, but his child had been born prematurely, and was very ill. It was horrible news to hear, but Silva was full of hope. It was good to know the truth too not just out of nosiness, but because of some of the scurrilous rumours that had been drifting around the internet, as is always the case in situations like this.

Suddenly, football was put in context. Gundogan not tracking back or City's failure to buy a third striker had never seemed more irrelevant. Silva shuttled back and forth between Spain and England, missing other matches when necessary, such as Crystal Palace and Newcastle. City's league dominance allowed such flexibility, but the league dominance was irrelevant - there are always more important things in life. The baby survived, and has fought his way to health and happiness.

When City won the league, the most touching tweet of all came from David, as he celebrated with a picture of him cradling his child. It was a beautiful moment during a wonderful day.

There are two things that I must add here. Firstly, credit to the club and Pep for how they handled the situation. You could argue that it is base levels of decency to allow a player off in such circumstances, but nevertheless it was reassuring to see a compassionate and understanding response from the club, and the togetherness that prompted tributes from certain players, such as Kevin De Bruyne after one particular goal.

But most importantly, though it hardly seemed possible, my opinion of David Silva has been lifted even further. Somehow. Silva must have been going through hell, but he never relented in his commitment to the side. Flying back to England he would step onto the pitch and put in a focused, skilful display as if nothing was amiss. He didn't have to. Many others would not have been able to cope, and we'd think no less of them for that.

But David Silva, throughout such a difficult time, never flinched once. He really is a giant of man.

I wish him and his family all the future happiness in the world.

OBSCENE! RAHEEM STERLING FLAUNTS WEALTH BY BRAZENLY ORDERING TWO KFC BUCKET MEALS IN FRONT OF STARTLED ONLOOKERS

By Showbiz Reporter

£50m striker Raheem Sterling has shocked locals in a Manchester suburb after flaunting his wealth once more in a KFC in the poverty-stricken town of Stockport.

Black Sterling, who is thought to earn over £150,000 a week, probably, sauntered into the fast food outlet at 6pm on Thursday evening.

FORGOT HIS ROOTS

Robert Dunn, 34, a bricklayer from Offerton, was chomping on a chicken nugget when Sterling strolled in.
"I saw his flash car screech into the car park and immediately guessed that it would be an arrogant footballer. And I was right."

Robert had got up to get a napkin when Sterling BARGED past him.
"He strolled in as if he owned the place. He didn't say 'do you know who I am?' but you could see it in his eyes. He didn't actually touch me, but he wasn't far off knocking me to the floor and spilling my Pepsi Max, which for some reason I had with me when looking for a napkin."

BRAZEN WEALTH

Coloured Sterling flaunted his wealth by ordering two bucket meals and extra fries on the side. He then further angered onlookers by DEMANDING a BBQ dip, and paying with cash, which may have been a £50 note.

He then angered staff further by REQUESTING information on where the straws were, changing his drink option, asking the over-worked counter staff to swap a gravy for coleslaw, then FAILED to put a straw wrapper in the bin. The wrapper was later binned by a flustered customer.

BITTER BERTIES

Evelyn McSporran, 47, who is between jobs, was APPALLED by his behavior.

"These footballers think they are above the rest of us. His attitude stunk. He was laughing and joking with friends, which seems pretty disrespectful when England haven't won anything in over 50 years and the country is on its arse."
"To be honest, I didn't even know who he was," said Evelyn. "I'm more into X Factor and renaissance paintings. I think there's a U in behaviour by the way."

Stockport is one of the poorest boroughs of Greater Manchester. The area is known for being where most of City fans come from, and the locals are renowned for their moustaches and poor fashion sense. And that's just the women etc. etc....

EMPTIHAD

Many think non-white Sterling should be keeping a lower profile, this latest incident coming just three years after his ACRIMONIOUS move to City from Liverpool, who made him the player he is. Sterling recently bought his 19th car of the year, and bought another house, when most struggle to buy one.

Carabao Cup Quarter Final – Leicester City 1 Manchester City 1 – Manchester City win 4-3 on penalties

City are going to Wembley! Oh no hang on, that's the other cup.

A stressful night in City's 4th most important trophy hunt.
Satisfying nevertheless, as City progress to the semi-final having barely hit 2nd gear throughout the tournament.

I watched this in the ground from the comfort of a corporate box of a Leicester-supporting friend. It was an interesting night, for sure.

City's weakened team was no surprise. But it's fair to say that the Leicester fans in the party were not impressed with the Claude Puel sending out a weakened team too. For them, this represented not only Leicester's best chance of a trophy, but also the best route into Europe. For Puel to thus relegate its importance did not go down well.

City's team: Bravo, Danilo, Adarabioyo, Mangala, Zinchenko, Gundogan, Yaya, Foden, Bernardo Silva, Jesus, Diaz

And because of the weakened side, the game was something of a mess. It was frustrating too, watching the blue hordes in the opposite corner, whilst I sat here restrained drinking crap lager. How ungrateful of me.

Always good to see our youngsters play, watch the develop, but there's always that feeling inside me of wanting to see our best team out there putting the opposition to the sword, even in the Carabao Cup. Stupid of me, but there you go.

As always, our youngsters did fine, but I find it difficult to assess past that. They are learning, and are not going to dominate matches at their age. It's just a case of wait and see. They were certainly not overawed, but I can't make conclusions on their career paths from a match like this.

City had that little extra class though, taking the lead after 26 minutes when Gundogan burst towards the penalty area and expertly laid it off for Bernardo Silva to slot home. With two further chances soon after, he could have added to his tally.

The 2nd half meandered nowhere in particular, at times seeming like both teams weren't overly keen to be there. Leicester brought on their big guns though, so maybe Puel did want this trophy after all. City did well to repel the twin threat of Vardy and Mahrez however.

And then we got our reminder of why this sport sometimes makes you tear your hair out and want to smash up items in your vicinity. Welcome back to an old friend, Bobby Madley.

By now Dele-Bashiru was on the pitch along with Nmecha, replacing Foden and Diaz.

And in the 81st minute, on came Kyle Walker. This is highly relevant.

But back to Madley. I try my hardest, I really do, not to slag off referees. I supported video technology because I acknowledge that referees are human, mistakes can be made, and the game has never been faster, so they need help.

Madley can go to hell though. The incompetence of this man is hard to put into words. Nothing will surpass his performance in the Everton league match, but this went close. I can only assume Kyle Walker has been sleeping with his wife, because there's no other logical reason for his repeated hatchet jobs on City's right back.

Firstly, the board went up for 8 minutes. In a game of no significant stoppages I can recall, this simply made no sense whatsoever. The Leicester fans I were with looked as puzzled as me.

And then the penalty decision, late on in that injury time. I am short-sighted and sat at the opposite end of the stadium, and I could see it was a dive. But not Madley. Everyone with me could see it was not a penalty. But not Madley. The man is a buffoon.

And so with that incompetence, 30 extra minutes of nerves and nail-biting in a game I had told myself didn't really matter. And for good measure, a yellow card for diving for Walker after he was brought down in the area. You really couldn't make this up.

But thankfully City seem to be quite good at penalties. Another shoot-out, another win. Bravo came to the rescue again, and as soon as Yaya stepped up, I wanted to tell everyone around me that he had never missed one, but thought better of it. It was made all the sweeter seeing Vardy miss his. I looked on enviously as the away fans celebrated wildly. City through, and I celebrated silently.

Oh, and one more thing Madley. We were told by our hosts that if the game did not go to extra-time, we would be going for some fancy steak dinner at a country house where the Leicester team were probably staying. So that went out the window. Idiot. Thankfully the Indian I had near Filbert Street was one of the best ever, so the night was saved.

Manchester City 4 Bournemouth 0

Another routine win, another notch on the winning run, and perhaps most importantly, a 13 point lead at the top, as United stumbled at the King Power stadium, drawing 2-2 with Leicester City. Fred Done has surely paid out on us now.

Aguero did what he does best, as speculation resurfaced about his relationship with Guardiola, scoring two and assisting another. As always, Pep reiterated afterwards that Sergio will decide when he leaves, and no one else. Savour every minute.

The visitors frustrated City for a while, but the result was rarely in doubt. Aguero headed in two, the first from a nice Fernandinho cross as Cook played him onside. Assisted a nice Sterling goal and Danilo even chipped in with the 4th as Sterling set him free. A stroll for City, and even at this stage the title race is beginning to look like a procession. As a natural pessimist however, I am of course not counting my chickens.

And thus City become the first English top-flight team to score 100 goals in a calendar year since Liverpool in 1982.

Of course this is the festive period, and there was simply no rest for any teams – next up was Newcastle United.

Newcastle United 0 Manchester City 1

A narrow victory it would seem, but as is always the case at the most hectic part of the season, the result is all that counts. Job done, as City continue to accumulate points, suffocating their rivals more with each passing game.

And because the games come thick and fast, how can we really evaluate players? We Brits love the festive programme, it's what makes this the best league in the world, so I am repeatedly told. Strip away the emotion though and it is truly ridiculous, and the December 2017 schedule most certainly had one game too many in it.

The calls for a winter break or an easier schedule are valid because playing this often quite simply increases the chance of player injury – and no one wants that, surely? A packed schedule also favours the big boys, as our squads go "deeper". Anyway, no doubt a break will eventually be brought in, and blizzards will hit the country two days after it ends.

The match itself did not long in my memory. Perhaps this was due to it being Boxing Day (well, almost) and the fact I was inebriated. So inebriated in fact that a cash machine swallowed my bank card as I slumped against it, I had to borrow money, then realised a week later you can get money out of a cash machine without a card. You learn something new every day.

Anyway, City got over the line in this one against an organised, defensive home side, a set up that clearly frustrated Guardiola. City still managed 21 shots and 78% possession, but it did not feel like we peppered their goal. City were clearly the dominant side however.

Sterling once more was the saviour with the crucial goal on the half-hour, and Newcastle only rallied late on, though Otamendi did have to make one goal-line clearance. City had more than enough chances to have put this bed earlier however, with De Bruyne striking the post and hitting another shot wide.

The only downside to the day was another injury to Kompany. Sadly this is little more than we expect from our captain by now. I expect that's another month or more out for him.

And that is 18 league wins on the bounce. Astonishing. The lead too at the top is extended to 15 points, and it was City's 11th away win in a row too. United had, quite hilariously, drawn 2-2 at home to Burnley the day before.

Random stat: Nicolas Otamendi completed 122 passes for Man City in this match - seven more than all the outfield players of Newcastle managed combined (115).

I still am not counting my chickens, but most neutrals will probably now accept that before the year is out, this title race is over.

Which is nice.

MUTV Listings

9:00: Bargain Hunt - Ed Woodward explains how United captured ex-academy player Paul Pogba for a mere £89m.

9:45: Escape To The Country – a selection of United fans explain their plans for the 14th May, the day of the trophy parade.

10:30: Flog It! – Transfer news – We discuss the imminent sales of Pogba, Fellaini, Rashford, Martial, Darmian, Blind, Smalling and many, many more.

11:00: Through The Keyhole – Hosted by Martin Edwards.

11:30: The Chase – A review of United's futile title challenge.

12:30: FILM: The Dark Knight – Video footage of Alex Ferguson watching Manchester United matches post-retirement.

14:00: FILM – 12 Angry Men – An exclusive "behind the scenes" look inside the United dressing room.

16:00: Great Railway Journeys – We tag along with a group of United fans as they travel to a home match.

17:00: Family Guy – An exclusive interview with Ryan Giggs

17:30: Billions – We examine just how much money the Glazers have leeched out of Manchester United.

18:00; Home And Away – Another exclusive interview with Ryan Giggs.

19:00: Top Gear – An exclusive investigation into how Manchester City doped their way to the Premier League title.

20:00: Last Of The Summer Whine – Coverage of Jose Mourinho's pre-season press conference.

23:00: FILM – Downfall – A look at the post-Ferguson years.

Crystal Palace 0 Manchester City 0

And so the year ended in rather brutal fashion, with a minute of action you'd struggle to find in the entirety of some other matches.

City finally hit a brick wall against a team that performed excellently and restricted City in terms of chances, if not possession.

It wasn't that surprising really – the schedule over Xmas and New Year is something I have already touched on, and records show that a team has very rarely taken full points over this period, however good they may be. Science has proved that a human body needs a certain amount of rest after strenuous activity. Playing Palace then Watford two days after does not allow such rest, and should not be allowed.

Apologies for repeating myself.

Still, I write this a day after the game, and it could have been much, much worse. Kevin De Bruyne has thankfully escaped serious injury, somehow, though Puncheon is out for the season. Karma you might say, but I wouldn't feel comfortable wishing serious injuries on anyone, not even a guy in court this week on assault charges. Still, I won't lose much sleep over his injury either.

As for Jesus, we are guessing at the amount of time he will be out, but his tears as he left the pitch suggested a season-ending injury, and the early diagnosis of a medial ligament injury that requires no surgery is probably the best we could have hoped for. After a few underwhelming performances let's hope that his words on Instagram are correct, and that 2018 is indeed his year.

As for Jon Moss, you begin to run out of words to describe refereeing performances like his. Refusing a physio onto the pitch for Jesus was a disgrace in itself, the penalty decision little better. Thank god justice was done, and bravo Ederson, so to speak.

One small point that might have been overlooked in the carnage of that last minute or two – when City broke, Aguero could have passed right to Sterling, who was hurtling forward in acres of space. Who knows, if he had, we might have had another famous last-minute winning goal. Aguero chose very badly. But never mind, it is hardly the end of the world.

This was City's first away goalless draw in the Premier League since March 2016 against Norwich City, ending a run of 34 matches in which at least one goal was scored.

Only two teams have won more Premier League points in a calendar year than City in 2017 (98) - Man Utd in 1993 (102) and Chelsea in 2005 (101).

Palace have only lost one of their past 10 Premier League games (W3 D6), having lost 13 of their 16 before this run.

Hodgson has now failed to see his side score in his past five Premier League matches against Man City (D2 L3), a goalless run that stands at 465 minutes.

This was Palace's fourth clean sheet in their past eight Premier League games, as many as they had managed in their 25 matches prior to this.

City goalkeepers have saved 10 of the past 17 penalties they've faced in all competitions, with four different goalkeepers saving those 10 (Joe Hart, Claudio Bravo, Willy Caballero and Ederson).

Wayne Hennessey was the first Palace goalkeeper since Nigel Martyn in May 1993 to keep a Premier League clean sheet against City.

Palace have missed five penalties since the start of last season, two more than any other Premier League side.

2018

Manchester City 3 Watford 1

Another balmy winter night in Manchester - where else would you rather be than at the Etihad, sat in the freezing cold as the roof supposed to protect you drips increasing amounts of water onto your head? Nowhere, that's where!

After the feisty end to the Palace match and the rare loss of points, I hoped that City would be fired up for this one, to reassert their domination of the league, and it was reassuring to see the old gang back together – well, most if it anyway. Delph back, Kevin De Bruyne indestructible, Silva back from Spain and John Stones returned too. The rest of the team picked itself.

Still, the weather was sporadically appalling, and I always worry that such conditions are a leveller, added to the ridiculous 1 day gap between games. So it was nice to get the 3rd quickest goal in our Premier League history, and the nerves were duly settled. Nice run from Sane, nice cross, and Sterling as always was in the right place.

An own goal later and a miss from Stones that should have nestled in the back of the net and City were cruising. De Bruyne hit the bar and the game was going how I had hoped. Watford had their chances though, and it didn't seem quite as inevitable as some previous games – Bournemouth for example.

But you know what? City won, that's all that matters – the Xmas schedule, the fatigue, the narrow avoidance of serious injuries, it all makes analysis irrelevant, when games come every few days, when players are dropping left, right and centre, and City yet again could have scored far more goals than they actually did.

And so after the third goal from Aguero, who was just about onside, it was no surprise that Pep made substitutions, and this seemed to unsettle the side, and the team tried to coast over the line. Thus, the last 10 minutes was a tad nervy, but job done. Aguero himself still underwhelmed for me, but with Jesus absent until an Easter resurrection, he will get his game time, and needs to show what he is made of.

Anyway, a new year, with new hope. It's already shaping up to be a belter. 2017 underwhelmed, but it got better as it progressed, because this is a team that is really stretching its legs now. Happy times ahead, hopefully.

Bluemoon Audio Script

And so another year comes to an end, a year that it's fair to say aged well like a fine wine or Susannah Hoffs. The bald fraud from Catalonia it turned out wasn't that flummoxed by the Premier League after all – it's probably worth reminiscing for a minute or two.

To be honest, if we're picking highlights of 2017, they are rather crammed into the last 4 months, though there's enough in that period alone to fill one of City's old season review DVDs or VHSs a few times over.

City's 5-3 win over Monaco was one of the most entertaining matches I had ever attended, it was everything being a football fan was about, but City crashed out on away goals after the 3nd leg, so in the end it counted for little.

City limped to 3rd place in the league, and there was more disappointment in a cup competition with the hugely underwhelming defeat to arsenal at Wembley in the FA Cup, Arsene Wenger once more getting just enough out of his team to retain his job. In the end though my city endured tragedy that really put things into perspective – it just didn't seem to matter that much for a while.

The summer saw the expected clear out, the old guard despatched to all corners of the globe, and West Ham. City's squad needed to be younger, and younger it became. Let's be honest, doubts had crept in amongst many that Pep didn't really understand this league, we'd fallen for some of the red-top bravado, the likes of Neil Custis desperate for him to fail, but with every new season comes hope, and City's summer signings certainly helped fuel that. This team seemed far more dynamic.

So, as for this season? Well, and I should warn you of a spoiler alert, it's gone quite well, all things considered. In fact, it has gone so well that it's hard to comprehend some of the statistics, it's hard to comprehend dropping 2 points at Crystal Palace as I'd kind of forgotten how that felt. I even felt a tad stressed at one point in the end, but for now the invincibles roll on. Even the powers that be are warming the balls in our favour now, and City couldn't have asked for pleasanter draws in the Champions League and Carabao Cup.

And what was different than what went before, from this manager or previous ones, was the improvement of existing players – there was hardly a player that has not pushed on this season, and what's more Pep was a manager who made changes during games, vital games that shifted tough positions in our favour, even though some of the changes were barely visible to the average football fan's eye.

City's success has naturally brought with it a natural backlash against such excellence. We've gone full circle from empty seats to bought success to denigrating the strength of the league to accusations of doping to corrupting the league to human rights and back to empty seats. It's been brilliant. The latest narrative has been to rewrite history and claim Mourinho has had a bigger building job than Pep, which is basically a lie, and the opposite of what many of these people were saying in August, when they predicted glory ahead for Jose, as he always wins the league in his 2nd season, remember.
And thus, as Mourinho slowly morphs into Michael Douglas in Falling Down, let's not forget the media reporting that United's board were feeding stories not long ago that they wanted him to stay for over a decade, yet as I write this, the Daily Mail fear he may resign at the end of the season. It's not as if he isn't clearly trying to engineer his exit anyway.

Whatever, City have effectively, once you take in goal difference, a 16 point lead in the league with 16 games to go. it's astonishing, so let's not be surprised that rival fans, especially United fans used to being the school ground bully, who helped set up the Champions League and the Premier League and Financial Fair Play to help maintain their own dominance and who used to hoover up all the best players from other clubs, are now scraping around for something to criticise, especially as their odious manager embarrasses the club he is supposed to serve on an almost daily basis, to the point that many United fans I have spoken to have had enough of his drivel and of his playing style too. Some would simply point out he's the perfect fit for his club. It's almost too good to be true – even in my wildest dreams, and when we were crap some of those dreams were very wild, could I have imagined a scenario like this. May it last for a long time.

So what of 2018?

A league, a trophy parade through town that will be much smaller than any of United's, and hopefully some cup glory too. A bright future for a bright team, as long as we don't sign Jonny Evans (I mean, seriously?!).

Jose Mourinho will morph further into Alan Partridge, locking himself in his hotel room for days at an end, bringing an over-sized plate to the all you can eat buffet and narrating scything put downs into his dictaphone, before emailing some cherry-picked stats and thoughts over to Duncan Castles. He'll treat himself to a new Vauxhall Zafira with heated seats to cheer himself up, but it won't work.

Duncan himself will publish a fascinating article for the Daily Record about how Jose Mourinho was the true success of the 2017/18 season, as he had more points per player born in Greater Manchester on a Tuesday than Pep, and by a long way. He was also hampered claims Duncan by a board that would only give him £400m to spend. Then in a long read that took him most of the year to write, Duncan will go through in excruciating detail every tactical foul and incorrect decision that went City's way during their triumphant season.

The World Cup will be enjoyed by all, because human rights aren't that important when it doesn't involve City, and England's players, knackered from 9 months of gruelling football, will bravely bow out on penalties in the first knockout round to an injury-ravaged Saudi Arabia.
Raheem Sterling, injured for the whole tournament, will cop most of the blame, and the Sun will run a front page exposé of him laughing a mere five days after England's defeat, whilst splashing the cash, brazen as you like, on a KFC bucket meal, with large fries.

Stan Collymore, after leaving a number of increasingly bizarre rants on Pep Guardiola's answer machine, will take out a full page advert in the

Metro claiming he's not bothered if Pep knows him, and he never rated him anyway.

And then there's next season. Giggsy given the United job until the end of the season, Pep's squad strengthened further, all players wanting to join little old Citeh, to work with Pep, to feel that fine rain that soaks you through. Imagine a manager with that lure. The future's bright, the futures blue, sky blue, laser blue, with a bit of maroon thrown in for good measure.

Arsene will still be there of course, he'll never leave, destined to spend eternity on the bench shouting at 4th officials and fiddling with his oversized coat zip. Conte will have gone, back to warmer climes, but Harry Redknapp will bemoan not replacing him, Sean Dyche too. Then City will start the season well, and once more the world will mourn the death of top flight football. And we'll laugh ourselves to sleep once more.

And so a happy new year to you all, may it be blessed with wealth, health, many many City wins, and much love to David Silva and his new born son.

(I was wrong about Arsene!)

FA Cup 3rd Round: Manchester City 4 Burnley 1

The FA Cup doesn't matter, eh? A capacity crowd, the highest crowd of that day's FA Cup matches, saw a game of two halves.
Kicked out of my normal seat in the 3rd tier of the south stand, I have to admit the ground looks even nicer from the other end.

Much of the debate during the week revolved around how Pep would use his squad over the subsequent three games – one FA Cup match, one Carabao Cup game, and of course the visit to Anfield.

As it happened, the team put out by Pep was stronger than I could have predicted, and Sean Dyche put out a pretty strong team too, despite warning of resting tired players. Thankfully both set of fans got to see a proper game.

The question is how do you explain the difference in intensity between the first and second halves? A half time roasting from Pep? Burnley as we know are supremely organised, and have conceded a mere 19 goals so far this season, and after this game, Pope has conceded the majority of his away goals to City. I didn't expect them to tear Burnley apart from the offset, but it was certainly an underwhelming first half, with passes going astray, and City failing to muster a single shot on target.

And whilst at half-time I was bemoaning my lot in life, and why City had to do this to me when I least expect it, City were not THAT bad. Burnley led through to an error from John Stones, and mistakes will happen with any player, and apart from a dangerous corner that Mee headed back across goal, the visitors threatened little throughout the game, apart from set pieces which is probably to be expected.

Little blame for Bravo for their goal, but his problem is more that he is a line-hogger. No coming out and narrowing the angle, he allows seemingly brilliant shots to repeatedly fly past him, and he seemed nervous passing out from the back too. I hope Ederson returns for all future games, but I'm not convinced, as Pep may reward the players who have played so far in the Carabao Cup.

As it turned out, the first half was a mere blip, because in the second half City were irresistible. Sane went from poor to brilliant. Aguero was on fire, Gundogan put in one of his best halves of football since Barcelona, his back-heel assist a thing of pure beauty, and he is now assembling quite a show reel of killer passes.

As for Burnley's complaint over City's quickly-taken free-kick to force an equaliser – laughable, and just desserts for trying to block, time-waste and stifle the game. Once City were in the lead soon after, the result seemed almost inevitable, quite a turn-around from my half-time mood.

And what the game showcased once more was City's ability to go through the gears and blow teams away. I felt at 4-1 that if the team had needed to score more goals, they would have done. Another opposition team pretty much gave up having gone behind. Long may it continue.

A quick note on Zinchenko too – whilst he was not one of the star performers, he seems comfortable in the team, and there's little higher praise than that, especially as he is playing out of position. I'm confident about his future at City.

And so on to the semi-final of the Carabao Cup. Strong team please Pep, let's put this to bed. Everyone is looking forward to the Liverpool match, but it's really not that important when you have a 15 point lead in the league, and when you have a 5 day gap too.

What really annoys United fans most? City are more attractive to players than United.

Not arrogant, just better, eh? City have finished above United for four years now, it's nothing new. City have won two titles. United fans may always struggle to accept a change in the power structure, but there's more to their latest outbursts, their desperation to find some mud to throw at the club fifteen points clear at the top of the table – it's not just the points situation itself.

No, I'd argue what really grinds their gears is the realisation of where both clubs lie right now in the wider scheme of things. That's what gnaws away at them – they can't just spend money to get themselves out of any tricky situation, they can't throw their weight around to get what they want. They are no longer the big cheese, not globally, not nationally, not even in their own city.

This is not me claiming City is a "bigger" club than United (we're not, and why would I care anyway?), it's a simple declaration of a fact – pretty much every player in the world bar Ibrahimovic wants to play for Pep Guardiola. They know that it would be in their interests to do so.

It's not the balmy Manchester climate, three restaurants or constant litter that draws the players, though bizarrely very few players have tried to engineer a move away from City in recent years, in fact a few have been almost impossible to budge. It is the manager, plus the project, plus healthy remuneration, though they'd get that wherever they went of course, and City no longer pay the highest wages. United do that, as they seem to have rebooted as Manchester City circa 2009.

I wasn't entirely comfortable with Pep's heated debate with Nathan Redmond after City beat Southampton recently, but let's be honest, if pretty much any other manager had done that there would probably have been a riot on the touchline. Pep has an aura though, and Redmond was probably delighted at such attention, and took everything on board.

Meanwhile across the city border, Mourinho whinges, deflects, embarrasses – on a daily basis.

United fans can talk about 20 league titles and "history" until the cows come home, it makes little difference. City have Pep, they have his playing style, they have a structure set up throughout the club to maintain standards long after he has departed.

Manchester City 2 Bristol City 1 – Carabao Cup Semi-Final 1st Leg

Yet again, at the death, City came up trumps. Amazing what happens when you put a striker on the pitch.

Lots of talk (zzzzzzzzzzzzzzzzzzzzzzzz) about City's failure to sell out the match, but what was most disappointing, but not that surprising really, was that much of the criticism was from City fans. I expect it from rival fans, what else have they got to beat us with after all, but when so many rival fans go on about the Emptyhad so much, it hardly helps when our own fans do too, especially as it's the "go-to" marker for a football w**ker to tell others that they should be attending a football match. If that's you, burn this book immediately, I don't want your custom anyway.

The fact is, three of City's worst performances, in a season of mostly remarkable performances, have been in this competition, and yet City could, and probably should still get to Wembley. Coincidence? Probably not. The intensity is not there, and as always, making wholesale changes even if what comes in is better than what the opposition has, badly affects the team's effectiveness. And the team acts like a chain –weaken one link and it has a ripple effect, which spreads through the team. Enough Clichés for you there? #valueformoney

So Zinchenko kept that left-back spot, Pep seemingly protecting Delph for the visit to Anfield, Bernardo Silva once more started but was moved around the pitch during the 90 minutes, never really settling, Sane flattered to deceive once more, and our striker-less formation never really got going, though with better finishing my viewpoint might be rather different.

The problems as always rippled out from Bravo and Mangala. Bravo made no obvious errors, but his nervousness when distributing was clear, and Mangala's lack of comfort on the ball was clear to see, which spread to Stones, and the two combined to gift Bristol City a penalty late in the first half.

But yet again there was an improvement post-break but nothing as profound as that witnessed just days before in the FA Cup. A superb kick from Bravo allowed De Bruyne to break, he fed Sterling, and Sterling, for the first time this season, assisted a De Bruyne goal.

Many would have expected the flood gates to open thereafter – I certainly did, but it wasn't to be. City dominated the ball, naturally, and the visitors rarely threatened themselves, unlike in the 1st half, but yet again it was another late, late show, a Bernardo Silva chip towards the far post, about the 30th that had been tried that match by a City player found Aguero, and the rest is history.

City take a narrow lead to what will be a tough 2nd leg.

RIP Twitter

Sad news elsewhere for the Hockin brand – early one Friday morning and my Twitter account disappeared forever. 6000 followers gone, some of whom actually existed.

Surely I had been reported, but by who? The previous night I had live-tweeted Alyson Rudd's appearance on the Times football podcast, but I was quite reserved, for once. Maybe it was the 3000 Duncan Castles retweets that did for me.

The only downside to a new account is that I am no longer blocked by Neil Custis, Stan Collymore et al. I'll give it a week.
#prayforHowie

CITY HAVE ARRIVED!!!!!

Kevin De Bruyne becomes the first player to be named in the UEFA Team of The Year for 2017.

God knows how Eden Hazard got in though. He's great, but has this really been a stellar year for him? Not convinced myself, but won't lose any sleep over it.

Liverpool 4 Manchester City 3

Stop all the clocks, cut off the telephone,
Prevent the dog from barking with the juicy bone.
Silence the tannoy and, with muffled drum,
Bring out the coffin. Let the mourners come.
Let aeroplanes circle moaning overhead
Scribbling in the sky the message: "The invincibles are dead!"
Put half and half scarves around the white necks of the public doves.
Let the Showsec stewards wear black cotton gloves.

Pep was my north stand, my south stand, my east stand and west,
My working week and Super Sunday rest,
My noon, my midnight, my talk, my terrace song.
I thought that unbeaten run would last forever; I was wrong.

The £400k a week stars are not wanted now; leave out every one.
Pack up the moon and dismantle Jihai Sun.
Pour away the ocean and sweep up the dead wood.
For no season now can come to any good.

Yep, Manchester City, little old Manchester City, lost a league game. It hurts, partly because we still can't play well at Anfield, but mostly because most of us are not only unused to the feeling of defeat, we can barely remember it and thus aren't coping that well compared to when losing was par for the course. It was good while it lasted, but it could never last forever.

I'd have preferred to lose at home to someone rubbish though, all things considered.

The only surprise in the line-up was David Silva starting, and finishing, on the bench, and he was missed, but there was talk of an illness preventing him playing for the full 90 minutes.

Let's hope it's another nine months before I have to wheel out that poem again, though I doubt it will be, a ridiculous amount of time between losses, ridiculous.

At 1-1, I thought City were taking control of the game. That second goal for Liverpool changed everything.

Can Firmino's push on Stones be both a foul and a mistake? It was a foul, it should have been a free-kick, and if it had happened the other way round, well…. I refer you to Martin Tyler still talking about payback for that Mane red card months ago that left Ederson poleaxed and resulting in him having to be stretchered off the pitch. That said, Stones should still do better, he was weak in a situation he should have been in total control of. At least fall to the ground and try and get a free kick.

And despite all the mistakes, all three finishes were sublime. All seven goals were sublime to be honest.

City lost the game not because they were outplayed for 90 minutes, because they weren't. No they lost because of 10 minutes of madness, partly caused by excellent pressing and a higher intensity from Liverpool.

If that game had gone on another five minutes, it would not have surprised me if City had not only equalised, but won the game. Sadly the comeback started too late.

So frustration by the bucket load, but this is hardly the end of the world. The celebrations by Liverpool fans showed what it means to beat City nowadays.

And the frustration is exacerbated because we know Liverpool cannot sustain that intensity for whole matches, and we saw the effect it had on them in the latter stages of the match. Sadly City had left themselves too much to do due to an error-prone 10 minutes.

And extra frustration after such intensity was handled well in the first half. City were growing into this game, and threw it away. But it's just one league game in a long season. The invincibles dream has died, but there are more important things to fight for than that.

Bluemoon Podcast Audio Script

Well it's good to get back to the real world – City lose a league match, Sanchez is going to United and we're about to sign Jonny Evans it seems – that's what you'd call coming back down to earth with a bump – it seems we don't always get our own way after all.

Still, would we want it easy? Would life get boring if game after game after game was won? Maybe Jonny Evans is pep's self-sabotage, to make things interesting. I jest of course - I don't have the arrogance of a United- supporting bigwig on Twitter to think City and Pep have got this football lark tied down yet – that winning run was amazing, but for me it was an outlier, and unlikely to be repeated in the foreseeable future. As for getting bored, when a few big trophies have been won I might get bored, should domination ever be an actual thing, but until then, I'm happy to see City win every game, be it a thrashing or yet another late winner – both have their own charms.

I also jest about Jonny Evans, who is an unexciting uninspiring signing, but then not every signing has to set the world alight – as a 4th choice central defender, his acquisition would be fine, as long as a top level central defender is also signed before the end of summer, assuming Mangala and Vinny will be gone after this season, which will surely be the case.

But back to that defeat, which was much easier to deal with by staying off social media for most of the subsequent evening. It's weird then that a lead reduced to 12 points gets me anxiously perusing the fixture list for City and United just to see what lies ahead. City should beat Newcastle and West Brom comfortably, and the lead might be back to 15 points or so by then if so, but slip up in these winnable games and the genetic disposition of many City fans demands considerable arse clenching.

Still, if you're that pessimistic, you can still get 50/1 on United for the league, Sanchez or no Sanchez. Games are running out, just 15 left, and if City are 15 ahead with 13 games to go, it would take relegation form to throw that lead away. And as next year is obviously Liverpool's year, it's even more important that City get a title under their belt this season.

Poems have already been written, books published and parade buses filled with petrol following Sunday's victory. No one can stop the Liverpool family and their white-toothed gurner-in-chief.

Over at Chelsea, the poisonous atmosphere that seems to hang over the club at least 50% of the time seems to have returned, Conte a dead man walking and the assertion I had a fortnight ago that they would finish 2nd seems like a lifetime ago – three consecutive 0-0 draws brings back horrific memories of Stuart Pearce teams and his not so lucky mascot by the dugout, the only season I've considered bringing a book to a football match. As for Arsenal, I almost feel sorry for their fans.
I said "almost".
Wenger is nothing more than a lingering bad smell now, sat slumped on the bench in his oversized coat, rising occasionally to shout abuse at the 4th official, his stubbornness dragging the club backwards at a rate of knots, throwing sly digs at City in press conferences as Rome burns. The mismanagement to allow your 2 best players to get to within 6 months of their contract expiring is staggering. Three if you add a fit Wilshere, and Claude and Troopz can hardly muster the energy to get angry any more. Sad times.

Whatever happens though, as United dangle £100m plus deals in front of 29 year olds who would be free transfers in the summer, in the cold light of day we can now probably dismiss the ridiculous talk some weeks ago of City dominating the game for years to come. Hopefully that will happen, but it seems rather premature to predict such things. There's too much money in the English game and too many savvy managers for one team to exert such total domination over everyone else.

Of course there must always be a narrative though, so that was a handy one as City extended the lead at the top of the table. Now there's new narratives, and they're just as ridiculous.
 Most attention has understandably revolved around the Sanchez saga, and like that time we signed Robbie Fowler after a protracted chase, the longer these things drag on, the more you want the player whether it's a good signing or not.
Sanchez is a level above the Robbie Fowler that arrived at City of course

but his defection to the red side is not some catastrophe. A 23 year old Sanchez or another player of similar skills and age would have hurt more but we'll get over it, probably by watching our team win a couple of trophies.

City have wasted many a million in the future, but that does not make them wrong for taking a stand now. We did not spend years undoing previous financial excess by slowly constructing sensible incentivised wage structure only to blow it wide open for a stroppy 29 year old. I'd have loved to see Sanchez at City, but it was never plausible once the stakes were raised.

United are simply City 2009 rebooted, playing anyone and anything to get themselves to the top of the pile. They're entitled to do what they want, but the past hypocrisy and high horses their fans all sat on, the moral high ground they occupied about not buying success seems as distant as the fanboy accounts proclaiming Mikhitaryan as the signing of the summer. With the figures involved too, I can't really blame Sanchez for going elsewhere – his loss, but a final payday, and his dogs are going to be treated like royalty. No pedigree chum for them.

As for Evans, some fans will see it in isolation and see it as terrible, which is understandable, but with further big signings, it is simply upgrading Mangala – not exciting, not pushing the squad onto new levels, but no disaster either. Pep sees something, and for once I trust a manager that he knows what he is doing.

What's more, Evans is more than good enough to play in the majority of league games that should be easily won by City, like our next two games, and thus offers great opportunities to keep Stones and Otamendi fresh. It's all about managing players over a gruelling 9 months.

But as this is the January window then this will be viewed as the most disastrous window ever for City, but January windows aren't as important as summer ones, and we're streets ahead in the league, close to Wembley in the Carabao Cup, have got highly winnable games in the other two cups and it will be fine.

A disastrous summer transfer window is another matter, but I simply don't agree that all of City's problems could have been sorted in one window last summer – by the end of this summer, this squad will be even better than we probably could have imagined. Those in charge mean business, serious business. They have a structure and a plan that is lacking across the city. Just think, if City win the league this season, as they surely must now, they will have finished above United in the league for five seasons in a row. That's pretty damn amazing.

And that's why seeing them win a big trophy now would be so, so hard to take. I survived 20 years of them winning everything, and now the thought of them outdoing City in anything fills me with dread, because I've almost got used to being better, become acclimatised to their incompetence, not that we haven't had our moments recently too. And that's why the Liverpool defeat was hard to take too – not just because it was Liverpool, because I'd almost forgotten what it felt like – so all things considered, that's not a bad position to be in, when all is said and done.

Elsewhere, Otamendi has signed a new extended contract, and everyone is happy about that – not something I thought I'd ever write a year ago. Fernandinho too, and naturally we're all happy with that too.

Manchester City 3 Newcastle United 1

"Where were you when you were shit?" sang the Newcastle fans, supporters of a club that used to get average gates of just over 16,000. Where were we? Watching City beat Newcastle as is the norm I imagine. I expected better from them, but football fans will always disappoint. Top banter though.

And so to a game that had elevated importance after the Anfield defeat. Hardly season-defining, but there was a real desire to get things back on track quickly and protect our very healthy lead at the top of the table, especially after United had won at Burnley earlier in the day.

No real surprises with the line-up. Zinchenko replaced the injured Delph who Pep has now said is "out for a while" which doesn't sound promising, after the early diagnosis suggested a speedy reply. But anyway, in a match where we expected most of the play to take part in the opposition half, Zinchenko made more sense than Danilo, as hopefully his defensive capabilities should not be needed that often.

And that is what happened – 80%+ possession in the first half, City looked fluid, the movement was good, and they dominated, without creating a raft of chances. Still, I was quite relaxed.

Sterling had a goal correctly disallowed – he was just ahead of the defender, but eventually the pressure told – did Aguero touch it? At first I thought not, but the replay on the screen in the ground seemed to suggest a slight deflection, and I doubt Aguero would just be able to claim the goal if not. Either way, another sumptuous cross from De Bruyne, who is simply a class above, though it should be noted pretty much all of City's 18 corners were atrocious, bar one chance that fell to Stones early doors.

The 2nd half seemed to be following the same pattern – a soft penalty for Sterling, but it was a penalty in the modern game, and Aguero's penalty was great, and even though the keeper went the right way, he could only get his fingertips on it. Surely game over.

But no, the team had to make us sweat again. Who was to blame as Newcastle hit back? Possibly Zinchenko, but he was simply outpaced and left exposed, in a move that felt very reminiscent of last season. Ederson probably went down too quickly too, and it was game on. And for 5 minutes or more, City panicked somewhat, and Newcastle sniffed an opportunity.

Thankfully the Ederson fumble that allowed a shot on goal was not costly, and instead we witnessed one of the great pieces of skill of this or any other season – a beautiful run from Sane that reminded us, as did his goal the previous week, of what he can offer once he becomes more consistent. Something to watch on a loop for hours.

And for Aguero, the perfect hat-trick, one with his head, one with his left foot and one with his right foot – the first in the Premier League since October 2015, which may well have been Aguero v Newcastle too! He loves playing against Newcastle, the criticism of him was put to bed for a few more days at least and the goal was one of the most celebrated of the season for the relief it brought to an anxious crowd. Game over.

Zinchenko, goal apart, was excellent, and justified his inclusion – yet again Pep seems to have trained a player to play left-back when they have never done it before. He was the only player in Europe's top five leagues to complete over 100 passes that weekend, and had a 94% pass completion rate.

And as sure as night follows day, Liverpool lose at Swansea on Monday night. They were probably still exhausted after last week's cup final.

Two minutes before United announce the Sanchez signing, and City announce a new extended contract for Kevin De Bruyne. Nice timing.

Elsewhere, the "class of 92" were kindly allocated every job going, a classic case of getting by because of who you know, not what you know. Thus Pip Neville somehow was appointed manager of the England women's team, for reasons that cannot exist within any logical or sane mind, and Ryan Giggs, a man for whom there are few depths he won't sink to, unless it's a managerial role in the lower leagues of course, took over the Welsh national side, presumably helped by a viral video that did the rounds showing him giving a pep talk during that rather brief period as United's caretaker manager. The clip was so tedious it wiped out insomnia in one fell swoop, the biggest medical breakthrough since the eradication of smallpox.

Anyway, if the jobs eat into their TV commitments, I'm all for it. Expect Nicky Butt to be announced as Barcelona manager sometime soon.

Alexis Sanchez –The Saga Is Over

January 22nd, 2018. The deed was done. No more conjecture, no more contradictory media reports, no more guff, no more. United signed Alexis Sanchez "from under City's noses", and that was that. Disappointment for sure, but when sifting through the many reports on how this had really played out, I wasn't overly distraught.
City need an extra attacking player, that much is clear. But as of January the league was close to wrapped up, the Carabao Cup is 4th priority, and I'm not sure how important the FA Cup would be taken either. So effectively a striker acquisition in January was for one reason only – to make a difference in the Champions League.

I'm sorry, but I'm not buying that. Any acquisition gives no guarantee of making a difference, and he might be unavailable anyway when the key ties come around. Having another top player always helps, but we can't say for certain Sanchez would have aided that mystical quadruple challenge.

Whatever, City certainly wanted Sanchez, and Wenger blocked the deal in the summer window. City went back in once January came around, but it seems things had changed. Like Dani Alves before, it appeared that a gentleman's agreement had meant nothing. Now Sanchez wanted more money as the transfer fee would have reduced as he got closer to being a free agent. The problem is, City are no longer a walkover. They told him and his agent (with his own astronomical demands) where to go and made their stance clear – come to us on the original terms we agreed, or forget it. Sanchez was so desperate to leave Arsenal he seems unprepared to wait until the summer when he would hold all the cards. United, as we know, the team whose players make history, not money, will pay anything to get one over City, even if it's a player they do not really need. They paid, up he went there.

Sanchez knew that coming to City meant winning the league, but I can understand if he felt this wouldn't really be a title for him to celebrate, to feel a part of, as City had the league almost tied up by January.

Nevertheless, I can say without prejudice that he moved to where the money was.

As for City, Mahrez rumours suddenly surfaced but that deal fell through too as the window slammed shut, Leicester City apparently asking for ludicrous amounts of money. Neither player is a spring chicken and City are right to walk away if they feel they are being ripped off. The club might have spent a lot of money in the past couple of years, but how many players would you say have lost value, how many have proved to be overvalued? Not many.

From podcast discussions and social media viewing it seems I am in the minority here, but I was glad eventually that both fell through. For me it's best to wait until the summer and get your number 1 target. Someone not about to hit their 30s, someone who would not potentially ruin what is clearly a dressing room with excellent morale. His wages he demanded were not viable – City would have had a queue of players rightly demanding parity.

This may reek of "never liked her anyway" type behaviour, but I do feel City might have dodged a bullet, and should always stick to their transfer guidelines, even if we miss out on some great players. Sanchez has stunk Old Trafford out too since his arrival, and will start next season as a 30-year old. We move on.

Towards the end of the season, the details of Sanchez's deal with United came to light, only reinforcing my view that City did the right thing, especially considering how he has unbalanced the team since his arrival, and the suspicion that his surly attitude would not be good for morale, at a time when morale is at an all-time high. Sanchez received a £6.7m signing-on fee, a pay packet of £391,000 a week, and even £75,000 for every match he starts. Utterly unworkable under City's wage structure. Another bullet dodged. #kaka #terry

Bristol City 2 Manchester City 3

We're the famous Man City.....

Job done, though with a performance that bordered on sloppy at times, but still showed the class of the boys in blue.

You'll never meet a poor bookie of course, and they had Bristol City at 16/1 to win the game – for them it was a done deal, but as a still-jaded City fan, it didn't feel that way.

Seems Pep didn't think so either, with a super-strong team announced an hour before kick-off, loyalty shown to Bravo and Bernardo Silva replacing Sterling – otherwise it was what you might term a "first-choice" team. It still puzzled me though that he didn't go for this line-up in the first leg and try and put the tie to bed, but perhaps he looked at the fixture list and decided this was the better time to go strong. Or perhaps the 1st leg performance of Bristol City had spooked him somewhat.

The descent of modern journalism continues down into the bottomless pit in which much of it resides. The Mirror, which it may surprise you used to be an OK newspaper, ran one of those articles whereby you take a tweet of someone expressing disgust/anger/vitriol and create a story around it. Thus we have an article on people criticising Leroy Sane "shushing" the home support after he scored the opening goal .This was the home crowd that had been booing and abusing him the whole match, for reasons that escape me. The click for hits is so desperate now, I've just scrolled past an article comparing the cost of Alexis Sanchez's car compared to those of the Yeovil town players. Just when you think they can't get any more pitiful, they make you reassess everything.

Speaking of booing – unless my ears deceived me, it seemed Aguero was also booed every time he touched the ball. Bizarre. Are the people of Bristol still harbouring grudges after the Falklands War?

Thanks to Kevin De Bruyne, and partly the man himself, David Silva has now won his last 24 games in a City shirt, a record in the league since football began in the 19th century.

And a pointless stat whilst we're at it, though it does hint at City's continued domination of the ball in attacking areas – the last 30 corners in City matches have all been to City. Imagine how destructive we would be if we were any good at them.

Off to Wembley I go, for my 8th visit this decade. Costly business supporting a good side.

And it is Arsenal at Wembley once more. You'd think that's the easier tie compared to Chelsea, but the head-to-heads in big games suggests otherwise. Something will have to give – Arsenal's recent Wembley record is pretty much immaculate, whilst Pep has won 9 out of 10 of his domestic cup finals, his only loss coming to a Jose Mourinho managed Real Madrid.

FA Cup 4th Round - Cardiff 0 Manchester City 2

A game that had everything we expect from a City match – by which I of course mean appalling officiating and horror tackles from the opposition that went totally unchecked. Nothing changes, nothing is done about it, and the referee involved will no doubt get a plum job next weekend.

But hey, City are through, after a thoroughly professional performance, in front of the stadium's record crowd, so that's the important thing here.

A fairly strong side (Bravo apart), though one devoid of strikers. It was up to City's young attacking players to provide the goals. Or so we thought. No David Silva, but Aguero did at least make the bench.

But that would be to once more underestimate Kevin De Bruyne. Not for the first time he had done his homework, and struck a free kick under a jumping wall and put city ahead after just 8 minutes.

Every time I see an appalling refereeing decision against Manchester City, I am thankful that at least I won't see anything that bad again, but by jove they prove me wrong every time. Boy did they excel themselves, twice, in under 20 minutes.

Firstly, Bernardo Silva launched a thunderbolt into the top corner to double the lead. Or so we all thought. But no, somehow the linesman had imagined an offence in his head and disallowed it. It wasn't just a mistake, it was amateurish beyond belief, to the point that you wondered how his career got this far. It was adjudged that Leroy Sane was offside and in the goalkeeper's line of sight. Two small problems with that. He wasn't offside, and he wasn't blocking the keeper's view. A keeper who got nowhere near the ball anyway.

Where is the communication? Let's be generous and accept the linesman made a mistake with the offside – the referee should have been able to see clearly that Sane did not inhibit the keeper. Just an appalling decision on every level.

Anyway, City soon doubled their lead. Bernardo Silva found space on the left and put in a superb cross, for Sterling to head home – his first headed goal since Boxing Day 2015.

The match officials hadn't finished there. Sane went on a jinking run up the pitch, and was clearly taken out by a horrific calf-high studs up challenge that could easily have ended Sane's season.

Result? A yellow card. Utter, utter incompetence, and again, how could one of two match officials not see the challenge for what it was?

A real discussion needs to be had on these horror tackles suffered by Manchester City players. Actually, scrap that, a discussion is not needed, what is needed for something tangible to actually be done before someone has a career wrecked, before someone's World Cup hopes are eradicated.

Needless to say Sane had to be substituted at half-time. Let's hope, as he walked off the pitch, that it is not too serious.

Hoilett shot narrowly over, but City utterly dominated the 2nd half. De Bruyne was on another planet. His through ball to Sterling should have registered an assist, but the keeper saved. Then De Bruyne set Bernardo Silva free and his shot was easily saved when he should have scored. Danilo too could easily have scored but his shot was poor too, after being sent through by who else but Kevin De Bruyne (not really, it was Gundogan).

Cardiff's thuggery continued – this is a Neil Warnock side after all, and it seemed too little too late when they eventually had a player sent off in injury time after Diaz had been hacked down. Again.

Naturally Neil Warnock saw nothing wrong with his team's actions, and suggested Pep should accept such things in England, which is rich considering a player's career could have been wrecked, and perhaps more pertinently, the match was played in Wales. God help us if this cretin, who is admittedly an excellent Championship manager, brings Cardiff up to the Premier League.

A private message popped into my inbox a few days later. It said Sane isn't as badly injured as is being portrayed, but that City wanted to make a point about how bad the tackle was. Let's hope so...

Next up – Wigan Athletic away. One of City's few remaining bogey teams.

City Sign Aymeric Laporte

As the transfer window deadline drew close and Jim White got his yellow ties back from the dry cleaners, City swooped and signed long-term target Aymeric Laporte. Another £50m signing, more weeping from the net spend weirdos.

Anyway, City had almost signed Laporte before of course, and not all were happy in going back for a player who had previously turned us down at the last minute. Ridiculous. Laporte had already explained that he was injured at the time, and young, and felt it better to stay where he was to develop. Perfectly acceptable logic.

As for the sort of player we are getting, a John Stones alternative would be my best guess. He has struggled recently but in a struggling team, but is a graceful ball-passer who fits the Pep template perfectly. I'm excited to see another young player hopefully develop at the club.

As for the timing, well it's not that often clubs make big signings in the January transfer window. However, this year is rather unique. Not only is there a World Cup of course, but the transfer window will now close before the season begins. Thus there is a very limited period of time in the summer to get deals sorted, and this feels to me like a summer deal done in advance. The Fred negotiations have a similar feel, though no deal was done in that instance, and City are thought to have cooled their interest since.

Anyway, next season will probably be the time to judge Laporte, but in the meantime he gives Pep more options and depth in defence. And makes the signing of Jonny Evans less likely, thank god.

Premier League: Manchester City 3 West Brom 0

Routine stuff as City go 15 points clear at the top of the table.

City were dominant, and for once it was Fernandinho that took centre stage. After City had tested Foster in the West Brom goals with a number of average efforts, Kevin De Bruyne was again on hand to supply the perfect pass to the Brazilian, who slipped it past the keeper.
De Bruyne himself was through and had a tame shot saved, and City were one better pass away from further goals on a number of occasions. De Bruyne clipped the bar from outside the area for good measure too.

And Fernandinho held centre stage for other reasons too - the Brazilian escaped any punishment for planting his foot onto the thigh of the prone Grzegorz Krychowiak in the first half.
Should he have been sent off? It's a tough one to call – he clearly lands studs on a prone player, but only he knows if he meant it or not – if he had been sent off, there would have been no appeal I would wager – but it's not *that* obvious that it's deliberate. The FA panel agreed anyway, with no further action forthcoming. Cue the conspiracy theorists.

As for the 2nd half – more of the same. Sterling cut inside and curled over with the goal at his mercy, a bad miss indeed, but it was only delaying the near-inevitable. More Foster saves, missed chances, obvious fouls ignored by the referee (standard), before De Bruyne supplied Sterling, he laid it back and Kevin swept it into the far corner of the net. That was pretty much game over.

There was even time for an audacious shot from Kevin De Bruyne from near the half-way line that appeared to clip the bar (or was saved – a corner was given but I'm not convinced), before Sterling set Aguero free to wrap up victory. Really routine stuff, and City march on.

And what's more, a nice debut for new boy Aymeric Laporte. Not tested unduly, he nevertheless put in an elegant performance, at times pinging diagonal balls to the likes of Sterling almost at will.

And back to that Fernandinho challenge –whilst that could be argued either way, that's not something you could say about Matt Phillip's appalling high challenge on substitute Brahim Diaz late on? Red card? Yeah, as if!

James McClean too tried, and failed, to halt the counter-attacking De Bruyne with a cynical sliding challenge just prior to the 2nd goal – opinions differed on the 93:20 podcast as to how bad that was, but cynical it most certainly was, but probably a strong yellow for me. Debate also flourished as to whether McClean could be carded, as the advantage was given. I stated what a friend who had been on a referee's course recently had said – that a player cannot once the game is waved on. Others pointed out that the FA law on the matter seems to contradict this, so I'm none the wiser.

As for West Brom, they offered little, as like many other teams, they could not keep hold of the ball for long enough, mustering a late chance for Sturridge that he squandered after something of a defensive mix-up.

- Man City have won their past 13 league games in a row against West Brom, their longest such run against a single opponent in their history.
- Indeed, this is also West Brom's longest losing streak against a single team in their league history.
- De Bruyne provided his 38th league assist since his Man City debut in September 2015, at least four more than any other player in Europe's big five leagues (Lionel Messi, Neymar and Mesut Ozil with 34).
- Sterling (14 goals, 6 assists) became the fourth Premier League player to have a hand in 20+ goals this season, after Mohamed Salah (25), Harry Kane (22) and Sergio Aguero (22).
- Aguero has had a hand in 12 goals in 11 Premier League games against the Baggies (8 goals, 4 assists).

Bluemoon Podcast Audio Script

Amidst all the wailing and gnashing of teeth over Manchester City football club, their human rights abuses, their oil money, their empty seats and their history, or lack of it, the buying of success, the lack of youth players and much more besides, there is one topic I've probably avoided until now. Size.

Men are very touchy about size of course, and it seems some include football clubs in that remit. Yes, the last refuge of the scoundrel is to fall back to how big their club is. So without further ado, let's cut straight to the chase.

No true football fan chooses a team because of their size, nor brags about it. Note the word true. Only insecure, bedroom-dwelling glory-hunters whose team are no longer the playground bully talk about club size. And no longer being the playground bully is key here. Because global reach is all that United fans have got right now. Now, football is cyclical of course, so that will change. City will not dominate for years and years to come in my opinion, though they're having a good crack at it according to the rumours as I write this. But size of club, as if this is something to brag about, is the final stand for these embittered losers with players' names in their twitter handle and a slavish devotion to Duncan Castles stats packs. Yeah, United might have lost 2-0 to Spurs to go 15 points behind hated rivals Manchester City, but just look at Alexis Sanchez's Instagram reach! Who's the real winner here? Oh yeah, that's right, it's Manchester City. It's the fans looking forward to hopefully seeing their team life that Premier League trophy sometime soon, it's the fans planning yet another trip to Wembley for a cup final, it's the fans raiding their piggy banks and checking down the back of the sofa to help pay for this mad, exciting journey.

What is so pitiful, to the extent that I do almost feel pity for these specimens, is that they probably believe what they say. When @simplyunited or @martial111 retweets social media interactions, shirt sales or simple revenue, they believe that this is something to be proud of, something that makes United better than everyone else. Not league tables, performances or actual achievements – that's so last year – no, they truly think that being the biggest, not the best, is something to crow about, it elevates their team above all others. DNA and all that. They have drummed it into themselves repeatedly and so incessantly that they now hold such opinions as fact. There's one small problem though. There's not a City fan on the planet that could give a damn about club size. Not one. It's almost as if, and I'm sticking my neck out here, we've got better things to worry about. Or perhaps enjoy would be a more apt word.

We all have different reasons for supporting our team – our dad's team being a prime reason – but if like me and like most you fell in love with the beautiful game as a child, you did not sit down as a 4 year old and think – "hmm, which club shall I attach myself to? Best make sure it's the one with the biggest revenue, the biggest stadium and the most fans in Ireland, Scandinavia and Singapore, so I can bask in reflective glory for the rest of my life." Nope, doesn't really work, does it? So how embarrassing it is to see such reasons occupy the entire life force of some United fans right now.

I don't have that photographic memory of childhood like some do – you only have to take part in a pub quiz with me to know that, when the children's TV round pops up – but knowing myself rather well by now after 40+ years, I'd say the reason I chose my team over the team that my father supported was perhaps linked to size too, in as much as I wanted to support the underdog, I already possessed the psyche and personality of a City fan – whether that's a good thing is a discussion for another time. Or maybe I just liked the colour blue.

Of course a lot of these fans hiding behind twitter accounts didn't sign up for City to be better than United – hell, they didn't sign up for them to be remotely close to United. The takeover was laughed off, the players marked as mercenaries, but the truth slowly dawned on them, brought into sharp focus after that FA Cup semi-final victory. With two league titles behind us, this shrieking is nothing new of course, but as a few journalists have noted recently, it seems to be on a different level this season. And so they retreat, to a place filled with memes, databases and social media stats, not the place we all grew up with, that made us fall in love for life – our spot on the terrace or seat in a ground, watching and praying for our team to do well, just this once. Their god is a Nottingham Forest fan who sits in a bedroom with a fake log fire behind him, monetizing his fake support, commentating as he watches a match, because who doesn't want to watch a man watching a match as opposed to actually watching the match yourself, as millions of comments scroll down the right side of the page from United fans who, like their god, has probably never been near the ground of the team they supposedly support so passionately.

And all of this reminds me of the knots rival fans are getting themselves in at the clear and obvious run of horrific tackles that have been inflicted on City players without proper punishment in recent weeks. Obviously rival fans can't accept this fact as being, well a fact, so have got in a right tizzy trying to excuse the appalling refereeing decisions, because the last thing a rival fan can do, the very last thing, is ever admit City have bad luck from match officials – the day rival fans admit this, hell will no doubt freeze over, and Bobby Madley will hopefully be entombed underneath the ice. No offence, Bobby.

I understand – I don't ever want to publically admit that any United players are any good nor proclaim to the masses that united, at any point in time, have a better team than City. But for such occasions, perhaps silence is thus the best option.

Anyway, you get the idea. I'd best go, I need to log onto a Rochdale message board and lord it over them about how much bigger my club is compared to theirs.

Burnley 1 Manchester City 1

Squeaky bum time as City's lead is cut to a meagre 13 points. Worrying times.

Burnley is never an easy game of course, especially this season. Vincent Kompany was drafted in to deal with the physical side of things, and the rest of the team almost picked itself, Bernardo Silva starting and Danilo getting the nod over Zinchenko at left-back.

The game was tough, as expected, but City sparkled away from the actual goal area. Burnley allowed very little space, but some of City's one-touch passing was mesmeric. Guardian journalist Sachin Nakhani suggested on Twitter that sometimes City almost have too many options when they break (I'm paraphrasing), and I'm inclined to agree. With multiple options not always the right decision is made, though it's easy to say that with hindsight. City's shots to goal ratio is the joint best in the division (along with United and Leicester), so it can't be that bad, but we still seem to be wasteful much of the time.

A beautiful goal by Danilo, and at that stage I thought it highly unlikely City could lose from this point, so was feeling good. The rest of the game though showed the cost of not taking chances. Burnley threatened themselves and in the 2nd half Ederson made one of the saves of the season, so there can be few complaints really about the end result. We as fans have to adapt to not winning every match, a crazy position to be in.

There's no avoiding that Sterling miss any longer. It was a terrible miss, not a lot more you can say. A truly terrible miss, and a costly one with an equalizer following not long afterwards.

There is a point to be made though about the consequences of it being Sterling missing rather than another player, as the consequences are different when it's him. Think of De Bruyne's miss v Chelsea last season, and think if the difference in attitude. Fact is, as witnessed every match day, there are still many who still don't want to praise Sterling for his efforts, and criticise him almost relentlessly.

Nevertheless, I think it was wrong to substitute him. Sterling has shown many a time that he can miss a chance and make amends for it soon after. I'd rather he had been given that chance again, as more than any other player at the club, he never hides.

As for the equalizer, goals happen, not everything has to be prevented. The mistake was Walker's of course, but the fact I have barely mentioned such a consistent player in his debut season so far shows just how rare these mistakes have been. The only time he has cost the team previously has tended to be down to incompetent refereeing rather than his own shortcomings.

Anyway, the gap is a huge 13 points and a much-needed week off for the players follows — well half the week at least. Enjoy it lads, let's hope you come back fresh and that Mahrez is still on strike. The Leicester game will be the only remaining league game in the month of February.

RAHEEM STERLING TURNS UP FOR TRAINING IN £70,000 NEW CAR DESPITE MISSING SITTER AGAINST BURNLEY

Feel The Noise

Elsewhere, Mr Happy himself, Jose Mourinho, again criticises the quiet Old Trafford crowd. Pep has done likewise in past. They should both shut up.

Yet again a manager criticises fans for a situation whilst displaying complete ignorance as to how we reached this point. If he's so bothered about atmosphere, campaign to his bosses for cheaper seats, standing areas and fewer corporate areas.
But we all know he'll never agree to that.
Would probably help if his team played more attractive football too. It's a strange world where we insist that people make noise whilst spectating. It really isn't compulsory, believe it or not.

United's capacity will actually be reduced next season, because of the enforcement of minimum standards and seat allocations for disabled support – good to see in the Premier League even if clubs had to be coerced – see also the push for living wages for all employees. Staggering that this is still an issue when you consider the money in the game.

Manchester City 5 Leicester City 1

A few days off for the City squad, and a week off playing matches, the hope was that they would return refreshed. After the tragedy of actually dropping points the previous week, and with Arsenal and Chelsea matches on the horizon (a distant one admittedly, this was the last league game of February), this game suddenly took on some importance.

Yeah, City are 1/200 for the league but still, it doesn't take much for us City fans to panic. A corner for the opposition is usually sufficient.

The team did not hold many surprises. David Silva had seemingly not recovered from his hip problems, and so the line-up was predictable, if we assume John Stones, just back from injury, was being held back for future games. Zinchenko though got the nod over Danilo.

Mahrez made the bench for Leicester. No surprise there either. Back in training the previous day, it would not have sent out a good message to the rest of the squad if he had started. Iheanacho was also on the bench.

And so with a storm brewing (well heavy rain forecast) and the opposition no slouches, it was reassuring to gain that early goal, even more so for Raheem Sterling to exorcise previous horrors after only two minutes. Thankfully he didn't miss this tap in, and naturally it was preceded by another inch-perfect Kevin De Bruyne cross. Obviously.

This gave the team breathing space, but despite dominating the ball, they did not really move on from there. They were on top though, and essentially it was an error that got Leicester level .Blame has been apportioned to a few City players for Vardy's equalizer — my scale of blame goes: Otamendi, Gundogan, Zinchenko, Laporte.

Otamendi's poor pass of course started everything. Zinchenko dived in, but probably realised he would not keep up with Vardy so thought it the only option. Gundogan had a better opportunity, but dived in too — wrong decision. Laporte shadowed Vardy and got a semi-block on the shot, but it continued in the same direction and into the bottom corner of the net.

So the early good work undone, and the rest of the first half panned out much like quite a few others. Proof that City games should be judged over 90 minutes, not 45. Sterling rounded the keeper after another exquisite De Bruyne pass, but his prod towards goal was deflected behind. Leicester's back 5 were stifling City, but not creating anything themselves.

And you should judge City matches over 90 minutes, because a tiring opposition in 2nd halves is a trend not to be ignored. City have scored as many goals in 2nd halves now as Arsenal and Manchester United have in total. And Puel gambled at half-time to try and create more up the field, going to a back four, taking Silva off, bringing on Danny Simpson and it all backfired. Maybe they would have lost heavily anyway, we shall never know.

The reason they have might have lost anyway was one of the most sublime moments of skill in a season of sublime moments. A pass from the left side of the penalty area across goal for Aguero to tap in doesn't sound like it should enter the pantheon of great assists, but this pass should. 99.9% of footballers would have used their left foot to put a ball across the area, but De Bruyne is not 99.9% of footballers. Instead he used his right foot in an instant, took out Maguire in an instant and City had their lead back, from a situation that did not appear super-threatening.

And after that, City took control, and Schmeichel fell to pieces. He obviously felt that playing out from the back was the only way the visitors could retain some possession and start threatening our defence, but he's no Ederson. But first a rocket from Aguero made it three, and the keeper can't take much blame for it, the power proving too much, though he got his body to it. His play-out play prior to that though created the chance, after Walker's chase-down of his own through ball. Next came his nadir, passing towards a defender, Aguero sniffed an opportunity, and sealed his hat-trick with a delightful chip. All was left was to finish it off with a thunderbolt from outside the area, power again beating Schmeichel even though it went in off the centre of the bar.

Job done, and the pressure off in the league until next month at the earliest. Mahrez finally got on, and Danilo came on soon after to deal with him, but the game was over by that stage even if Aguero still had work to do.

Aguero is a key example of why we shouldn't assess single halves in matches. Barely above average in the first half, he was unstoppable in the second. The leading scorer in Europe in 2018, almost in the top 10 of all-time Premier League scorers, and outscoring the likes of Suaraz, Messi, Ronaldo and Neymar over the season as a whole.

Do we ask too much of him? He's the greatest striker I have ever seen, he has his lulls, but every player not called Messi (or De Bruyne) does, and his stats are ridiculous. The greatest goals per minute ratio of them all, this will be the 5th season in a row he has scored at least 28 goals for City. The only question is whether he fits into a Pep system, but hopefully the manager's views have mellowed on that front. You can have all the money in the world, it is still an ominous task replacing his goals.

Shout out to Kyle Walker, who chased down his own failed pass to create one of the goals. It's unfair I've mentioned him so little this season so far (repeating myself), apart from a solitary mistake against Burnley, but he has just been so consistently good that it's pretty much passed everyone by in a season of superstar performances and record-breaking stats. An absolute steal, whatever the price.

There's a movement to have Salah considered as a key contender for Player of The Year alongside De Bruyne. He's been magnificent, but come on. The voting is done early by players, anytime now in fact, and I can say without bias that if De Bruyne does not win it this season the whole system is utterly discredited and I will cry and cry and cry.

This was, however, the first time De Bruyne has been credited with three assists in a single game for City. Still, if colleagues hadn't been so wasteful in the past, it should probably have been about the tenth time.

And the next day United waved the white flag, losing to a Newcastle United team that hadn't won at home in four months. The visitors were abject. City go 16 points clear, and the fat lady has not only cleared her throat, the microphone is on and she's good to go. Never felt more like singing the blues……..

No time to relax though, because it was time for the knockout stages of the Champions League.

Mourinho v Guardiola

What coping mechanisms do you employ when a bald fraud's oil-funded bunch of merry mercenaries are running away with the league title? What do you do when this team is your nearest rival (whilst pretending they're not your "biggest" rival), when you have both spent bucket-loads of cash but only they are excelling, and when even your Emptyhad jibes seem as laboured and tired as Wayne Rooney after emerging at dawn from a packed Saga coach? Well you change the narrative once more of course and you Claim that Jose Mourinho, who took over United in the same summer as Pep Guardiola, after both teams had finished the previous season on the same number of points, inherited a weaker side and has had the bigger building job, a Claim that seems to have been widely accepted by all and sundry.

But is it really true?

Finishing level on points does not tell the whole story, naturally. Teams over-achieve, teams under-achieve, they suffer bad luck, good luck, bad injuries, bad decisions. It's a guide, but it does not offer a definitive conclusion on the strength of the relative squads. It should however, not be dismissed. Both Pep Guardiola and Jose Mourinho had plenty of work to do on squads with many problems, and both had a nice warm-up period to plan before taking up the reins, though Jose had bugger all else to do, unlike Pep, who had the small matter of managing Bayern Munich. Pep's appointment was announced many months before Jose's, but have little doubt that the Portuguese eye-gouger knew he was going to United for some time.

City stumbled over the finishing line the previous season with a dire 1-1 draw at Swansea City. Only five of City's starters that day are still at the Club, and one of that five is the oft-maligned Mangala. City lined up with Hart, Navas, Sagna, Mangala, Clichy, Fernando and Iheanacho. On the bench were Kolarov, Nasri, Bony, Caballero, Demichelis, and the already-fading Yaya Toure. The line-up tells you everything you need to know – City had a huge rebuilding job to do, with a keeper Pep thought was not fit for purpose (which was, sadly, correct, and it took him two bites of the cherry to sort that), a rapidly-ageing full-back rota that would be replaced wholesale, a Club captain who could not stay fit for two weeks at a time, and now can't again, and a host of problems elsewhere, especially up front, with a raft of excluded players almost unsellable because of their hefty wages. There was work to be done, not least because those that stayed plus all new arrivals had to accept and incorporate the Pep way into their playing style, a system they will never have encountered before, a complicated system that leaves little room for error.

And that is precisely what the City players have now done.

Across the city, the narrative would have you believe that the United team that finished the 2015/16 season level on points with City were a bunch of average, uninspiring plucky part-timers with barely a top-class player amongst them. The Moyes and Van Gaal years had left something of a mess, there's little doubt about that, but to Claim there was a lack of talent is laughable.

Oh but you had a world-Class spine exclaim United fans! We had Silva, De Bruyne, Aguero and sometimes we had Kompany too. Hardly the basis for City "terrifying Europe" and the excellent Fernandinho, who struggles to get a regular gig for Brazil hints at great coaching and utilisation rather than being bought in to guarantee instant success (how many a Spurs fan laughed as they brought in Paulinho around the same time).

United? Of course they have the world's best keeper and in front of him the future of the England defence for a decade, or so I was told. Let's not forget that Phil Jones was the new Duncan Edwards. They'd spent £30m on Luke Shaw, the most expensive teenager ever, until they broke their own record on Martial. They had the bright young thing of English football, Rashford, they had the player of the year Mata recruited at just shy of £40m, they had Schneiderlin. They had players that had been there and done it, won leagues and cups. Young, Valencia were top class, that was the narrative then. Many of the old guard are still at the club and still playing. If they were not fit for purpose, what does this tell us about the job Mourinho and Woodward have done if they remain at the club and get ample playing time? Is this not what the narrative should be?

Whatever the truth, United immediately brought in an old youth player for £90m to help that "spine". Bailly added to that spine, Ibrahimovic too, with the Bundesliga top assister Mkhitaryan thrown in for good measure. Both of Mourinho's seasons have started with many in the football media world tipping them to win the title.

But of course this is not just about who built the squad better right now - this gap, this chasm, is about more and that was really rankles with many across the divide. It's about improvement of players at your disposal, and one of the two managers is streets ahead. Because on current form, by judging how players are performing right now and in previous months, after Jose got six big-money targets he had instructed Woodward to acquire, how many United players would currently get into City's team? Two, if we're full of Christmas spirit. City's form might be a blip, an outlier, maybe that view will change, but does it feel like it will to you? Meanwhile United fans are saddled with a manager most of them despise but must pretend to have some affection for, playing in a way that goes against what's in their DNA, whatever that means. Trapped.
Won two trophies though!

The narrative works by re-writing history, by re-evaluating how good players are. Walker's a waste of money, but now City are successful because we splurged money on full-backs. Sterling's only asset is pace, but now of course he's brilliant, but you'd expect that after what City paid for him.

It's classic deflection. United's squad was probably slightly worse than City's in the summer of 2016, it lacked a sparkle, though both underwhelmed to a great degree. Look at that squad for the Swansea squad once more and marvel at how far we have come. But, if United were missing a top-class spine and more, they have had three transfer windows since then, and endless cash, to rectify previous errors. To use it as an excuse for failure eighteen months down the line is rather desperate. They could have bought a Salah or a Kevin De Bruyne, though naturally Mourinho would soon sell them on anyway.

Schneiderlin was supposed to be that rock at the base of the midfield, the engine-room like Gareth Barry was for us. They've got Matic now anyway, who Chelsea were fools for letting go, so everyone proclaimed. Juan Mata was signed for big money as reigning Football Player of the Year. Martial was the next big thing in French football, Duncan Castles told me so. All these players are not rubbish, they cannot be dismissed as poor players that left United at a disadvantage; they were players that could have succeeded at United (as two of them still might) if coached properly. But now history can view a raft of expensively-imported players at Old Trafford as average at best, simply because they were not a success. Schweinsteiger, Depay, Di Maria, Januzaj - all were going to bring back the glory years to Old Trafford. But alas, no. Their FIFA rating downgraded, the general consensus now reached that Mourinho needs another season to get this rabble in shape. A narrative conveniently changes when things don't go so well.

Don't fall for it, this coping mechanism. I understand why it happens and it happens in the modern glare of social media. Thank god I didn't have to frequent Twitter in the 1990s. The number of appalling decisions made by my football club would drive anyone to drink. But in those days you could forget about football for most of the week, away from the water-cooler or playground. Not anymore, if you enjoy perusing the internet. Any failure is magnified again and again and again, every signing, every kick of the ball scrutinised to death. And you need a comfort blanket when you're not the best anymore, when you can't buy all the best players and lord it over all and sundry. You seek reassuring views, views that make you believe that better times may be around the corner. And that's what is happening right now. Jose Mourinho and Pep Guardiola both had to turn underwhelming squads into world-beaters, with ample resources at their disposal. They both had the same remit. Guardiola had a tough first season, Mourinho too but won a couple of lesser trophies, so came out ahead.
But now it is a one-horse race, for now. Historical records are being broken, one team is a juggernaut. One of the two managers is doing a

far better job, one club has a plan, a structure throughout the Club that is designed for continual success – hey one club even has a women's team too. One club is just run better. The other has a manager poisoning the atmosphere as he always does, only this time a season ahead of schedule, before arranging his release to PSG. And this has not all come about because one manager had a bigger building job, it's come about because of the way they went about that building job, and where it has left them now. That's just the way it is. Accept it, because as always with football, it will change – but don't re-write history in the process.

Champions League: Basel 0 Manchester City 4

I'll be honest, I wasn't expecting that. The biggest ever away win by an English side in the knockout stages in the history of the Champions League, and surely the tie has been put to bed with the 2nd tie still to come.

On a cold Swiss night, City were overwhelming favourites, but Basel had put 4 of the last 5 English visitors to the sword – they were not to be pithily dismissed.

The line-up certainly put some of my predictions in the trash bin. Kompany started, and from nowhere, Fabian Delph was fit and in the starting line-up. Great to see.

The bottom line is that this was a mismatch most of the time – City's one-touch passing and movement is back to its best, their domination of possession (74% on this occasion) suffocating, and the home team could not cope, until City eased off with four goals in the (onion) bag. The team is imperious right now.

Wigan 1 Manchester City 0 – FA Cup 5th Round

I keep trying to write match thoughts on this game, then stopping. It's too annoying to go over old ground.

And I doubt you want to recall the night's events either, so I might as well cut my losses and run.

So to be brief – City are out of the FA Cup, and whatever the circumstances, wherever the club is on its journey, this hurts. I'd hate to be a club that did not consider the FA Cup important as despite how it has been messed about and disrespected by the FA and managers alike down the years, it is still special to me, the oldest cup competition in the world. And I think of the great away days to Aston Villa or Huddersfield (match excepted), Middlesbrough and the likes, and there's no experience like it – cup away days are the best.

And whilst I can't say with any certainty that Pep and the players have disrespected the competition, putting Bravo in net tells you all you need to know. What's more, if this was a league game with something big at stake, could you really see City losing this? Lose just a few percent of intensity in players, and this is the result.

Otherwise, everything went wrong on the night, one of those nights you just want to forget as quickly as possible. A red card? It was on the edge of one, so you can't really complain or at least call it a miscarriage of justice, but I've seen so many similar or worse tackles against City players go unpunished this season that I don't even have the energy to get angry about it all. Throw in the fact the goal was offside, helped by Walker's inexplicable decision to leave the through ball, the pitch invasion trouble and the tedious mentions of how City's quadruple claims had been quashed when no one had ever talked about it, and the night was complete.

29 shots, 82% possession, no goals. Wigan defended superbly, and now are probably our only bogey team. Let's hope we don't get them in the cup anytime soon.

Yellow Ribbons And Arab Despots – Pep Guardiola's Moral Compass

Credit to Pep Guardiola, who managed to get himself in trouble via a novel method – wearing a yellow ribbon.

First, I should remind you why Pep wears a yellow ribbon, one he had been wearing for quite a while on the touchline, before the FA told him to stop. Guardiola is wearing the yellow ribbon in support of the Catalan politicians who were jailed during the region's fight for independence last month. Speaking about the situation after Man City's win over Napoli, the Citizens boss said: "I hope that the politicians in prison can leave as soon as possible for their families."

"If it can happen to them then it can happen to us. For giving an opinion. People shouldn't be confused and think it couldn't happen to them, because it can."

Many think the ribbon is to support independence itself, but that is not the case.

Anyway, the FA considers the ribbon a political symbol, and these are not allowed on apparel on the touchline. Unfortunately the FA can never be trusted to do much right, and the utterly ridiculous saga over poppies on shirts proved that. UEFA are fine with the ribbon being worn, but the FA take a different view. Hence he has been told to remove it when on the touchline., Pep's cause not helped by Jose Mourinho whinging about it the week before.

Pep will accept the charge, but whether he continues to wear the ribbon remains to be seen. You can imagine he would, and that will give the FA bigwigs a real dilemma.

A separate charge that the nation, now suddenly keen about human rights around the globe, put to Pep was that he was something of a hypocrite for being picky about his human rights concerns, considering who his club's owners were. Not really. It's not that unusual to be passionate about concerns closer to home – Pep is a passionate Catalan, so this is an issue that will mean the most to him. After all, are you as concerned about human rights in Burma as human rights in England? Thought not. But in reality, he's hardly going to criticise his bosses. He will have his views, but they will remain private, as you'd expect.

Most importantly, Pep has missed a trick here. He should go the Morrissey route (not the racism and all that) by having a bunch of yellow daffs hanging out his back pocket each match. Problem solved.

But never mind, because the club had other things to think about – City were off to Wembley again.

Carabao Cup Final – Manchester City 3 Arsenal 0

Have you ever sat/stood at a cup final, relaxed, hoping your team didn't score any more goals? Well I did this weekend? More on why later.

So not a Champions League final, but the chance for Pep's first trophy, and the first trophy at City for quite a few players too.
A chance to win the trophy for the third time in five years, to forget Wigan, to forget #yellowribbongate, to celebrate this great team. Fingers crossed.

City would put out the better team, we knew that before the team-sheets were released, but that is only half the story, and victory would have to be earned. The defeat at Wigan was still clear in our minds, Arsenal's record against City is better than most, as is Wenger's record at Wembley. Having said that, Pep's final record is one game (Real Madrid) away from perfection, so something had to give.

And a trip to Wembley never gets boring. Virgin trains heated to the temperature of a tandoor oven makes me regret travelling occasionally, but still, it was worth it, the dread of that early alarm call, the train down and a few light beverages to quench one's thirst, the drinks in London requiring a re-mortgage of your house, the walk down Wembley Way, the maniac that always seems to be sat in close vicinity, it's all part of the experience.

And so to the team. Surprises? Not really – Sterling was not fit to play, or even make the bench, the main talking point being the inclusion of Kompany, as we all knew Bravo would start. Gundogan over Bernardo Silva and Danilo over Zinchenko were the only other decisions to be made, but none were particularly surprising nor controversial.

But what a strange first half. Tepid, almost. Wenger reverted back to a back three, and the midfield seemed congested. Passes were misplaced, especially by Gundogan.

The big early chance fell to Arsenal, though Aubameyang seemed offside to me. Still, kudos to Walker for his recovery tackle and Bravo for doing the rest. Early scare, disaster averted, and that was probably the only big chance Arsenal created all afternoon.

When we considered how City may score goals, we probably didn't envisage a long ball from Bravo, but this is a team full of surprises. Aided by some abject defending from Mustafi, the rest is history. As for talk of a foul, give over. Aguero simply stood still. With Ospina off his line, Aguero did the rest, and City had that crucial lead. Surprisingly it was Aguero's first goal in a final.

The rest of the half didn't really sparkle, but the emphasis was on Arsenal to do something, as they trailed, but they had little to offer. Aubameyang was shackled by Kompany on numerous occasions, and the only apparent threat, a ball over the top, did not present Arsenal with a route back into the game.

With Fernandinho picking up a hamstring strain just after half-time though, there was concern that this would leave the defence lacking protection, but there was no reason to worry. Bernardo came on, played well, and once Kompany had doubled the lead in the 2nd half, Arsenal had nothing. There was even time for Silva to add a great third goal after a good pass from Danilo, and how great to see the old guard score the goals.

As for calls of offside for the 2nd goal, there was no case to answer, as Sane, who does need to stop goal-hanging, did not impede Ospina in any shape or form. If you think that was offside, you need to learn the laws of football properly.

And how great to see Vincent Kompany manically celebrate a goal again, reminiscent of THAT goal against United in 2012. What a day for him and whatever happens in the future, I'm deeply grateful he got at least one more day like this. Now lift that Premier League trophy for us at least one more time Vincent.

After that, as I mentioned earlier, I was happy to see City close the game down, as I had a couple of pounds on Aguero 1st goal and a 3-0 scoreline. A nice £400 for four of us that almost covered a couple of rounds in London.

And good to see Phil Foden get on the pitch too. That's one more trophy than James Milner has won since he left City.

So a trophy in the bag, and a good night (and terrible curry) to follow, before we dragged our sore heads back north the following morning, dodging the three snowflakes that threatened to bring the capital to a standstill.

A quick note on the Arsenal fans not staying until the end – I've no problem with that –as a fan-base we can hardly criticise on that front, we leave in droves when we're winning, but they are being abjectly managed right now, their performance lifeless, as City move away from them at considerable speed. I wouldn't have stayed, just like I didn't after Wigan beat us.

We need to talk about Jack Wilshere, a man chiselled out of the same bitter, paranoid shell as his manager. After the game, as you probably are aware, he posted a few of his special thoughts on Instagram, thoughts that make you wonder if Wenger had stolen his phone, or at least hacked his social media accounts. He bemoaned the perfectly legitimate first goal, called the 2nd goal offside, and suggested Fernandinho should have been sent off late in the first half when Wilshere dived over his stationary leg. Apart from all his points being incorrect, he was spot on, to be fair. What's your next conspiracy theory, Jack? Expect him to claim that jet fuel can't metal beams.

Leaving aside the legitimacy of his points, what is more damning is making such thoughts public. It is deeply embarrassing, but probably not that surprising when we consider who his coach is. This petty, hissy-fit whining makes him look more of a moron than he already did, which is impressive, considering he also tried to get a City player booked by kicking a free kick at him deliberately. If Arsenal football club pertains to greatness once more in the future, players like Wilshere should be first out of the door, the epitome of everything wrong with that club right now.

Cranks of the day – as always there was one around me – this time sat to my right. He called the City team white boys all game, kept repeating his mantra about how David Silva was the best player ever and that De Bruyne was overrated, slagged Gundogan constantly ("he's shit), and constantly called the Arsenal fans and match officials "Munichs". Apart from that he was fine.

As for the opposition, how bizarre and rather unsettling to walk into a pub later that night to hear a group of fans singing "who's that lying on the runway?"
A group of Arsenal fans, that is.
We had a good chat later nevertheless, and were sent on our way with the words "two years ago when there weren't any cameras around, we'd have battered you!"
Yeah right. The only thing they'd have battered us with was a plate of couscous and a few Wenger Out banners.

The Continued Bad Treatment Of Football Fans

Once we had all expressed our strong political opinions on the situation in Catalonia, and showed our support with yellow ribbons, inflatable oak trees and a vow to go on hunger strike to support our beleaguered boss, it was good to get down to an actual football match on Sunday, even nicer to win a trophy at the end of it, the first trophy of many hopefully for pep and quite a few of the players at city.

As I stood in an endless queue though after the match, stuck at a human traffic light before I was eventually allowed to get on a tube, there was something else that struck me too. The utter stupidity that saw me watch a cup final at 4:30pm on a Sunday afternoon. Nothing new of course – as I made my way to Wembley in May 2011, to see if my team could win its first trophy of my supporting life, news filtered through that United had won the league with a draw at Blackburn. Welcome to the future, where special days at Wembley are downgraded to being just part of the day's wider entertainment. Super Sunday, Mega Monday, stupendous Saturday. Cup finals used to mean something, they were a big event – I'd sit there in full City kit watching the other teams strive for glory, watching the teams arrive, soaking up the atmosphere of the special day. I dreamt of going once in my life, now cup finals are inconveniencing me. Not sure why I sat there in full City kit aged 23 either, to be honest.

I stayed over in London, but it's just as well. If City had won in a similar manner to their previous league cup final, i.e. on penalties, you'd have been lucky to reach the tube before 8pm. Good luck getting back to Manchester then.

The FA doesn't care one jot, just like the Premier League, Carabao, BT Sport, Sky or whoever was involved in us reaching such a situation. City are due to play a derby on an early Saturday evening – there could be a league title to be won, against our bitterest rivals, but hey, what's the worst that could happen? Spurs away – yeah, lets' put that at 7:45pm on a Saturday, trains back from the capital are notoriously frequent, reliable, and run throughout the night, so what's the worst that could happen? Whilst we're at it, let's send Brighton fans up to Old Trafford to play their FA Cup quarter-final match at the same time.

And when I say that City are playing United at tea time on a Saturday evening, that is naturally subject to change again, so don't go actually planning your life, or anything similarly stupid. That is where we are at now – rearranged games that are still somehow subject to change. What's next? Well the Premier League teams may escape this particular change, but as of next season, we will see 5:55pm Champions League kick off games, another kick in the private parts for all working football fans. Still, nice of UEFA to change the rules so that 4th place in the league goes automatically into the group stage as of next season too, now that teams like United and Liverpool are fighting for that spot rather than City. Complete coincidence of course, and I wish Phil Townsend, the latest United executive to move to a new job at UEFA, all the best in his new rule.

But back to us proles. Yeah, it's not a revelation for me to point out to you all that football is no longer for fans in grounds. Football is for the man or woman in the pub, it's for the armchair fan, designed to provide wall-to-wall coverage for those far from the actual action. Games stacked one after another to sate those that need wall-to-wall action. That's assuming United aren't playing, obviously.

There's no bigger indication of football moving away from match-going fans for me than VAR, which I always thought was a great idea and a necessary for the game of football – now I'm not so sure, though it can improve, that's what trials are for after all, and some will never accept it however well it goes. But at Wembley, I saw the down-side in action, kind of. When Aguero lobbed Ospina to put City ahead, I celebrated manically along with everyone else around me, including the crank sat next to me. But then I stopped. Because it suddenly dawned on me that I could know for sure that City were actually winning the match. Mustafi was complaining to the referee, there was plenty of activity on the touchline too. Maybe there always is, and I just hadn't given it much attention in the past. But now, well a goal could be reviewed and retrospectively disallowed. Until that ball was carried back to the centre circle, I couldn't be sure, and no one really knew whether there was a review or not. Apparently I have read that VAR was used seamlessly for Kompany's goal, but being in the ground I couldn't possibly know that. You have to be watching on TV to get the inside track nowadays. Let's not even get started on the Spurs match, because whilst during that bizarre first half most decisions, if not all, were correct, it would no doubt have left the people in the actual ground dumbfounded. Bit harsh booking son too for stopping during his penalty run-up.

But anyway, finally back to those pesky kick off times. The problem is a particularly British one. When Borussia Dortmund recently played on a Monday night for what I think was the first time, 25,000 fans didn't turn up, out of protest. If City fans did that, the banter brigade would explode in glee. Carrick4united or simplymartial would probably go blind with the over-excitement such a protest would cause. But of course we keep turning up, on the whole, however much we are messed about, another TV deal for staggering amounts is on the way, and the wheels keep turning, the bubbles refuse to burst. This is the future. Games at midnight refereed by robots in a studio all to satisfy the lucrative Asian market and united fans in Singapore and cork. Welcome to a brave new world.

Arsenal 0 Manchester City 3

See previous review.

Well not really – this was even better, even easier.

As the "beast from the east" ravaged the country, talk was of this game not going ahead. It did, hence this match report, but the message didn't seem to reach most Arsenal fans, who stayed away in droves. Can't say I blame them.

Before this game, that I would have secretly have been happy to see called off, it was agreed on the 9320 podcast that 4 points would be a good return for the next two tough games, enough certainly to pretty much end any talk of a title race. 4 points would mean a 14 point lead at the top, if United won on Monday night at Crystal Palace, and with just 9 games to go. The fact is that City only need to maintain relegation form to win their third Premier League title. Even the world's greatest pessimist (me) must admit it's over now.

Though if we lose to Chelsea... (shut up Howard)

Was that the greatest half of them all? Well the caveat must be the level of the opposition, but having taken that into account, the answer may still be yes. Just look at the goals. I almost felt sorry for Arsenal and their fans at one point. Almost.

Arsenal started brightly, but once City moved through the gears, the result was rarely in doubt. City have only won 1 in 32 at Arsenal, their home form remains strong, and they did show a response to Sunday, until City seized control. A beautiful curled shot from Bernardo Silva started the rout, then David Silva finished off a silky move. Sane scored the third, the best move of the lot, even if the finish was the messiest of the three by a long, long way.

I'm not even convinced this was one of Arsenal's poorer performances. I'm not sure there was much they could do.

When Arsenal threatened, Ederson was a match for it all, the flourish being another penalty save. That's 5 penalty saves from 9 from City keepers, and Ederson once saved an Aubameyang penalty whilst Benfica keeper too.

The history of football is littered with teams that have a large half-time lead not adding to the tally in the 2nd half, and this was no different. City eased off the throttle, and saved their energy for battles ahead, closing down the game.

And all without Stones, Laporte, Delph, Mendy, Fernandinho, Jesus, Sterling and more.

With 10 games to go, City match the points tally of United's title-winning team of 1996/97.

To put it another way - this is a special team.

And another special word for Arsene Wenger, who for some reason seemed to feel the need to have a passionate conversation with Pep Guardiola as they came out for the match. Or the need to lecture him is how it looked to me. The look on Pep's face is priceless, the look you'd expect from a drunk uncle telling you how he once cracked the Enigma machine in an afternoon, but was told to never tell anyone about it. Whatever he was saying, Pep clearly wasn't interested, but is enough of a gentleman to take it and walk away.

Manchester City 1 Chelsea 0

Well surely that is it. Job done, the title on the way? I'm not counting my chickens until it's mathematically impossible to mess it up. But still, surely....?

Still, what a week. A trophy, 2 league wins, 3 clean sheets, the march continues.

But what a strange match. A training exercise between a team in possession and one without. Chelsea came to restrict, and at half-time you could argue it was working just fine. But their attacking intent was so non-existent that it felt like delaying the inevitable. And so when the Bernardo Silva shinned City into the lead almost immediately after half-time, the game was 90% over as a contest.

For a neutral, this would hardly have made for compelling football. Still, that not City's concern, especially when only one team wants to play.

Another good performance from Sergio Aguero, without scoring – proof that is game is about more than goals nowadays.

And never have I felt more relaxed with a single-goal lead against a big rival as the game neared the end. Alonso managed to shoot wide, but the danger seemed non-existent.

There's little point saying more. City won, and that's all that matters. The title is now in the bag, and it's time to count down to the moment when it is definite. Could it be on derby day? Surely not.

Paul Pogba

(read in the style of David Attenborough)

It's 2027. In a block at United's training ground, we see one of nature's most enigmatic occurrences – a herd of midfielders collected together over a 10 year period to "free" Paul Pogba. Estimates on numbers vary, but most agree the number is at least 20. Together they cost over £1.4 billion, but by now, they are almost worthless. Their task, to allow Paul Pogba more freedom to dab, get new haircuts and occasionally play some nice football, has failed miserably, on the last point at least.
The colony started out with a single member, known only as Matic, but twice a year, the pack leader would add to the numbers in order to allow Pogba to reach his full potential. First came Veratti, a wild animal not suited to the pack. Pogba was not freed, but changed his hair colour with increasing frequency, like a threatened chameleon. Next came Fred, but Pogba remained in his shell.
Over the course of 9 years, 74 more midfielders have been added to the pack, but all to avail. Now they live in isolation in a wing at Carrington, where they survive on dance videos, Instagram posts and wining second-tier trophies.
Sadly the pack has hit hard times. Numbers are threatened, and conservationists predict that within 15 years there may be no dabbers left in the UK. This is why we need your help.

Just £5 will buy enough hair dye to change Pogba's hair colour three times.
£10 would provide one bursary for Dab University.
£20 would allow Jesse Lingard to make more Instagram posts.

Please help today. Every donation makes a difference. Please help those less fortunate than you.

Champions League: Manchester City 1 Basel 2.

What can you say? Nothing really. The crowd was bigger than I expected. The match didn't matter. City played worse than usual having made wholesale changes, which is usual. Foden got a run-out, the youngest ever English player in the knock-out stages of a Champions League. Also the youngest starter in an English team. City started well. They defended badly at times. We can take nothing from the player performances in what was close to a dead rubber. City were never in danger of going out. City thus qualify for the quarter-finals of the Champions League with the minimum of fuss. The trams were rubbish as always after the game. I had cheese on toast then went to bed.

Raheem Sterling

I wrote this article in January 2017 – I found it interesting to re-visit as Sterling progresses through his best ever season. After all, some of the same questions still linger.

Apart from trying to quantify just how big Wayne Rooney's decline has been over the past couple of years (it's big), there are few players that create such discussion and such disagreement than a specific 22 year old English attacking midfielder. Why this is so can be hard to pin down, but the disagreements from fans of other teams does not bother me in the slightest – most of those who dismiss him as a great player could write their football knowledge on the back of a stamp.

What's more disconcerting is the criticism he gets from City fans, those that watch him every week. He's clearly not perfect, and world class performances week in, week out would have stopped such an occurrence, but how many players reach that level consistently? No, the criticisms hint at something else apart from how well he plays. And it's worrying, because when you sit in the ground and listen to a vocal minority who cannot wait to criticise him for every mistake, it makes you wonder why you bother and where this attitude comes from.

So I thought I would list what I think are the reasons for why an unassuming footballer who has done very little to deserve real headlines can be so divisive.

He's crap.

What?!

Well let's be frank. There are City fans out there that think that a young player directly involved in 39 of our goals since he joined 18 months ago has no other asset except speed.

Now he does have flaws, they are plain for all to see, flaws that expose him at times. He is hesitant at times in the area, lacking decisiveness, I feel he lacks physicality (not an essential trait, but still) and his shooting is clearly a major weakness that needs work.

And yet he is often our brightest attacking spark, his positional sense, football intelligence and movement is incredible for someone who has just turned 22, and the stats show him in a good light too. He also never hides. Two international managers and two club managers – in other words, every manager he has played for – rate him and play/played him regularly. But hey, what would they know?

And it is weird how those that don't rate him shout the loudest after a bad performance, but are nowhere to be seen when he excels – and let's not forget, even during last season's disappointments, when many players failed to live up to expectations, and when he was abused wherever he went, Sterling was probably our best player in the Champions League.

And yet even with his clear improvement this season, perhaps the biggest improvement of any player under Pep, the warmth remains elusive from many.

"If he can't handle a bit of booing then he's in the wrong game" is an opinion I've heard many times. I bet they wouldn't be so dismissive if it was David Silva who had been booed for 12 months.

So in summary, man up Raheem, you snowflake.

Liverpool's hatchet job rubbed off on some of us.

Raheem Sterling is clearly an ambitious man who believes in himself, and like many thousands of footballers before him, and many thousands in the future, he wished to leave his football club for another one. We all know what transpired, and the Liverpool media cabal went to work, as did the club's own PR department - thus he was booed for an entire season by every set of fans he encountered.

And if Norwich fans believed that he was a money-grabbing snake who went on strike to force a move and betrayed the Club that had nurtured him from an embryo to the man he is today, then I would bet all the money in the world that some City fans have their doubts about his character too.

It's also part of the natural hypocrisy of the football fan who would happily drive an underperforming player out of a club, but cry betrayal if a good player requests a change in their career situation.

Other players are excused because....

A clear theme that you will see on message boards and social media is fellow City players receiving a fraction of the criticism that Sterling does should their form falter. One clear example is Sergio Aguero. I'd say there's a certain logic to this. Aguero has been there and done it, like other players whose form has dipped sometimes, such as David Silva or Yaya Toure. They've delivered historic moments and trophies, so they get leeway when they don't hit the heights. Aguero especially has got credit in the bank, for obvious reasons. It's not really fair, as Sterling hasn't had the chance yet to create history, but that's life.

The transfer fee.

I think this is definitely relevant. If Kelechi Ihenacho and Raheem Sterling played side by side for a season and both flattered to deceive, then Sterling would get the vast majority of the criticism and abuse. With a large transfer fee comes expectations, and standards. Players are often bought for potential, but as Sterling had already come close to winning a title at Liverpool, we sometimes forget that he still very young and far from his peak years, and at the price we paid some of us expect instant results, the complete player.
It's a bit harsh as the fee is simply the price at which Liverpool were prepared to sell, and what's more they did not want to, and there is the English premium to factor in, but it's hard sometimes to analyse a player without detaching yourself from what he has cost the club. If fans could do that, they'd have much less of a problem with a player who has been no worse than a host of other City players, and often much better. Personally I see what he could become in a few years – and it's bloody exciting.

Which begs the question?
Why does John Stones, six months older, just as expensive an acquisition, and regularly left out of the City side after a string of costly mistakes, attract far less vitriol than Raheem Sterling? Answers on a

postcard please.

Perhaps it's because of……….

The particular flaws in Sterling's game are what wind fans up the most.

Bit leftfield this, but hear me out. Sterling's flaws in his game are the type that frustrate, especially in a team that underperformed last season and appears to waste its chances this. Thus holding onto the ball when he should shoot or going to ground when you think he should also shoot or simply missing a good chance with a scuffed shot are the sort of situations that have fans tearing their hair out, if they have any left. As I have also mentioned elsewhere, whilst Raheem is no waif, I do not think he is overly-physical, and getting regularly barged off the ball by bigger, more physical opposition players, in a league that is extremely physical anyway, also rubs fans up the wrong way. The last thing we want though is him bulking up in the gym and losing the positive sides to his game.

On the other hand, I would offer an unproven theory that many fans see the mistake of John Stones as a by-product of the Pep system that requires panic-inducing passing sequences across our own area and is high-risk, always offering the chance of a horrendous mistake, so it's not really his fault.

Perception is all. After all, missing a sitter is more "obvious" than failing to pick up an opposition player at a corner or not tracking a run.

It's just a theory.

The colour of his skin.

The (non-white)elephant in the room.

I cannot state that this is a problem amongst City fans, nor can I claim to know how you all think, but there has clearly been an undercurrent in certain sections of the press, and amongst rival fans, a feeling that Sterling is being treated differently because he is a young, black man with money, despite the fact that apart from purchasing a nice house and car, as all top footballers do, he really has not been flaunting his wealth. But when the media repeats a narrative enough times, as the Express do for example with immigrants or impending arctic blasts, then it seeps into the psyche, even when simply parting the curtains reveals a peasant sunny day with a light south-westerly breeze.

I digress.

As I said, I think there are more relevant reasons for City fans' negative analysis of the player than this, and this is more a perception amongst the general public, and the odd right-wing tabloid editor.

A victim of an underachieving Club

The last two and a half years have not been the greatest in our history, if you accept the much higher expectations. The league cup victory was nice, but we are aiming higher than that nowadays.

And thus when times are hard, the knives come out, and as alluded to earlier, a City team must always have a scapegoat, and Sterling fits the bill nicely, having not been part of our previous successes.

Obviously Aleksandar Kolarov is also available for this role as and when required.

He runs funny.

It's amazing what little justification is needed to dislike a player. Even his sideburns last season had people tutting. Still, I'd happily see Daniel Sturridge sent to prison for 20 years for a crime he did not commit simply due to his goal celebration.

Yep, football fans are weird, illogical beasts. People are weird. The world's currently really weird.

Maybe it's that simple when it boils down to it.

Whatever, players, amazingly, tend to react positively when supported, when cheered on, as teams as a whole do.

Something to consider, eh? Because it's getting rather tiresome hearing one player get it in the neck for most of this team's ills. Sterling's attitude and willingness to learn and improve is spot on, and I think he can work on his weaknesses and become England's best wide player in a generation.

Show him some love, you won't regret it.

Stoke City 0 Manchester City 2

Something finally clicked in my brain after this win. I essentially knew after winning at Arsenal that the league was won. But, but, but....what if City lost to Chelsea, then Everton, United, and then they had Spurs too?! This was less likely than Luke Shaw winning slimmer of the year, but still that little doubt persisted. Then City beat Chelsea, and the league really was won, but, but, but...still those tricky games to come, and if the lead was as much as halved, panic could crop in. Again, rubbish, but still the lingering doubt persisted –it's what we do as City fans, after all. Hashtag typical city.
Anyway, that's gone now. City have won the league. It's obvious, it's undeniable.

There's not much to say really. City did it on a wet, cold night in Stoke, and they did it comfortably. Professional, dominant, and effective enough to cruise over the finish line. This is how titles are won.

With Jesus starting up front with Aguero absent, the likes of Bernardo Silva and Gundogan found themselves on the bench, to be brought on later in the game. It was the old Sane/Sterling/Fernandinho/KDB/David Silva combo that is usually so effective.

In the end it was two goals, but it could have been much more. And as is often the case, one player decides to shine even more than those around him. Across much of the season, that player has been Kevin De Bruyne, but he has almost taken something of a back seat in recent weeks as David Silva has elevated himself to new levels. Of course it's always good to see him score too, even better to see him score a brace.

And what a comprehensive endorsement of his professionalism and commitment to the cause that he has produced such stellar performances at a time of considerable turmoil in his private life. I couldn't love him more if I tried.

The first goal was a goal of real beauty. A beautiful through ball from Jesus, a pin-point cross from Sterling and a laser-like finish from Silva with a defender on each side. The second involved Jesus too as the provider, but was a result of incessant pressing that has served the team so well this season.

Stoke, battling for their Premier League lives, could produce little of note in attack, and once the second goal went in, there was little hope for them. The game was gone, and the title race was emphatically over. Don't go dusting down that trophy parade bus just yet, but we all know it will be needed in the coming months.

There's no denying it now. City are going to win the league for the first time in four years. All that talk of Pep not adapting to the Premier League, all that talk of how pretty passing won't cut the mustard in the England, all the media types willing Pep to fail in England. All white noise. It seems Pep knew what he was doing after all, and was not going to compromise for anyone.

It leaves one remaining question – when will they win it? And it is now looking distinctly possible that City could win the title against Manchester United. Oh my.

One final point – I wish I was as "fat" as Luke Shaw.

Let's All Laugh At United

I did a pub quiz on Tuesday night – we came 9th, pretty disappointing, but then I was a tad distracted. Yes, my worst ever pub quiz performance is being laid squarely at the feet of Jose Mourinho. Probably worth it, all things considered. The United v Sevilla game was on the TV, on silent, and I tried not to look up that often, waiting for the inevitable United goal. As you probably know by now, it never came, but we did get to see the greatest goalkeeper in the world, ever, create one of the great howlers of modern times. The quiz didn't seem too important after the hilarity of the match.

It's easy to mock as a City fan right now, so I took time out from enjoying pub life to do my usual retweets on twitter like the sad man that I am. Just doing my duty. Of course on the subject of mocking, us City fans have got a lot of catching up to do, and I've always held back because it will always come back and bite you on the behind eventually.
That Aguero goal is followed by a United title win, and there's always a game against Wigan on the horizon to bring us bitter berties back down to earth with a bump. Just mercilessly mocking United is puerile, it reeks of banter, the worst word in the English language, but mocking the swathes of deluded reds and other fans who put themselves out there to be shot at with their proclamations and superiority is fair game.
And for some reason, maybe because they were dominant for so long and now don't know what to do now they are no longer the playground bullies, at a time of social media explosion, United seem to have the worst fan accounts and so called expert commentators of anyone. A more blinkered, prejudiced, arrogant band of weirdos you will struggle to find. They really are a strange breed, and ripe for the dry humour I think many City fans carry off so well.
Everything they say contradicts itself – bemoaning glory hunter fans whilst mocking our empty seats. Bemoaning the price of football whilst again mocking empty seats. Excusing their empty seats because the ground's a bit bigger. Excusing their endless spending sprees against City's spending because it's organic whilst City have been self-sufficient for years. Hating Mourinho until he became their manager, then claiming it's just what the club needed after the Moyes and Van Gaal

years. Calling City small and United big, thus essentially outing themselves as glory hunters who only follow their team because of their size and global fan base. Wildly claiming every signing as the best and their players as the best but then excusing failure as they can't compete with City's wild spending. And the arrogance. Boy, the arrogance. They just don't get it. The Busby Babes, history, DNA, it means nothing when considering how to be successful right now, and in the future. Who's signing the mercenaries now, eh?

So desperate to put one over City, they signed a player on extortionate wages who would have been free in the summer and who Mourinho quickly turned into the new Bebe. Some achievement.

I retweet very specific things, and as I have pointed out to many a United fan, by retweeting or commenting on specific posts or opinions, I am not attacking Manchester United the football club, but specific people who said specific things – and most the time I'm attacking or highlighting the terrible standard of journalism that pervades the sport nowadays, an industry desperate for hits and thus advertising revenue. An industry that has left us with the Daily Mirror writing articles about every Paul Scholes or Gary Neville comment or tweet, a paper that writes daily articles entitled like : "Manchester United fans loved what Paul Pogba did during the Liverpool match". It's putrid, desperate stuff. But then there's the United arm of the industry. Being a United PR lickspittle is a whole industry, and a very lucrative one at that. Commenting on United and fighting their cause makes you more money than commenting on City, or Aston Villa, or Nottingham Forest. City still don't have that fan base, and probably won't for at least a decade, maybe more, maybe never. United sell. Right from the bottom, from the twitter accounts spewing drivel on an hourly basis, to the fans pretending to be United fans for financial reasons who have bizarrely made a career out of sitting in a bedroom commenting on a match they can see but you can't and being so pathetically pro-United and thus anti-City that it's clear they're just trying too hard and probably don't care that much about any of it really, as long as they get loads of hits.

The pro-united newspaper journalists are harder to work out though, as it's hard to know what they're getting out of it. Neil Custis is a Newcastle

United fan who is staggeringly pro-Mourinho and thus by extension pro-United, and clearly hates City and their oil money – always great to have a newspaper's Manchester correspondent batting for your side, eh? Anyway, Neil finds it impossible to criticise, so instead, when Mourinho does something appalling, as he is wont to do regularly nowadays, like denigrate the club's history or simply play a style of football that would send an insomniac into a coma, Custis does not dare criticise, but instead asks others what they think. Naturally he's not quite so reticent in criticising City, despite the fact they are playing football on a different planet to their neighbours right now. After all, if David Moyes had said some of the things Mourinho did this week, he would not only have lost his job immediately, but have been run out of town, had fatwas from the Men In Black and been ridiculed for life. But of course Jose Mourinho is different.

It's hard not to mock these sort of people when they are little more than the Pravda wing of a football club. Comical Ali stating everything is ok whilst everything crumbles behind him, fiddling whilst Rome burns. City fans don't want to become "them" or what we thought they represented during their glory years – not arrogant, just better and all that. But maybe we are in danger of falling into that category. Do we care? Do we mind if we are seen as arrogant, rather than everyone's 2nd club because we always messed everything up? Probably not. But I hope we don't lose our identity, that made us what we were, the gallows humour that flowed through the fan base through those many lean years. But also, perhaps we should make some hay whilst the sun shines, enjoy the ride and point out the utter hypocrisy and outright lies of others. Above all, it's a good laugh most of the time, though I would never resort to personal insults or low digs – their own words are normally good enough to make a point.

It's a strange time to be a City fan at the moment – it's almost hard to comprehend a 16 point gap at the top of the table, whilst simultaneously wondering if we'll still mess it up. It's hard to comprehend being one of the favourites for the Champions League, it's hard to comprehend that the squad should be even stronger next season. And hardest of all to comprehend, and the hardest thing of all for United fans to accept, though deep down they know it's true, is that the club of mis-shaped stands, botched takeovers, calamity buys, relegations and much, much more is now the club going places, the club with a clear identity, a clear philosophy, and a planning process 8 years in the making coming to fruition, whilst United stagger from one misfit to another, spending money randomly to try and reassert the playground hierarchy. So laugh all you want every time they mess up, it won't last forever. And it' what they would have done to us.

Week Of Destiny

And so everything I had feared might happen, did so. Liverpool in the Champions League. Feared not just because of their strength of their team, though they pose more problems than they should, but because what followed was as inevitable as night following day. Buckle up for the ride, it may be best to stay off the internet for a few weeks. Yes, it's like 2013/14 all over again, the Liverpool PR machine rolled out. History, five times, history, empty seats, history, atmosphere, history. The fan base is a cult, there's really no better word to describe them.

And right in the middle of those two games is the Manchester derby. Suddenly it doesn't seem as important, but beat Everton and it really, really is.

And that is what happened.

Everton 1 Manchester City 3

And then there was one.

One game.

Against United.

It has happened – City will win the league if they beat Manchester United next weekend.

Oh my.

Let's start with the hot debate of the moment – the hypothetical question over whether you'd rather win the league against United, or beat Liverpool over two legs. Answering both is not permitted in this hypothetical land.

After considerable thought, I went against the tide and plumped for winning the league. That's because whilst losing to Liverpool would indeed make the internet unbearable for the foreseeable future, it guarantees nothing – beat Liverpool and City still have two huge hurdles between them and the trophy. Beating United of course wins us a title that we're guaranteed of anyway, but the stars have aligned to give us bitter blues a rare opportunity. For all of United's dominance, they never won the title by beating City, they never relegated us either. Denis Law didn't relegate United either in 1974, they would have gone down anyway. So this could be a once-in-a-lifetime opportunity. It may not happen again. Nothing will beat the 93:20 moment, but winning the title at home to United would be a worthy runner-up.

Having said all that, I wouldn't wish to disagree with those that think Liverpool is bigger. There is after all a trophy to compete for, and the sanity of social media to preserve. And it is no surprise of Pep prioritises that, with news emerging that he may rest key players against United.

As for the match, it was as close to a walk in the park as you could hope against a team we struggle against so often. Sam Allardyce obliged by playing 4-4-2 and by putting Rooney in midfield, and Laporte played at left-back. It was fluid as ever though, with Walker pretty much a right winger, Sterling central, Sane hogging the touchline but moving infield often, and De Bruyne slightly more withdrawn than usual. Whatever it was, it worked.

After the 3-0 win at Arsenal in the league, the question was asked if that was the greatest half of goals ever, before City cruised through the 2nd half. The same question can be asked here. Sane's volley, his move to take Ederson's goal kick and help create the 2nd goal for Jesus, and the pin-point cross from Sterling to complete the first-half rout. All beautiful goals in different ways.

82% possession, the greatest share of the ball by an away side in Premier League history. Fernandinho with the most touches ever, almost as much possession as the whole of the home side. New records fall, and we shrug our shoulders as they are so commonplace. City become the third team to beat all other teams at least once in a season, and equalled the record of 13 away wins.

Oh, there's more. in the first half, both De Bruyne (61) and Fernandinho (62) completed more passes than Everton (59)... in the 57 minutes Rooney and Schneiderlin played together, they managed eight completed passes between them.

Everton rallied after Bolasie squeezed the ball in off the post, but it was short-lived. City wrestled back control of the ball, and saw the game out without really breaking sweat. This is football on another level, that keeps previously troublesome teams like Everton at arm's length.

Was this line up a dress rehearsal for Liverpool? Possibly, though only time will tell. Laporte seems the only serious option for left-back, and a withdrawn De Bruyne might help track Liverpool's midfield runners. Pep might want the game stretched to the wings, to avoid midfield carnage, and he has to decide if Sterling is up for the fight, and whether Kompany is fit for another game. Jesus was back to his industrious best, and with Aguero still on the cusp of full fitness, he will probably retain his place. The nerves are kicking in as I type these words.

THE WEEK FROM HELL

Liverpool 3 Manchester City 0

I'll be honest, it's hard to write about this match. And you probably don't want to read about it anyway. After weeks of crowing about European heritage, atmosphere and a lot more besides, I really wanted this one to go well, more than was good for my health. But it didn't. It went terribly.

In a way it was good to get round to the actual football, rather than the talk that preceded it. But Pep Guardiola, who has not been to a Champions League final in 7 years, may well have overthought this one.

Adding Gundogan into midfield simply did not work. And by the time this was acted upon, it was too late.

For all the poor play, and the admission that City deserved this one, there were to be no breaks during this hellish week, that's for sure. Salah was offside for the first goal, but nothing was given. Sane was about 3mm offside when crossing for Jesus to hit home in the second half, if at all, and that was given. Robertson slid through Sterling to get a ball in the second half – no chance of a penalty being given by a referee more interested in his own reflection than refereeing the game fairly.

So City succumbed again to a blast of pressure. They controlled the early part of the game, but as soon as the goal went in, it was a different game, just like when Liverpool scored their 2nd in the league game. City became sloppy, clearances were rushed, spaces left for Salah to exploit, runners not tracked, the intensity down. And just as disappointing, Silva and De Bruyne could not impact on the game. A sobering night.

And at half-time I probably would have snapped your hand off for no more goals – that's how embarrassing I feared it might be. Liverpool sat back though and protected what they had, City dominated possession, but could not fashion chances, so in its own way this half was just as disappointing. There were the close calls mentioned above, but the precious away goal remained elusive. Can you really see Liverpool not scoring in the 2nd leg. It seems inevitable to me, and I'm normally such an optimistic chap.

And Pep will have to answer to the repeated criticism that once again in a crunch Champions League game, he overthought things. Sterling was left out, which for me was the wrong decision in a season where he has come of age, whilst the inclusion of Gundogan was a failure without doubt, and you cannot pin all the blame on the player.

Something inside me wants to avoid all that carnage outside the crowd. Let's cut to the chase - Liverpool football club were fully complicit in everything that happened to the City coach – they knew exactly how it would play out, streets full of braying yobs launching missiles at the coach to the extent that a replacement coach had to be called for the journey home. It was all planned. The police stood by, did nothing, then we got a mock sincere apology about it all. Job done. And if any other team's supporters had acted like this (see West Ham v United), then the media response would have been rather different.
Sometimes you can't fight the tide.

So mission impossible next week it seems – City can score plenty, I have no doubt about that, but keeping a clean sheet seems unlikely. If Liverpool score, City require 5, and that's asking for too much.

Still, can we please win the league v United instead? I care about that more anyway. Honest.

Manchester City 2 Manchester United 3

No, we can't.

It took me five days to get over this. I was still snapping at people after our Champions League exit.

We all have different opinions on what is more important in a season, but I'll repeat what I have no doubt already stated – an opportunity might not present itself like this again. Hey, we'll get knocked out of more Champions Leagues in the future, and the fact it was against Liverpool makes it more painful, but it was not the end of the world. Likewise, City are winning the league whatever this result had been. But to win it against United? Well that's a story to be told for many years.

Or not. If City had just played terribly, or United had dug in for a draw, I'd have been very disappointed, but got over it. No, it was the nature of the defeat that really hurt. At half-time, even I thought it was game over. The fat lady was clearing her throat, the cork was being loosened in the champagne bottle. Where on earth did that 2nd half come from?

The City team will have known that United would rally after that 1st half embarrassment, but where was the reaction? United definitely stepped up their game, but they weren't that good. A fully-focused City team at its peak should withstand that pressure with ease.

I don't have the energy or inclination for blame. What's happened has happened. Of course City should have been out of sight by half-time, and surely United would not have rallied if three or four down. Sterling missed chances again, and we know and he knows he must work hard on that aspect of his game. He's given too much this season for me to be angry though. Naturally a small section of fans want him drummed out of the club.

Even taking that profligacy into account, even after the United comeback, this game still had frustration galore to provide. How on earth a penalty was not awarded for Ashley Young's hatchet job on

Sergio Aguero will leave me baffled for the rest of my life. It was a red card offence, and Martin Atkinson waves play on. It's impossible to comprehend. So many times this season, so many times.

And then Sterling proves that he is cursed, sticking out a leg a yard out to a shot that was probably going in anyway, and somehow deflecting it onto the post.

Everything that could have gone wrong seems to have done in the past few days – all the little decisions, the fine lines, the bounce of the ball, seems to have gone against City, coupled with poor play naturally.

So it wasn't to be. Gutted.
The only consolation? There's two. City will win the league, and when that moment arrives, and when Vinny lifts that trophy, this will all be forgotten, hopefully.
Secondly, we do tend to play United in April most seasons, so let's hope this opportunity is not once in a lifetime.

Sometimes things don't go your way. You move on. The season has been so good, we've almost forgotten how to cope with days like this, but then this scenario was hardly normal. Ah well, until next time.

And coming back to this, well after the event I will repeat the above point once more. We have to accept as a fan base, now that we are spoilt, that City will have bad days, our manager will not win every battle, nor every trophy. Other teams will have glory, their days in the sun, and that's how football is, and should be.

WHY MUST YOUNG BLACK MEN WITH MONEY FLAUNT THEIR WEALTH BEFORE OUR EYES? SUN EXCLUSIVE (*please paraphrase this and use picture of Raheem Sterling with piece – Ed*)

Manchester City 1 Liverpool 2

They say things happen in threes, and so it has come to pass. One week, three terrible results.

I never expected anything from this game, so it was the easiest result to take, in a way. And at least there was a response from City.

There's no glory to be taken from failure, not after this club's ascent, but I was proud of the team response in the first half. It just proved not to be enough. The first leg proved crucial.

And I do wonder, the general consensus being that it was better to be away in the 2nd leg, how this would have played out if City had been at home first. That home advantage in the first leg allowed Liverpool to virtually kill the tie. Perhaps it wouldn't have made any difference at all – we'll never know.

And whilst it's easy to criticise Pep, and justifiable too, I do have to admire his *cojones*. A bold, risky formation, and it worked for a while. City battered Liverpool first half, but could not get the goals that Liverpool did in a similar situation.

And yet, and yet – what if Sane's goal had been correctly allowed? Again, we will never know. But I can safely assume the Liverpool team will have been a bag of nerves at half-time.

Anyway, in the end, the defending was not good enough over the two legs, and Liverpool's front line and pressing midfield forced the mistakes.

The positives now the dust has settled – there may have been a lack of an end product in the first halves of the last two games, but some of the domination over what are now our two main rivals was a joy to behold, and hopefully a sign of what the future holds. Away from the desperate disappointment of the past week, one thing is clear. City have the best team in the country. A young, team that will only get better. The journey has only just begun.

Before the Liverpool v Roma semi-final, there were ugly clashes outside Anfield and its environs, mainly started by Roma fans. This probably would have happened whatever had occurred before the City game – Italian fans are hardly averse to such behaviour, and they have a long memory too, but Liverpool football club and its fans needs to take a look at itself too. It facilitated an atmosphere of intimidation in the previous round, passing it off as passion. Don't act all surprised then when there is a reaction against such rhetoric. And think about how you act in future. Not that you will, obviously. It wasn't your fault, after all.

Tottenham Hotspur 1 Manchester City 3

I'll be honest. I'd written this game off. After a tough ten days or so, with players out, the team looking leggy sand the home side's recent record, it seemed this was the wrong game to target, when considering getting the league title wrapped up. Regroup, beat Swansea, West Ham etc and move on. What do I know, eh?

So Fernandinho suspended, Aguero still not fit, Stones mysteriously unavailable (he didn't seem particularly concussed in the pub the following evening) and up against a Spurs side undefeated since they last played City.

In came Laporte in place of the rather erratic Otamendi. Kompany was his partner, and it was great to see Delph too.

And within five minutes of the game starting, my preconceptions had evaporated. City were bright, inventive and confident. No malaise from previous games, it seemed the squad had regrouped and was focused on the task ahead. Determined to put everything behind them and sew up the title. Little did we know just how quickly they'd do that. A Sane volley onto the post and a De Bruyne shot past the far post was an early sign of things to come.

Many commented post-match that Spurs simply didn't turn up. How convenient that they only seem to do this when playing City. Just maybe City made them look average. The home side seemed unsure as to whether they should press City's back-line, despite their own high defensive line, and this played into City's hands somewhat. But the City team were up for the battle anyway, no doubt about that.

And thus with the host's very high line, City's young, energetic front line could reap the rewards. The only surprise is that the breakthrough came from a Vincent Kompany long ball. Jesus ran onto it, and coolly slotted home.

And soon it was two. A penalty? Not quite.
A decision that went City's way - remember this date in history!
Still, the challenge from Lloris on Raheem Sterling was on the edge of a

red card due to his raised studs, so swings and roundabouts, especially considering that Davies should have walked just minutes later for a nasty, deliberate foul on Kompany. Yellow card for Davies, no retrospective action therefore, and another nasty challenge gone without fair punishment. It was ever thus.

City were dominant, but their dodgy period followed in the lead up to half-time. The goal itself was slightly fortunate, but City switched off again, and the composure seemed to desert them briefly.

So a single goal lead at half-time almost felt disappointing. But it wasn't to prove a 2nd half problem on this occasion. The BBC match report talked of concerted pressure from Spurs in the 2nd half, but whilst drink had been taken, that is not how I remember it. A rare Spurs foray into our penalty area ended when Kompany stepped on Alli's foot (kudos to him for that), and City looked comfortable. Profligacy threatened a deserved victory though with Jesus missing a one-on-one and Sterling having two shots deflected behind when he should have done much better, but eventually Lloris palmed a shot out tamely, and Sterling walloped the ball into the net. It capped a poor night for the Spurs keeper, and the game was seen out comfortably by the visitors. An unexpected three points for me, and thoughts turned to winning the league at home to Swansea the following week.

And what a performance it was. Mastery of the ball once more, incisive attacking, and all of Spurs' danger men kept extremely quiet – I almost forgot Kane was playing to be honest. It was the first time Spurs had lost by more than a goal at home in three and a half years, and of course their first defeat since they last played City in December.

And City's domination of the league can be seen by their superb record against the rest of the top six, averaging about 2.4 points per game, and having won at United, Arsenal, Spurs and Chelsea. And of course, City have beaten every other team in the league at once, only the third Premier League team to do so.

Man of the Match? Plenty to choose from. Kompany was majestic, Delph was great, Laporte classy and seemed a natural fit alongside Vincent, and Silva was his usual self. But despite no goals and no assists, it was De Bruyne that really purred for me. He seemed to be back to his best.

And of course we cannot move on without mentioning THAT flick to send Sterling through on goal. If Raheem had scored it would have been an assist to perhaps rival Silva for the 6th at Old Trafford. Sexy football.

A special mention for Gundogan, often derided as a weak link in this special team. That is unfair. In many ways he is still in his rehabilitation process after one serious injury that was not his first. It will take a lot of time even if he has been match fit for a while. He is also a fine player, and should not be derided for not being David Silva or Kevin De Bruyne. And in the context of this game, the biggest praise you could give him is that Fernandinho was not missed. City dominated in midfield, and Gundogan was key to that.

And so on to Swansea, assuming that United beat West Brom and Bournemouth. Which they surely will...

Oh, hang on.......

BREAKING NEWS

MANCHESTER CITY ARE THE 2017/18 PREMIER LEAGUE CHAMPIONS!!!!!!!

Yep, typical United, party poopers for all eternity, losing at home to the bottom club to hand City the title as our manager played golf, and others probably had a quiet Sunday night planned watching Countryfile. Well, put it on series record, cos there's a party in Hale. With five games to spare, City have won the league at a canter.

The narrative has been skewed in recent weeks, the dream path of winning the league against United and European glory seems a distant memory, but never take anything away from the moment that your team is proclaimed league champions. However it happens, I will never remotely tire of such a moment, at such an achievement.

And for United fans, keep telling yourself that this was actually a good thing, for City to win the league when not playing. You're not fooling anyone. If you were at Old Trafford, knowing that as that full-time whistle went your team's defeat had handed the title to your cross-city rivals will have been demoralising. So even if this was not the perfect way to win the league, it was still hilarious.

Top desperate ways to have a go on City on social media after they secured league?

Number of fans outside ground celebrating, attacking players for going to the pub to celebrate with fans, the money spent, obvs, and of course that cringe-worthy video released by a sponsor (if you've seen it, you'll know which one I mean).

Debate about who should be manager of the year continues. I won't lose any sleep over who wins, and I doubt Pep will either, but those that argue that Sean Dyche should win it presumably think that the league-winning manager should never win it, unless it is won by shock outsiders rather than a cash-rich team. After all, every year a manager of a "smaller" club will do really well, but almost every year the award is generally given to the manager of the title-winning team. Except, when City win it, the narrative changes. Three non-title winning managers have won the award over the past decade – I don't need to point out to you who won the league on two of those occasions. City have secured their third title in seven years, and it is plausible will end the season with no Manager Of The Year awards, no Player Of The Year Awards or even Young Player Of The Year Awards (Kane astonishingly nominated in that and the senior category). Funny how the rules change when City are involved.

Anyway, whilst Duncan Castles writes a withering piece on how this season is actually a failure for City, consider this simple fact:
Jose Mourinho has spent €881m at Real Madrid, Chelsea and Manchester United in the last 7 seasons without winning the Champions League.

(and won two league titles in those seven years compared to Guardiola's four in the last five)

Two stats stand out above all others this week – if Ederson had not made a single save all season, and let every shot on target in, City would still be in a European place. And if we took away all of Aguero's and Jesus's goals, City would still be top of the league.

In addition – City were top of the league for more days this season than United have been in the past five years.

Special shout out to the unique Alyson Rudd, who predicted pre-season that City would not finish in the top four.
Then on a mid-season Times podcast, she gave City a half-term report

score of B, as they were performing as you would expect them to, and nothing more.

That's the journalist who predicted City would not finish in the top four.

So to recap what we've read online this season: a ridiculous price to pay for an untested keeper, paid way over the odds for an average right-back, £50m for a forward player whose only asset is pace, spent good money on an injury-prone German player, £50m on a central defender who can't defend, keep playing an Argentinean defender who is a liability. Delph will sit on the bench along with Sterling – careers of English players ruined by City again.

And yet we appear to be sixteen points clear and champions. Funny that.

Good news and bad news during the week that followed. Sergio Aguero's season seems to be over as he has surgery on his knee meniscus, whatever that is. Not too serious hopefully to prevent world Cup participation. City though will not be facing a transfer ban as rumoured in the press, after CAS ruled they had done nothing wrong in the transfer of 16 year old Benjamin Garre.

The PFA named their team of the year this week as well, and there were five City players in the team. FYI, United haven't had an outfield player in the team since 2013. Just saying.

The five were Otamendi, Walker, De Bruyne, Silva and Aguero, seemingly getting his lifetime achievement award after being previously ignored. You could argue for 10 City players to be honest, and 10 player of other teams who have been omitted. I don't really care, if I'm honest.

Which brings me to the PFA Player Of The Year – it was obvious in recent weeks and even months that the momentum was with Salah, and he duly won. Basically Salah or De Bruyne were worthy winners. There are strong cases for both, the players voted, that's that. Hopefully De

Bruyne ain't that bothered after winning the league. Those who call the decision outrageous need to take their blinkers off. Stats don't tell the whole story and for me De Bruyne was a key inspiration between a record-breaking league title, but then I *would* say that. It is however an award that favours attacking players – only 1 goalkeeper has won it after all. The further forward you play, the greater your chances. I doubt Baresi in his pomp would ever win the award over the league's top scorer.

On a happier note, Sane won Young Player Of The Year. He's the first City player to do so since Peter Barnes in 1976, and the first player to win the award in a title-winning league since Ronaldo in 2007.
And yet personally, I think Sterling had the better season, even with his misses. Opinions, eh?

Arsene Wenger has gone!

Well not quite, he'll be going at season-end. RIP Arsenal Fan TV.
You'll already have seen my opinions on Wenger earlier in this book, but it truly is the end of an era, and let's not forget or underestimate just how much he transformed English football after arriving from Monaco all those decades ago.

Manchester City 5 Swansea City 0

What a strange feeling. For the first time for any of us, we got to watch our team as champions, before the end of the season. A relaxed affair and a celebration to boot. The sun even popped out at times too, which was nice.

One dilemma as the mini-heatwave spluttered to an end was thin or thick coat? I do not expect to have to make such tough decisions in mid-April. Damn you climate change.

The only relatively interesting talking point leading up to this match was how Pep would approach it. Would he throw in the kids, or take this game as seriously as any other, with records to be broken and perhaps an obligation to other teams fighting relegation to put out a strong side?

The "play the kids" brigade were to be disappointed, as Pep went strong. Danilo came in for Walker, Gundogan was naturally in as Fernandinho was finishing his two-match suspension and Bernardo Silva replaced Sane, but you could hardly call this a weakened side.

Theories that Bravo could start to get his appearance tally up (currently standing at 1, when Ederson viciously head-butted Mane's foot) were false, and from the moment the game started you knew that not only was this side not weak, but that the players were not on the beach. They were up for it.

Of course first we got to greet the champions, and there was a good, relaxed atmosphere in the ground. The guard of honour was a bit limp – to be honest, I was expecting the Swansea players to be holding huge knives over the approaching City players, creating a covered walkway, the knives glittering in the Mancunian sunshine. You can probably tell I've not seen a lot of guard of honours.

Anyway, back to the match. I can be brief – City dominated form start to finish, bar one free header placed tamely over the bar in the 2nd half (that would have won me £60, damn!). More records were broken – possession hit 83%, over 1000 passes were attempted and almost 950 were successful. Phil Foden touched the ball more in 19 minutes than any Swansea player did during the whole match. Andy King played 90 minutes in Swansea's central midfield, and completed 11 passes. Ilkay Gundogan played 90 minutes in Manchester City's central midfield, and completed 138 passes; that's two fewer than Swansea's entire team.

What's more, if City had conceded a goal for every shot on target faced at home this season (i.e. if Bravo had been in nets #banter), then they would still be top of the league.

And the goals were classic City. Flicks, movement, lose marker, tap in. City score a vast majority of their goals from close in, evidence of precise passing and movement.

But special mention of course to Kevin. Another thunderbolt, he has scored more goals from outside the area than any other player.

And City got to wheel out the perfect trio of substitutions. Some time for Yaya, some time for Foden, and a welcome return for Mendy. I cared not one jot how well he played, my only concern being that he saw out the game without incident.

And what a shame the heading of Jesus is a work in progress (I'll give him benefit of doubt and assume he meant that 5th goal) as it would have been a great assist for Foden. Surely more game time for him next season?

And perhaps it's best that the next time an Aguero-less City get a penalty, Gundogan takes it over Jesus. He's German, it's a no-brainer.

I chose a thick coat. Bad, bad decision.

Bluemoon Podcast Audio Script

As I sighed heavily and turned the channel over, as Liverpool popped in their 5th goal against Roma, deciding that now was a good time to catch up with Homeland, my thoughts turned to a question I had posed on a previous podcast. With United in a cup final, and Liverpool seemingly close to European glory, could their achievements lessen City's achievements this season?

I guess what I'm basically saying is that I have got greedy. The past few years have hardly been laden with success for City. It wasn't that bad either, as our history goes, but for the money spent, it was hardly a raging success either. There was a comfort that United seemed intent on messing up most opportunities that their wealth presented them, stumbling around searching for an identity after Alex Ferguson retired, trying to work out where they last saw their DNA.
Was it on the mantelpiece? In the bowl in the kitchen? Keep looking United, you'll work it out one day.

Anyway, this season has been rather different for City. We've been imperious in the league, on a different level to everyone else, and there is talk of one of the great sides emerging, records are being broken hourly, or so it seems, and all is rather good, if you ignore certain cup competitions. And this is where the greed comes in. City have the best squad, of that I have no doubt. I just want the records to show that, the honours handed out to prove that City were the best. I want City to have the limelight, and no one else. And if Liverpool win the Champions League, you can rest assured our league title win, which might include 100 points and a goal difference greater than any other team's points total, will be pushed to one side, reduced to a footnote as we endure a summer of book releases, DVDs, talk of history and poetry. Endless, endless poetry.

I've been here before though. I've used up all my get out of jail cards, so can't complain if things don't go my or our way for once. When City were 2-1 down to QPR – you may remember the match – I cashed in all my favours to a god I don't believe in. Just let us win this match god, and

I swear I'll never ask the football gods for anything again.
I kept my promise, for 2 years, but then we were up against Liverpool
and I could not have envisaged or anticipated just how horrific them
winning the league would be. I mean, the last two weeks have been a
timely reminder. I found some new get out of jail cards down the back of
the sofa, found religion once more, and amazingly the football gods
delivered once again. I was happy now.
Two titles, done in amazing fashion, I could relax now. What will be will
be, and all that. I'll never ask for anything again, I promised. Nor think
the world is against me if City fail to win a particular competition.

Except it didn't really work out like that. I cashed in one final card for
the penalty shoot-out against Liverpool – I'm not sure I could handle
even losing a League Cup to them. But I'm out of cards, which was
proved to be the case when City let their lead slip in the derby. City are
on their own now, forced to forge their own path to success without my
help, without those cards, my lucky socks or my lucky turnstile.
So with no lives left, I may have to accept that other teams might be on
the rise too, that glorious nights lie ahead for Liverpool or even United
and that the world does not revolve around City, not even for one
season. That I can't just ask for one more thing to fall City's way. Shame.

But nevertheless, if I did attain godly powers, it is a strange situation
that I'd choose United winning the FA Cup if I had to let 1 of the 2 teams
win a trophy. The fact is, much as I'd really rather it did not happen, and
see Mourinho have a trophy-less season, an FA Cup win would not
overshadow City's season. A Champions League trophy certainly would.

I know I shouldn't care. I am happy at that league win, and the league is
what I care about most. Win that ever year and I die happy. Even every
other year.
But if City are overshadowed by events in Kiev in late May, we as a fan
base should not despair. The results might have been bad, but the first
half performances against United and Liverpool were, I hope, a small
window into the future. A reminder that even during a bad week, this
team is a class above all others. Liverpool might be designed and
managed specifically to do well in the Champions League or other cup

competitions, as long as they don't draw West Brom, but can you really see that intense style bringing consistent results over a Premier League season? Hopefully not.

As for United, what it must feel like to be them right now, the unthinkable on the brink of happening – a league title and Champions League for their two most hated rivals. I'm not sure an FA Cup would make up for that. So it could be worse I guess.

I've run out of favours from the footballing gods, so United will win the FA Cup, and Liverpool the Champions League. I'll try and go camping for both so I've got no internet access. I'll accept we've had a good season and nothing else matters, move on, enjoy the World Cup knowing England haven't got a cat in hell's chance, then look forward to the next season with renewed optimism and hope, and the Men In Black picking off families on Wembley Way before and after the Community Shield. Exciting times ahead for sure. And that's the key to future happiness for me – enjoy my own team's successes and don't let anything else dampen that.

STAN COLLYMORE – WHY PEP NEEDS TO STOP OBSESSING OVER ME AND MOVE ON!

West Ham United 1 Manchester City 4

A continuation of a theme – watching a match I wasn't sure how much to care about. I could never fail to care about a match though, so every West Ham attack still got me agitated.

For West Ham, suddenly this match meant a lot more. Southampton finally won a football game the previous day, so West Ham, amongst others, had been sucked right into the relegation battle. Three points clear of Southampton, with a worse goal difference, just. A defeat would not help, but a thrashing could pose additional problems come the end of the season.

Their remaining games? Leicester away, United and Everton at home. Not the kindest fixture list, and the prospect of needing something on the last day will get the nerves jangling.

Another strong side from Pep. No surprises there .David Silva was allowed more leave back in Spain, so Gundogan retained his place. The front free were as expected. It was good to see Laporte getting game time too – no Kompany in the squad, and rumours of a minor knee injury. Let's hope it is just minor, and a precaution when dealing with a fragile man.

Of greater interest perhaps was Moyes choosing two full backs, Zabaleta and Evra, with a combined age of 134, to go up against Sterling and Sane. Good luck with that.

Another guard of honour, which I was not expecting. Still no knives held over the players though. Disappointing.

It took City 12 minutes to take the lead. To be honest though, the timings were irrelevant, because from early on in the game, I felt this game was only going one way. If West Ham had scored, I'd bet on City scoring two in response. The team were professional once more, even if there were glimmers of sloppiness and profligacy.

Strange to talk of profligacy once more about a team that will break all scoring records known to man (and woman). Scary for other teams too.

The first two goals did owe a debt to look and West Ham incompetence. Evra deflected Sane's shot, and then we had the most fitting goal of all.

Yes, City's 100th Premier League goal was scored by Pablo Zabaleta. Once a blue, always a blue.

It all started from a lovely Fernandinho through ball to Sterling. He eventually got a shot away that was blocked, but eventually an overlapping De Bruyne put in a low cross, Adrian parried it and Rice spooned it off Pablo to double City's lead.

It was all too easy to be honest. Throughout this match, you felt City could have scored double if the need had been there. But as with the Spurs match, there was a wobbly period in the lead up to half-time.

There's no doubt that it should have been a penalty to West Ham for a foul by Gundogan, shortly after Ederson had parried a Lanzini cross. However, Cresswell scored from the resultant free kick, so it made no difference. In fact, Ederson is probably more likely to save a penalty.

No mistake from Ederson for the goal, but you could possibly file under "he'll be slightly disappointed with that". He was probably a bit aware of crashing into the post head-first.

But how bizarre that the Sky commentary team seemed intent on revisiting the non-award of the penalty, as if West Ham had been cheated out of further reward. They scored from the free-kick. IT DIDN'T MATTER.

Anyway, little to worry about. City came out in the second half and dominated the rest of the match. Ten shots to City without reply at one point, that tally will only have increased by the end of the match. Once the third goal went in, West Ham were done.

And a lovely goal too, a poacher's goal, set up by Sterling for the hard-working Jesus. Then he set up Fernandinho too as West Ham fell to pieces, having a one-on-one saved prior to that after a poor Adrian goal kick.

On came Danilo, Yaya and most notably Nmecha, which was great to see. Suprisingly no Foden though, who I was led to believe had been promised game time during every match this season.

A special shout out to the match officials, and one of the most magnificently incompetent displays of the season. Now I don't think that two middling fouls by Otamendi in quick succession in the first half really merited a red card, but you have "seen them given". Maybe we should be thankful therefore. Anyway, Lanzini was clearly offside when receiving a pass that Ederson then parried in the first half. Not given. Fernandes was yards offside when receiving the ball that led eventually to their goal. Not given.

There were other decisions that appeared to have been made entirely via the medium of guesswork, but there's only one that require special treatment.

It takes a special level of incompetence to see Sterling have his legs taken away from under him via a sliding tackle and then award West Ham a free kick. Astonishing. Raheem Sterling must truly wonder what he did in a previous life, but this has gone well beyond a joke now. We should be thankful I guess that the decision was not important in the context of not only this match but the season as a whole.

So job done, against a poor side. More records tumbling, City matching the away wins record (15), and soon to surpass the goals record too surely. Most Premier League wins in a season too.
But hey, not that special a team eh?

From football365.com: *The first team in Premier League history to reach 100 goals on two separate occasions, Pep Guardiola's team have now scored three or more goals in 20 of their 35 league games this season (Manchester United have done so 20 times since January 2016).*

Most impressive of all is the variety in City's attack. On Sunday, three different City players scored in the same match for the third league game in a row and the 23rd time in all competitions this season. That's absolutely ludicrous.

It was sad to see Pablo Zabaleta in such a struggling side. I thought it would be a good move for him, but he deserved better than this side and this manager. I hope West Ham stay up for his sake and for the sake of the fans, a club we seem to have quite an affinity with.

Next up Huddersfield, a team also deep in trouble after a home defeat to Everton, and the small matter of the trophy presentation. There are even rumours it might be warm and sunny. I'll believe it when I see it, but already another coat dilemma looms on the horizon.

Season ticket prices for the 2018/19 season have been announced. And would you believe it – City have repeated last season's rises. I'm disappointed, but can't say I am surprised. For my full feelings, just read my article at the beginning of the book.

We discussed this on the 93:20 podcast that very night. The general thought as to why the club would do this, seemed to come down to this: City want the club to be a global force, and they see prices as needing to be aligned to that –small incremental rises are better than freezing prices for a few seasons then imposing a big rise on everyone. Either way, it's an idiotic decision made by people who are supposed to be extremely intelligent. They obviously are not *that* bothered about capacity crowds or atmosphere, as they continue to drive away the working class support that provide the foundations for this club, and always have.

And for what? The wages of a loan player for a month, 1/100th of the money received for an official wine partner. Utter nonsense.

I wouldn't mind as much if the money went to fixing a leak in the south stand roof or for more staff, but it won't.

Manchester City 0 Huddersfield Town 0

The only remaining question for the season was answered pretty comprehensively – at what point would City ease up and coast into the summer?

Huddersfield were 40/1 in places to win this match, but perhaps this performance was not all that surprising. A trophy to lift post-match and a night of partying, playing a side scrapping desperately for survival.

And recalling how City struggled earlier in the season against Huddersfield, managed by a Klopp disciple, it is perhaps even less surprising. No 10 goal haul this time around.

And how nice to see the sun shining brightly on a sweltering day. Sunburn was inevitable, I never learn. Has the ground ever looked more beautiful though, on a day of celebration?

To be honest, the main focus of attention for parts of the first half was a faulty fire alarm system, and the general feeling that whoever was in charge of the tannoy had fallen asleep on the control board. Bing bong, bing bong.

City seemed to start brightly, but soon tailed off in their intensity. In fact, Huddersfield could easily have led in the opening 45 minutes, with one clever free kick resulting in a tame shot easily saved by Ederson, one sliced shot and a good save from Ederson from Pritchard from long range.

In the second half City dominated the ball, but a well-organised, intense-pressing Huddersfield side held firm. Aided by some inept Mike Dean refereeing near the end, they could even have snatched all three points, Dean hilariously claiming Malone got the ball as he barged a City player off the ball. One point may be enough though, giving Huddersfield a three-point buffer with two games remaining.

The performance was part of a day of celebration - kids on the pitch with players, a trophy presentation, the sun out. It felt almost like a testimonial, so the performance that followed was understandable.

Players wanting to make the perfect pass, put on a show for loved ones, it lacked the need or desire to win. If City needed to win, I'd have little doubt they would have done.

Richard Keys bemoaned City's desire to win, suggesting this was unfair on Huddersfield's relegation rivals. Like most thoughts channelled through Key's fat, hairy fingers, it is utter drivel. City have already put two relegation candidates to the sword in recent week. The trophy has to be presented at some point, so this occasion was merited. What's more, this is just the luck of the fixture calendar – plenty of teams have rested sides around Champions League commitments or eased off once their season does not matter anymore. That's life. The criticism would have some merit if the City players had strolled around the pitch not giving a damn, but that was not the case and Pep would never allow it to be the case.

So a boring draw, but the main event to follow. How frustrating then to see another pitch invasion. Now, I am not against pitch invasions per se, but we had one after Swansea. What need was there for another one, bar people wanting a "look at me, I'm on the pitch!" moment? Grumpy old man behaviour from me perhaps, but I want to see my team lift the Premier League trophy, not see you avoiding rugby tackles from stewards. Fuck off the pitch and think of someone else for once in your life.

The less said about the musical interlude, the better. Let the fans make the noise, not tannoy announcers and bands.

Typical City, knocking the trophy over. Sergio Ramos knows a good repair shop if needed.

But grumpiness aside, Vincent Kompany strode up and lifted the Premier League trophy aloft for the third time. All those nine months of hope, expectancy, joy, nerves, sorrow, disappointment and more, all banished in an instance. That bad week is done, it's gone – City are champions, and breaking records galore along the way. Drink it in.

One leftfield thought – how do players who have not appeared much feel, being in the middle of such huge celebrations? An imposter? Embarrassed?

I'm not saying they should, I just think it must be something of a surreal experience. They are free to enjoy themselves, and it will help inspire them to strive for even greater rewards in the future.

By Tuesday I resembled a beetroot left on a radiator for three weeks. Can't wait for it to rain again.

Ederson was still on the lash on Monday morning – we can safely assume Bravo starts against Brighton. David Silva is back in Spain, so he's out too. This could be a weak side for the Yaya Toure tribute night. Those remaining records may have to wait for now.

A quick note on the Huddersfield fans staying behind to watch the trophy presentation. This was trumpeted by some as some as a noble act, the antithesis of Arsenal fans or United fans leaving early when their team lost a final or a match where a trophy would be presented.

This is an argument that simply does not add up. Why would Huddersfield fans not stay behind? They won an unexpected point that may see them stay up, the sun was out, they were happy. They will never win the Premier League themselves (I imagine) so they might as well enjoy themselves.

Which is hardly the same as Arsenal fans staying behind at Wembley to see us lift the Carabao Cup, is it? Do you think City fans would have stayed behind to clap the winning team, to clap any team, especially teams they have tribal rivalries with, teams they compete for titles with? Of course not, we'd be in the pub before you could say "Pep out".

Alex Ferguson & Common Decency

The night before the Huddersfield match, news emerged that Alex Ferguson was seriously ill in hospital. Naturally this brought out all forms of humanity. It really doesn't need a lecture from me to tell you how to react. Any adult should know how to behave with common decency. Should, but don't.

How much you hate(d) Alex Ferguson is utterly irrelevant to any argument. Ferguson was not a serial killer, dictator, rapist, murderer or corrupt politician selling arms to despots. He was a football manager. Hate him all you want – I considered him a bully and a control freak – but do not celebrate the potential death of someone you dislike, someone who is a husband, father, grandfather and friend to other human beings. To be blunt – fucking grow up, because if I mocked the death of one of your loved ones, you wouldn't take it very well, and nor should you.

He was undoubtedly, a brilliant manager, and that's probably what irks most for many rival fans. And his personality no doubt played a part in that success – away from football, he was generally considered a nice man.

And the sad thing is that, considering that we all die eventually, I hope Alex Ferguson dies in the summer of whichever year his number is up. Horrible thought to consider really, isn't it?

But then could football fans across the country, and in some places especially, be trusted to hold a minute's silence or applause before a match? You can answer that for yourself, no doubt.

Get well soon Alex.

The Greatest Team

Naturally thoughts turned to talk of whether this City side can be considered one of the greats of the Premier League era (football of course beginning in 1992). In fact, the discussion has existed since it was clear City were running away with the league.
And also naturally came the backlash from wounded United or Arsenal fans (and the odd Chelsea fan) mortified that their greatest teams could ever be eclipsed, especially by these moneyed mercenaries put together for the price of a small country's GDP.

First off, I must state I don't give two hoots what fans in general think of City's current side. But nevertheless, I have to laugh at some of the counter-arguments being bandied about when anyone dare suggest this City side is one of the best.

One argument regularly put forward is that city must prove themselves over multiple seasons to be truly defined as a great team. Fair enough, yet City are then thus defined as inferior to teams who had amazing individual seasons – so which is it? Using this argument, we must then discount Arsenal's Invincibles, United's treble-winning side and a good couple of Chelsea sides too.

And even if we allow the criteria to allow for single-season achievements, still the arguments don't add up. Let's consider first the Arsenal team of 2003-04. Now apparently one loss makes you worse than a team with no losses, which is a novel way to interpret greatness or who is better.
Let's also look at the bare statistics. That Arsenal team got 90 points. City got 100! Arsenal scored 73 goals that season. City have scored 106. Arsenal conceded 26 goals, City 27. Arsenal's goal difference was +47, City's is +79. Arsenal won 26 league games, City have won 32. Whichever way you look at it bar number of defeats, City invariably come out on top. More points, more goals, more wins. You cannot judge a team on losses without also looking at wins.

And if greatness must include other competitions, then Arsenal don't come out of that well at all. Arsenal exited the semi-final stage of the Football League Cup and the FA Cup to eventual winners Middlesbrough and Manchester United, respectively. In Europe, Arsenal lost two of their opening three UEFA Champions League group stage matches, 3–0 at home to Internazionale and 2–1 away to Dynamo Kyiv, but eventually finished top of the group. Arsenal ultimately reached the quarter-final stage of the Champions League, where they were eliminated by London rivals Chelsea. And they'd have lost in the league too if Van Nistelrooy was better at penalties.

I could do the same with United's treble-winning side. Winning a treble of course puts them right at the top of the pile, but their league title win was secured with 79 points, 80 goals, and a goal difference over 30 goals inferior to City's current one. You get the gist. How strange that fans of other teams want to rank greatness on specific metrics rather than the one important thing – league tables, and the points won within said table.

The argument boils down to one thing for me – which team would come out on top if they all competed together now? I've no doubt City would win the league, comfortably. Fans of other teams will of course disagree.

Manchester City 3 Brighton 1

The most wins in Premier League history. The joint top most wins in the top flight of English football. The most points in a Premier League season. The most goals scored in a Premier League season. The most consecutive victories. The most away wins.
This is YOUR Manchester City.

A "weakened" team selected by Pep, which was not surprising after Sunday night's partying. Perhaps this was a team selected on who had sobered up and who had not. No English players – they were probably booked into the Betty Ford clinic.

I won't comment too much on the match – what's the point? City won, and are still on for 100 points, that's the key thing. Sane got a hat-trick of assists, and was electric, there was some clinical finishing, and Danilo was excellent, a rare chance for him to shine gratefully taken.

The less said about Claudio Bravo however the better. No appalling mistake for the first goal, I would after all expect most keepers to come out and try and block the attacking player, but he failed to block the cross adequately and was woeful spilling a week second half cross-come-shot. He will never be good enough for us, it's that simple really.

And still no Foden off the bench. Weird. He remains on four appearances, and whilst he may be bring saved for Southampton, why not just bring him on for 2 minutes? He could break his leg tomorrow. It makes no sense to me to keep him stalled – you could call it keeping him grounded, but he doesn't appear to be the sort needing such attention.

An interesting note on Bernardo Silva – whilst he has been eased into this side, and thus appeared off the bench regularly in the early parts of the season, he has still clocked up more appearances than any other (outfield) player this season, and has 9 goals and 9 assists. That's impressive stuff. What's more, he just seems to get better with each week, which bodes well as one by one our legends depart. That ball control, and a certain type of artistry I crave more of.

Quite a few angry people on Twitter appalled that there were empty seats in the stadium, the thought being that any real fan would crawl over broken glass to say goodbye to Toure. Some people are weird. It may amaze you to discover that some people have more important things going on in their life than clapping Yaya Toure. I appreciated and enjoyed the opportunity to say goodbye to a club legend, but I wouldn't have dropped everything to do it, be it my employment, nor travel across the country whilst there was a rail strike on. People can prioritise as they see fit without having to justify their decisions to fans who think they're better than you.

It would help not having a family stand though behind the net, as there will always be gaps for a midweek game, especially when the kick-off is put back to 8pm.

As for Yaya Toure, he had a quietly efficient send-off but there was no fairytale ending with a penalty or free kick scorcher, though he had one shot saved late on. The turbo boosts were rare, but got the crowd up when they did occur. I will speak more about Toure at the end of the book – just to say that the send-off was excellent and well-judged. City have handled these quite well, and they might get plenty of practice in the coming years.

A summer of Dmitri Seluk "going to war" with City no doubt follows, and no one at City could give a f**k what he's got to say.

Southampton 0 Manchester City 1

Oh my god. The season that gave us so much still had one little gift left. Or a hundred gifts if you will. Manchester City are English football's first ever centurions. They may be its last, too.

And in a way, it had to be this way. On the same date as THE Aguero goal, and against a team that had its heart broken late on already earlier this season, it was meant to be.

And yet the team line-up did not give out the impression that Pep was desperate for 100 points. Bravo bafflingly in net again, and a random selection elsewhere – missing this time around were the likes of Walker, Otamendi, David Silva, Jesus, Kompany and there was no Mendy in the squad at all.

Stone and Laporte were the defence this time around, which makes me happy. No strikers, so Sterling was the false 9, or whatever you want to call it.

And it played out as if one team needed it more than the other, as has been the case in all matches in recent weeks - Southampton needed a disastrous sequence of events to occur for them to be relegated, it was never plausible, but they still had to approach the match as if their survival was on the line, and they did. I thought they played well.

City were not worse, but the urgency was not really there. A half-time rollicking from Pep seemed to stir them up somewhat, and as the game progressed City threatened more and more – which is not difficult, as for the first time this season they could not muster a shot on target in a dull first half. Sterling hit the woodwork and Stones went close too with a header, whilst Fernandinho had to clear off the line – Bravo was right to come out though to try and stop the shot.

And so the game seemed to be meandering to a disappointing 0-0 draw, the season over with City ending on 98 points, winning the league by 17 points. Southampton were taking their time, and whilst City seemed intent in trying to get that winning goal, you hardly felt it was inevitable, or even probable.

But then…

De Bruyne who had one of his sloppiest hours of football, had cranked up his intensity as the game progressed and as injury time ran out, launched a delightful ball forward.

And as delightful as it may have been, 95% of professional footballers would not have been able to bring the ball under control. Gabriel Jesus could though, and one delightful lob later, I was bouncing off walls, Jesus was in the crowd, and the City bench celebrated as if the league had just been won. Seems 100 points does mean a lot to them after all.

Shame the goal wasn't quite scored after 93:20 minutes, but I reckon the referee would have blown by then. The goal was almost the last kick of the game.

So history made again. The Centurions. An astonishing achievement. Just reward for a team that outclassed everyone else, and for Pep, who showed that his vision can conquer any league.

Look, getting one hundred points was not *that* important, it was not the be-all-and-end-all, but reaching 100 points gives the team definition, it gives them a title, a specific achievement that we've not seen before, when all around want to denigrate the idea that this is not one of the great Premier League teams. This team won 100 points in one season. A hundred points. Stick that in your pipe.
A signature achievement as one journalist termed it and it somehow seems even better that they achieved the round 100 points, and no more.

50 points at home, 50 points away. A nice symmetry, and a sign of the consistency of this team.

City were behind for just 153 minutes this season, the lowest amount of time in Premier League history. They were top for 240 days during the season.

With Kevin's assist, he tops the Premier League assist league for the season, edging out Sane, and gets a nice little playmaker trophy for his troubles. You can stick your PFA Player of the Year awards up your arse. Sideways.

Good for Foden and Diaz to get on the pitch and get their 5th appearance. Foden, the player Pep has ruined by not playing (#sarcasm) is the youngest player to win a Premier League winning. Good too for them to be on the pitch and be part of that euphoric ending.

And special kudos to Ederson, who is becoming quite the character at City. Days after a world record for the longest drop-kick, the Brazilian somehow managed to get himself booked even though he wasn't playing – receiving a yellow card for celebrating the goal with the fans and players.

And wasn't that just a perfect way to end the season? To end such an astonishing season. Better than blowing Southampton away 5-0, I reckon.

And in the evening – an additional two year contract extension for Ederson, taking him up to 7 years, or to 2025 to phrase it another way. Wow. That's faith in a goalkeeper, and faith that works both ways. Has there ever been a longer playing contract for a City player? I doubt it, but well deserved after a superb debut season in England.

Out went Pablo Maffeo however, signing for Stuttgart for about £9m. A shame, I thought he could return as backup and be a part of the squad, but I won't pretend to have seen much of him playing. What's more, he had only a year left on his contract so couldn't be loaned once more, and it seems City have included sell-on clauses and perhaps buy-back options too should he continue to develop in the future.

So that is that. The season is over. It's been a blast.

All that was left was for Sheikh Mansour to once more sort out the Manchester weather (is there anything this man can't do?) and for a selection of blues to take over the city centre for an evening and salute our rather inebriated players. A fitting end to the season.

I didn't attend, finishing this book instead, and rather regretted it as I watched online. I thought I had done my celebrating at the Swansea and Huddersfield matches, but it would have been good to be there and mingle with other giddy blues.

Anyway, onwards and upwards blues. Onwards and upwards.

Best Moments of The Season (in no particular order)

1. That time City players hit it off United players for 2 minutes at the end of the derby. It was joyful to watch, City expertly winding down the clock in one corner of the pitch as United players manfully tried to get the ball back. The City players just knew they were better. Quite simply, they were taking the p**s. No surprise then that they bought confetti with them to Old Trafford as part of the post-match celebrations.

A consolation prize of a glass of milk to throw over Jose Mourinho for Kyle Walker, who at one point kept kicking back the ball handed to him by a ball boy, then gave angry glances towards the referee as if it was the ball boy's fault.

2. Guardiola's squeal of joy after City beat Chelsea 1-0 at the Etihad. He seemed rather pleased. Of all the matches this season, you would not think this one ranked high on his list of important victories. But perhaps he realised when that whistle went that the title was definitively tied down.

3. Full time: Manchester United 0 West Brom 1. Well naturally - it was the moment City won the league. Not the way we would have wanted it, but that moment, the moment when your team becomes champions, is always amazing.

4. The moment Raheem Stering's shot curled into the top corner to win the match v Southampton. I haven't celebrated this hard very often. It was not that important a game, but the nature of victory demanded joyous celebrations, especially considering the wrongly disallowed goal from the same player just a minute before. Moments like that are why I am a football fan.

5. Pep serenading the City section after the penalty shoot-out win at Leicester. I don't demand a special connection with my club's manager – I'm more interested in how good a job he does. However, a connection is always savoured, and this was a

moment we would not have experienced from our previous manager. Pep's a proper bert now.

6. De Bruyne's pass to Sane at home to Stoke. Making the impossible possible. Feel free to nominate his pass in the 1st half instead.

7. The noise when De Bruyne's thunderbolt hit the back of the net at Stamford Bridge. The purest of sounds.

8. The trophy presentation for the Carabao Cup. Any trophy, at Wembley, is a magical moment. Drink it in.

9. Vinny lifting the Premier League trophy after the Huddersfield match. No further explanation needed.

10. And of course, Jesus popping in that goal with the last kick of the season. What a way to end a mad 10 months.

Top 5 Team Performances Of The Season

5. Manchester City 7 Stoke City 2

Perhaps a tonking of a team that would spend most of the season battling relegation does not deserve a place on the list. I'd argue otherwise however, as it is not often you see seven goals – if you're a City fan, it's the 2nd time in the Premier League years.
And the goals, oh the goals. Divine.
And the passing, oh the passing. Even more divine.
There was a lot of extremely sexy football on show this day.
(just pips the 6-0 battering of Watford, cos of Kevin's passing range)

4. Manchester City 5 Liverpool 0

Yes, the visitors had a player cruelly sent off after Ederson head-butted Mane's foot, but let's not take away from what a destructive performance this was. One of my favourite recollections of the season was the dejection on the Liverpool players as they trudged back up the field after each 2nd half goal. Beautiful, and the whining of injustice afterwards made it all the sweeter.

3. Manchester United 1 Manchester City 2

The victory that perhaps shut down the title race at such an early stage – City went 11 points clear, and never looked back. It's not the score that matters, in a game where United almost snatched an equaliser late on, but the nature of the performance. The goals were scrappy too, but City were just a class above their neighbours. It was a clear indication of the direction both managers were taking their team, and I couldn't have been happier.

2. Chelsea 0 Manchester City 1

Again, forget the score. This was all about the domination of the current league champions on their own patch. It was a real statement of intent, and even though it was only September, a clear a sign as anything that City were the team to beat this season. Fortunately most weren't capable of such a feat. I know this will be number 1 for many, but there was one bigger performance for me……

1. Napoli 2 Manchester City 4

A result that ultimately didn't count for as much as others, but what a performance. City arrived in Naples to play the league leaders, who were on fire at the time. Napoli came out and battered City for a short while, but the team showed utter resilience, fought back and picked off the home team. It was a magnificent game for the neutral, and a real statement of intent for Pep's team.

On another day, the choices would probably change. The 2 games against Spurs were unlucky to miss out. So were a lot of games – it was that type of season.

End Of Season Player Ratings

Below are the ratings for City's senior squad. I've omitted youth players. I don't know how to allocate a score for an occasional appearance for Adarabioyo or especially Nmecha and even Diaz. It's good to see them develop, but I'm not going to score them. If I *had* to then Foden would get a 9/10 for his development, and his role in national glory at youth level.

Ederson – 8.5/10

There is one unresolved question for me about Ederson – just how good a shot-stopper is he? After all, City's domination of the ball throughout much of the season was so complete he was not the busiest in respect of stopping balls going into his net. However, that should not divert from his many other qualities, qualities I have not witnessed before from a City keeper, or any other team's, to be honest.
Ederson is an outfield player wearing gloves in all but name, and his skill with the ball at his feet was integral to City's success this season.
We as a fan base panicked last season every time the ball was passed across our own area, though that was with Claudio Bravo in net, and for all his faults, he was no mug with the ball at his feet. But this season, that panic has subsided, because we know what our new number 1 is capable of. And his skill with the ball has proved a headache for opposition managers all season, never knowing whether to press or sit back, aware that Ederson can pass through, in front of or around them. With Pep as his guide, he has changed how I look at goalkeepers.
He only loses a point or so because, as alluded to earlier, he still needs to prove himself at the bread and butter stuff too. Still, with only one glaring error this season that springs to mind (and one in pre-season, and perhaps one in a dead rubber) in his first season in the country, he was a crucial, crucial signing, and worth every penny. Many scoffed at the transfer fee. They're not scoffing now.

No wonder he's been tied down for 7 years.

Claudio Bravo – 5/10.

The rumour is that Claudio Bravo is happy at City, amazingly. His family is settled, and he has no desire at the age of 35 to move on to a new club. You can't really blame him on his wages. Anyway, his role has been as cup keeper, and he carried out the Caballero role admirably in the Carabao Cup. Without him we wouldn't have got past Wolves, and he captained a steady ship throughout the competition. There is still no confidence though that he can step in and be a capable deputy to Ederson in any match of real importance, but the ability must be there when you consider his career. Who knows what the future holds? Let's cut to the chase though – it hasn't worked out, and it would be best for all sides if he moved on in the summer, and we perhaps bring back Gunn as No. 2, or get in a wise old head as back up.

Benjamin Mendy – 5/10

Points for keeping up morale in the camp, we obviously cannot rate a player that sadly spent the vast majority of the season in rehabilitation. Let's hope that by the time the World Cup comes around he is in that French squad and that we can see a lot more of him next season.

Fabian Delph – 8/10

One of the surprise packages of the season. I've always rated him as a player, and felt that if he kept fit he had a role to play in this squad, during a long, arduous season. I just never envisaged that role being as a left-back. Still, injuries are part of his life, and his involvement has been far from constant, but considering that a move to Stoke was a possibility last summer, I think he deserves a high score for how his season has panned out. His performance at Wembley v Spurs as City unknowingly clinched the league was the perfect demonstration of his worth. And as soon as Mendy suffered his injury, he became a vital cog in this league team.

Kyle Walker – 8.5/10

£50m for a full back. How the world mocked City's capture of Walker last summer. Imagine how much he'd be worth if he could cross mused

Gary Lineker, taking a rare break from political insights. Well he'd be worth £50m Gary, in case you're still wondering. I've always found it baffling why there is this faux outrage that players in certain players in certain positions can command a hefty transfer fee. Why shouldn't a full back cost as much as a striker or a midfielder? Kyle Walker is as important to how City function as Paul Pogba is at United, and that would be true even if Pogba was playing well. Full backs are important, just like keepers.

Doubts about Walker specifically proved ill-founded under the tutelage of Pep. Concerns about defensive discipline, and the usual drivel about pace getting him out of bad decision-making. After all, we were all reminded that Kieran Trippier is twice the player Walker will ever be. Anyway, it was an understated season of consistent excellence from Kyle Walker. Disciplined defending and barely a single mistake (Burnley away springs to mind, plus at Anfield in the Champions League) he was the consummate professional who fulfilled his role in an well-oiled machine and was rarely talked about because he just did what he did. Pep's system needed players like Walker to work, and work it most certainly did.

John Stones – 6.5/10

A tough mark to allocate, and seems harsh, but then again...
There was a point well into this season when John Stones was heading towards a 9/10, and the Stones/Otamendi axis looked like a partnership to carry us forward for years. Then Stones got injured, was out for 6 weeks, and never quite got his form back. Then he got concussed and was unavailable for a period again. The next time I saw him was drunk in a Hale pub. Then he got another rinjury.

All managers seem to rate John Stones, including the England manager, and so do I. An elegant, classy player whose style fits the Pep ethos perfectly. At one point this season, he had the highest pass completion rate in Europe's top five leagues. But the key to his future is of course consistency, to cut out mistakes and make that early season form a norm. He has the attitude, time, and manager to succeed, so here's hoping.

Nicolas Otamendi – 8.5/10

Another "interesting" season for the most polarising of players. When City went through their week of hell against Liverpool and Manchester United, Otamendi was at the centre of the storm, his old self reincarnated, games full of poor decision-making, rash slides and sloppy play. But that has not been the definition of his season, far from it. I don't think he'll ever be truly appreciated by all, but for much of the middle part of the season, with Stones absent and Kompany as injury-prone as ever, he kept the defence together, and showed his best form at the club. Even after their second half collapse to United, City had the tightest defence in the league. Much of that is due to our suffocation of opposition teams, but Otamendi must take credit for some of that statistic too. His early season partnership with Stones was also important in allowing City to move away from the rest at the top of the table. An important first team player, and he even pops up with the odd goal too.

Made the PFA Team Of The Year, so must be doing something right. Also made more passes than anyone, in any team, showing how vital he was to connecting defence to midfield. I'm still not convinced he is one of the world's best defenders, far from it, but Pep got the best out of him most of the time.

Vincent Kompany – 7.5/10.

When we look back on this season, I think that perhaps our club captain should get a much higher mark, because he contributed more than I thought possible. But at the end of the day, his contributions were often fleeting, growing as the season progressed, eventually regaining full fitness, putting in captains' performances, and culminating in him proudly lifting the Premier League trophy for the third time. Legend. There are still regrets. He's still liable to get injured at the drop of a hat, his goal against United in the league should have been the precursor to winning the league but ultimately counted for nothing, and he could not guide the team to Champions League glory. He might not be a Pep type of player, but his presence of a pitch still inspired those around him like no other.

Danilo – 7/10

A squad player who did his bit during the season, but never truly shone. Where was his best position? Right back we would naturally assume, but Walker rarely missed a game. The left-back slot was of course available for most of the season, and he was ok there, but never truly prospered, though it was natural for him to play there. Who knows what the future holds? Worth retaining for his utility, let's hope season two gives him more of a chance to shine. He certainly was not a bad performer though, and his lack of appreciation is more due to the high standards of the team he was part of. Fellow pod contributors disagree with me, thinking he is rubbish, so not sure this score will get much support. Twenty two appearances through the season, and not many mistakes I can think of. Would like to see if he can develop, but I want Maffeo back too.

Aymeric Laporte – 6/10

An average score because I don't feel he has had the opportunity to shine yet. With a summer World Cup and a transfer window that will now close before the 2018/19 season commences, there is a tight window for summer transfer business. Thus, this always felt like a summer transfer that was brought forward. Thus, he will be judged next season when he has settled in and understood what is expected from him. His appearance at left-back against Liverpool did not really work, but his early appearances and his partnership with Kompany v Spurs showed great promise, and we look like we have another classy footballer. Like Stones his true worth will be decided on pure defending and consistency.

Ilkay Gundogan – 7/10

A player who seems to be a victim of the brilliance of others. Gundogan, should it need pointing out, is an excellent footballer. What he isn't is Kevin De Bruyne or David Silva. For me, he is a player who despite remaining fit for quite a while now, is still completing his rehabilitation, a man learning to trust his own body again.
Whatever, he has been good this season, without dazzling. His inclusion at Anfield was a disaster in the Champions League, but that's on Pep as

much as the player himself. In his preferred position, he is a consistent
performer, and it was interesting to see that Pep trusted him in the
Champions League. A good squad player to have, it's a sign of how far
we have come that we perhaps doubt a player of his calibre.
Some will disagree, saying he has rarely risen above average, but that's
opinions for you. He's had bad games, but so have more revered
members of the squad.

Fernandinho – 9/10

Too generous? Not generous enough? I don't know. What I do know is
that Fernandinho, the classiest footballer I've ever shared a birthday
with (apologies Cesc Fabregas), has been consistently brilliant
throughout the season, a vital cog that has allowed the attacking players
to shine. He's essentially done what he's done for years, but added
precision of passing to his game, or at least improved the passing to
levels Pep demands. He was everywhere, a machine that just performed
week-in, week-out with little fanfare and little attention from outside
the club. The next challenge for the club is not only to replace David
Silva at some point, but to replace Fernandinho too – and transfer talk is
already revolving around who that player will be.

Zinchenko – 6.5/10

Are City and Zinchenko two ships that pass in the night? Zinchenko
finally got his chance both in the Carabao Cup and standing in at left-
back, and did a perfectly good job, all things considered. I like him, he is
a lively player, but in the end he seem to fade out of Pepe's plans,
making only a couple of handful of appearances, and as his natural
position is one that City have a wealth of talent in, you wonder if he has
a future at the club. My hunch is not, which is a shame, because I'd be
interested in seeing if he develops. Perhaps a loan move is on the cards
for next season.

David Silva – 9/10

There's very little that hasn't already been said, so I won't. Just the
greatest. And considering what he went through in his personal life for a

significant section of the season, perhaps he should get the perfect score. In fact, just thinking about him no longer playing for us has made me gag. Hide his passport Pep.

Bernardo Silva – 8/10

I think Bernardo deserves a great score. This was a leftfield signing early in the summer that had me buzzing. I assumed he was going to United, after all. City had a well-performing, settled squad, so there was no rush to integrate Bernardo, but after a few fleeting unspectacular glimpses of him, he has grown and grown with every passing week. He now looks like the player I hoped he would be. One of those players to which a football seems glued to, he has contributed greatly to City's success this season. His stats may not quite blow you away as much as some of his colleagues, but he has chipped in with goals and assists. It's great to have him, and he is the perfect example of the spectacular depth of this squad.
Seems a genuinely nice guy too, and the butt of the dressing room jokes.

Yaya Toure – 5/10

A rather disappointing, drab end to his City career. I agreed with his contract extension last summer, as he had a purple patch towards the end of the season, and keeping him on for one more season was a low-risk decision. However, it just hasn't worked out. Pep says Yaya knows why, which suggests that he has not applied himself sufficiently, and when he has had a brief chance, he has hardly suggested otherwise. Thankfully the league was won early, and Yaya could have some game time, and a goodbye from us. Sadly though, expect a summer of his agent telling us all what a nasty man Pep is after biting his lip for a year now.

Kevin De Bruyne – 9.3/10

I've cheated by drilling down into decimal points to ensure KDB is my player of the season. Fine lines and all that. I could go on for hours about his skill, his drive, his poise, his passing, his pin-point crossing, his vision and more besides, but you know all this already. He was the driving force in this team steamrolling the league. His standards dropped slightly as City exited the Champions League and lost the derby (fatigue?), but his consistency was rarely in doubt. Even after a hatchet job at Selhurst Park that made me fear for his future, he started the next match. His desire to win was unequalled and most of all, he was Pep's man on the pitch.

You see, Pep wanted an extra player in his "group of leaders" at the start of the season, and De Bruyne was the one brought in. Now I think he has as much influence on the pitch as Kompany. A top class player that dragged the team onto another level this season, adjusted to Pep's demands and change of roles and never looked back.

Oh, and….Kevin De Bruyne is the first player to ever provide 15+ assists in consecutive seasons in Premier League history.

Raheem Sterling – 9/10

Some are going to look at that rating and think I've been drinking since dawn. I myself gave it three glances, and I wrote it. But sod it, I stick by it. It's strange in a way that I give such a rating to a player that is still not rated by some City fans – ratings like this are normally obvious – David Silva, peak Yaya, Kevin.

Anyway, Raheem Sterling misses big chances. He lacks composure in front of goal sometimes, is aware of this, aware that work is needed to develop this side of his game. That apart, his season has still been stellar. This team of superstars lacks something when Sterling is not playing. He has doubled his season goal-scoring record, contributed plenty of assists on top, scored clutch goal after clutch goal, and his stats would be even better if certain referees didn't pursue a certain agenda against him. Absolutely crucial to this season's success, a player who knew where to be, whose positional awareness and football intelligence was second to none. Sort the shooting out and he's a world elite star.

For now, he's Raheem Sterling, and he's top of the league.

Leroy Sané - 8.5/10

It was Leroy that won Young Player Of The Year, but I think his season wasn't quite as stellar as Raheem's, superb as it was. Splitting hairs anyway, as Sane showed he has a huge future, and City are blessed with two top class, young wide players who should only improve further with age. Sane had his little dips, but when on form was unplayable out on the left flank. An exciting player that is capable of anything. Nice to see a City player win an award anyway.

And with a hat-trick of assists against Brighton, Sane drew level with De Bruyne on 15 assists for the season. What do I know, eh?

It should also be noted that Sane was involved in more goals this season than any German player in Europe's top five leagues. So yeah, he's pretty good.

Sergio Aguero – 8.5/10

Rating players really is difficult sometimes, and let's face it, pointless (no pun intended). A Premier League great, who pitched in with 30 goals and we shrug our shoulders and move on. We wonder if his time is up at City, wonder if he fits "the system", wonder if Pep doesn't rate him. Thirty goals! And that's with injury curtailing his season, with him missing plenty of time on the pitch during the course of the season. We should have two more seasons from him before he returns to his homeland, and we should sit back and appreciate every minute. Only when he is absent do you truly comprehend what he brings to this team and the gap he leaves when not there.

And he did meet Pep's demands. On podcasts all season questions were asked if he would work the channels and the front line as Pep demanded, or whether he could work with Jesus on the pitch. Well he didn't definitively answer all questions posed, but he worked his arse off and he kept scoring. He adjusted his game as others in the squad had, and he got on with it. A car crash curtailed his season, and understandably shook his confidence, but he was soon back doing what he does best – namely breaking the all-time goal-scoring record at Manchester City.

All in all, my rating is probably harsh, but hey, I've got to take points off players somewhere!

And he did only start 22 league games.

Jesus – 7.5/10

A tough one this. It has felt like a second successive fractured season for Jesus, but his reputation remains high for club and country. And that's fair enough for a 21 year old. The middle of the season included a long goal drought and another significant injury that hampered his progress. On his return he admitted that he feared further injuries, so you can understand how this might inhibit him on the pitch. Like Gundogan, he has to learn to trust his body again. 12 goals from 26 games, and 24 goals or assists in his 25 starts in league games. Pep loves his style, a "link" player who fits the team's ethos. He works the line, presses and his passing is possibly underrated too. But he still has developing and improving to do yet before we can begin to consider him getting in the team ahead of someone like Aguero. An injury-free season is what is needed after the summer. And hopefully he stars for Brazil in June and July too. Still, he ended the season pretty well, and for that moment of class alone, probably deserves an extra point.

Pep Guardiola – 9/10

It has not been the perfect season. The FA Cup defeat still craws, and the Champions League defeat to Liverpool was partly down to Pep. But the wider picture needs to be looked at. Pep has had money to burn, but he has used it well. His ideas have come to fruition in his 2nd season, and his side walked the league, breaking pretty much every record going in the process.

Manchester City now has the best squad in its history, perhaps led by its best ever manager. History will judge that. It can, and probably will, get better. A man's vision is being recognised, and it is breath-taking to witness.

Many wondered if Pep could adapt to the Premier League, or if the Premier League would adapt to him. He has answered the questions. Even the national side is trying to play like City now. That is a measure of the influence Pep brings wherever he goes. And despite the odd disappointments this season (like any season – the quadruple was never more than a pipe dream), it has been a stunning season. The future is bright, the future is sky blue. The key now is to defend a title, which has not happened for a decade, strengthen in the summer, and place this team in the pantheon of greats.

As an aside, let's look at that City squad, and let's estimate their current market value. I've been cautious, conservative, factoring in lower prices for goalkeepers and the like. Obviously age is a factor for a few players too. Off the top of my head, this is what I think each player would go for if sold right now:

Ederson - £45m, Bravo - £20m, Kompany - £5m, Otamendi - £30m, Stones - £35m, Laporte - £45m, Mendy - £50m, Walker - £50m, Delph - £25m, Fernandinho - £15m, Silva - £15m, Gundogan - £30m, De Bruyne - £150m, Sane - £90m, Sterling - £75m, Jesus - £60m, Aguero - £20m, Bernardo Silva - £60m, Danilo - £30m, Zinchenko - £15m.

Twenty players there, valued by me at £870m! Some loss of value on older players (Aguero going back to Argentina, Silva getting on, etc), but that is some value. Only Stones would struggle to recoup his transfer value, but a fit Stones can recover from that.
You may disagree with my valuations, but the point stands. This is a phenomenal squad. Pep made great players even better.

Journalist Q & A

1. With the title seemingly sewn up by the start of the year, has this been one of the drabbest Premier League seasons to cover as a journalist/football fan?

James Ducker: Drab? Manchester City may have sauntered to the title and turned what is supposed to be the most competitive league in Europe into a version of the Scottish top flight but the quality of their football has been arresting and, for this observer whose job it is to cover Manchester, a privilege to report on at times. It's hard to beat a nip and tuck title race or a frenetic relegation battle that goes to the final day, but while there have been better and more entertaining campaigns than this, it certainly hasn't been drab. Some of the games between the top six have been the best I can remember - Liverpool 4 City 3, City 2 Manchester United 3, City 4 Spurs 1, Arsenal 1 United 3, Arsenal 3 Liverpool 3, Arsenal 2 Chelsea 2, Chelsea 1 Spurs 3 and so on. Plenty of thrillers in there.

Oliver Kay: It feels as if proper title races have gone out of fashion. There have been so many one-horse races over recent seasons. We won't remember too many classic tussles this season, but we will remember the quality of City's football, which has been superb.

Mark Ogden: I'm not sure I'd describe it as drab. Some of the football played by City, Spurs and Liverpool has been exceptional, a real raising of standards, but it has been predictable in the Premier League due to City's dominance.

Simon Mullock: Not for me. I think a lot of people – especially some of my fellow football hacks - have had their eyes opened by the way Guardiola has imposed his philosophy on the Premier League when the common perception was that he couldn't do it his way. I'm hoping it will prove to be a watershed moment for English football and that other top-flight managers will come up with something a bit more sophisticated than sitting 11 players behind the ball in the hope they'll get lucky.

2. Did you think at the start of the season that this would be one of the most competitive seasons yet?

James Ducker: I can barely remember what I did last week, let alone what I thought at the start of the season but I'm sure I expected the title race to be more competitive than it ultimately proved. Arsenal's demise doesn't surprise me in the slightest but I expected Chelsea to make a better job of their title defence, even if problems were brewing there last summer, and I thought Spurs would make a better fist of things after their strong showing in the second half of last season. United? Second is a marked improvement on last season's sixth but their football has been hard to warm to and there have been some wretched defeats. The bottom half of the table has been very competitive – only five points separate 10th and 17th.

Oliver Kay: We've seen and heard a lot of revisionism since the start of the season. I tipped City to win the league – I even placed a disappointingly small bet on them breaking the Premier League goalscoring record – but I don't think I or anyone else was expecting them to win it by 20-odd points. For a team to be so far ahead of the rest, you would imagine everyone else must have been terribly disappointing (as indeed has been the case in a few of the recent one-horse races), yet Liverpool and Tottenham fans are delighted with their progress. Many United fans (not all) will tell you this season has been a season of great progress. Chelsea looked strong until the New Year. Yet City have won it by a country mile with a record number of goals. That's seriously impressive, no matter how desperate people might be try to "normalise" it.

Sam Lee: I thought United would be closer but Guardiola gelled the City team together better than I expected. Didn't expect too much from anybody else.

Mark Ogden: I thought City and United would dominate, so I was half-right! But as disappointing as United have been, they're still second, which again highlights the lack of quality in the league. This is not a good United team by any means, but they're still runners-up.

As for next season, I can't see beyond City, United and Liverpool. Spurs look to have missed their moment, Arsenal are in a mess and Chelsea's recent signings suggest that Abramovich is losing interest.

Simon Mullock: I quietly thought that City would win the title with plenty to spare – but I've still been amazed at how dominant they've been. If you looked at the relative individual merits of the City, United, Chelsea, Tottenham squads last summer there didn't seem to be a lot in it. But the improvement Guardiola has coached from his players, both individually and collectively, has been amazing.

3. Now it has finished - is the quality of this league very good, or is there a huge chasm between a few teams and the rest?

James Ducker: I think a lot of teams in the bottom half of the table are probably pretty interchangeable with many sides in the top half of the Championship. The three promoted clubs, Huddersfield, Brighton and Newcastle have all stayed up and it wouldn't surprise me at all if Wolves and Cardiff stayed up next season. The gulf between the top six and the rest seems wider than ever, even accounting for Arsenal's worst season for a very long time. It's almost like a mini league within a league and I suspect that chasm will become increasingly pronounced over the coming years and perhaps, in time, lead to a breakaway.

Oliver Kay: There's a huge gap. And it's a big problem throughout Europe. It's the way the game has gone over the two past decades – Champions League income, the big "brand" clubs getting bigger and more powerful, the petrodollar clubs emerging – and it leaves an unassailable gap between the super-rich clubs and the rest. I know we had that crazy season in 2015/16, when Leicester came from nowhere to win it, but that was the exception. A "big six" club can perform miserably, going through the motions, and still finish above the best of the rest, which in this case is a Burnley team competing at its very limits. Smaller clubs might have two or three years of punching above their weight, but ultimately their best players move to clubs higher up the food chain, reality sinks in and they drop down again. It's not healthy – and what really isn't healthy is that those bigger, richer clubs are demanding a greater share of the TV money in future. City are one of the main movers behind that. You'll have detected my admiration for the football they're playing, but I can't stand City's the-rich-must-get-richer attitude. It's the kind of big-club arrogance the club and indeed their fans always hated when they were on the other side of the debate.

Sam Lee: There's a huge chasm, yeah. Anything below the top six is generally poor, and even then Arsenal are on some kind of island of their own - better than the teams below them but nowhere near the five above. I think the relegation battle goes to show the lack of coaching in the top flight. The teams in the bottom three (as it stands today) have got better quality players than Newcastle, Huddersfield and Brighton, but those teams have done enough, in the cases of Newcastle and Brighton a lot of that is down to their coaching. In reality, however, while avoiding relegation is obviously an achievement, a lot of the bottom half have been shocking, and while they will stay up, they are merely less bad than the bottom three, who are truly terrible. So yeah, a lack of quality and a lack of quality coaching.

Mark Ogden: I think the league is weaker than it has been for a while and that has been highlighted by City's huge winning margin. That is not to take anything away from City, who have been off the scale at times, because you can only beat what is in front of you.
It's not City's fault if teams like Newcastle and Chelsea (Chelsea!!) decide to play for a draw before a ball has even been kicked.

Simon Mullock: I think the top five teams are as strong as they have ever been in the Premier League. A little bit of a myth has developed that in every season there was always three or four teams good enough to win the title, when in reality it was usually a shoot-out between two clubs or just one team running away with it. The fact that United can beat every team in the division at least once – and still be miles off the top points-wise illustrates how high the bar has been raised. Liverpool are in the Champions League Final, Tottenham battered Real Madrid and were the better team for two-and-a-half hours of their two games against Juventus, while Chelsea can still beat anyone on their day.

Unfortunately, the standard of teams outside the top five has really dropped off. Arsenal are even more Arsenal than they've ever been and Burnley have broken into the top seven playing an extremely functional style. That's not a criticism, because I think Sean Dyche is doing a brilliant job with the resources at his disposal. But Everton in eighth says a lot about the in-depth quality of the Premier League.

4. Your thoughts on Pep - spent a lot, run away with league. How do you quantify his level of success this season?

James Ducker: Spending a lot of money certainly helps but it's no guarantee of success. United have spent more than £615 million since Sir Alex Ferguson retired five years ago and still look a long way off being a title or Champions League winning side. Even City, for several years before Guardiola arrived, were flailing in the transfer market. Under Guardiola, they've bought well in the main and clearly identified the areas of the side that needed surgery but it's the uplift he's brought in players he inherited that has stood out for me. It's not just player with clear scope for improvement, though, like Nicolas Otamendi or Raheem Sterling. It's the improvement in players who were already top drawer - David Silva being the most obvious example. He's 32 now and has just had the best season of his career. What Guardiola has done this season in the Premier League is extraordinary.

Oliver Kay: Absolutely superb. Yes he has spent a lot, but they haven't just run away with the league, as other teams have done in recent years. It has been a masterclass. They have played his way – the way so many were people so desperate to tell him wasn't possible in the Premier League – and they have dominated from start to finish. I know there are a lot of Pep-deniers out there who like to think he has done nothing more than wave a few big cheques around, but that's ludicrous. Look at the way they play. His philosophy and vision shines through everything they do. That's coaching, not chequebook management.

Sam Lee: Plenty of people were saying his style could never work over here and even his biggest admirers probably didn't think he could get it to work so impressively, so quickly, so let's not put it down to money or the quality of his players. As we've seen countless times, money does not guarantee success, and the kind of performances that City have put in so regularly are testament to Guardiola's coaching ability.

Mark Ogden: He also spent a lot of money the year before and came fourth, so it's not all about money. He signed good players and made them better – that's not a bad formula, is it?

Sometimes, people can over-complicate their analysis and attempt to identify some hidden X-factor, but ultimately, it's a simple game and Pep has transformed City by making his players better.

Players don't get better if you confuse them or bombard them with tactical changes – just look how United performed under Louis van Gaal!

Simon Mullock: Guardiola has spent a fortune and there's no getting around the fact that if he hadn't been given the money then City wouldn't be champions. But it's a bit lazy to suggest that winning the title by almost 20 points is all about the dough when you compare Guardiola's spending to what Mourinho has wasted.

And the reality is that almost every single City player has improved. Think of the current values of Raheem Sterling, Kyle Walker, Gabriel Jesus and Ederson and compare them with how much United would get back for Paul Pogba, Nemanja Matic and Victor Lindelof.

5. Does Pep have an issue with the Champions League? Does he overthink things sometimes?

James Ducker: I was pretty critical of the performance over two legs of the quarter final defeat to Liverpool and the concern for Guardiola is how, for the past five seasons now, his teams (first Bayern Munich, now City) have conceded flurries of goals in 15, 20 minutes bursts and ended up losing a significant number of games pretty heavily. I admire and love his determination to play on the front foot but he's not been to the Champions League final since last winning it with Barcelona in 2011 so maybe there are small adjustments he needs to make. I suspect City will go close in the competition next season, though.

Oliver Kay: One thing I couldn't understand was that when City went out, some suggested it was because he wasn't flexible enough – no Plan B etc. If anything, I thought the problem was that he veered away from Plan A, because he was fearful of Liverpool's forward line. I felt before the first leg at Anfield that Jurgen Klopp must have been delighted when he saw the City team – Gundogan out wide, Laporte at left-back, no Sterling. I felt he did overthink that. It was the one time all season he showed fear, which perhaps planted a seed of uncertainty in his players' minds.

As for whether he has an issue with the Champions League, no I don't think he does. He hasn't won it since 2011, but it's a knockout tournament and the best team doesn't always win. Are Zidane and Ancelotti better coaches/managers than Guardiola? You would struggle to persuade me so.

Sam Lee: I'm not sure he has any more of an issue with the Champions League as any other manager (apart from Zidane, incredibly). He overthinks things at times, yeah, but the argument regarding him in the Champions League has always been skewed - he's won two but even going back three or four years that was seemingly not going to be enough. Those standards were never applied to Ferguson, for example, who is widely (and fairly) regarded as the best ever. If you look at his record since leaving Barcelona he had two blow-outs (one where he abandoned his usual tactics, one where he went more radical than ever (overthinking), and one which was very unlucky, the kind you get in cups. At City he was in his overhaul season, which I think is fair enough, and this year he overthought it at Anfield.

Mark Ogden: I wouldn't say that he over-thinks, I just believe that you come up against great coaches and great players at the business end of the Champions League and the ties can go either way.

It's fine margins. City would have gone on to knock Liverpool out if that goal had stood before half-time at the Etihad, but it didn't and Liverpool recovered.

Maybe Pep needs to be a bit more cautious in the latter stages. You can't be cavalier against teams that can hurt you, and are prepared to take you on in a way that the majority of the Premier League clubs are too frightened to do.

His Bayern teams also suffered heavy defeats in the semi-finals under Pep, so maybe his flaw is that he doesn't think enough about the defensive side of the game when faced with top opponents.

Simon Mullock: It's easy to suggest that the Champions League has become Pep's Achilles heel. But in a way a lot of that is down to the ease with which he won the European title at Barcelona. But the biggest games are decided by the smallest margins and I really do think Guardiola was spooked when he was drawn against Klopp's Liverpool. His mantra has always been that he sticks by his belief no matter what. But after successive defeats at Anfield in the Premier League, he tried to change too much for that first leg because I think he thought Klopp had his number. For once, City didn't look organised and by the they settled, they were 3-0 down and it was game over. Even so, he was still only a couple of dodgy refereeing decisions away from turning it around.

6. Salah a worthy winner for Player of the Year?

James Ducker: Yes, he's had a wonderful season, but I think Kevin De Bruyne or David Silva would have been worthy winners, too. I voted for De Bruyne in the FWA awards on the basis that he has been the driving force in a team that has steamrollered the opposition and set a new Premier League points record. But Salah is a far, far, far, far, far more worthy winner than David Ginola when he won the award in the year United won the treble.

Oliver Kay: Yes – just as De Bruyne would have been. I felt all season I was going to go for De Bruyne for the Football Writers' Association's award, but Salah's performances in the final month or so swung it for me, particularly in the Champions League. I don't know why so many City fans have been so outraged by this. It's an individual award. It's subjective. The vote was a tight one. De Bruyne has been exceptionally good. So has Salah. They can't both win.

Sam Lee: Just about. But De Bruyne would've been too.

Mark Ogden: Absolutely. Kevin De Bruyne would also have been a worthy winner, too.
I voted for Salah because he stepped up a gear when it really mattered and became unstoppable with his goals.
De Bruyne flat-lined a bit after the end of January and it coincided with City's mini-slump and it is about what the player does from August to May, so Salah deserved it in the end.
He is a potential Ballon d'Or winner this year and, to be honest, it needed something that special to beat De Bruyne.

Simon Mullock: It's hard to argue against anyone who scores 40-plus goals in a season but I'm still going to put the case for why I voted for Kevin De Bruyne. I've seen strikers have hugely prolific seasons before - Shearer, Cole, Ronaldo – but what I have never witnessed is a midfielder dominate an entire season with the majesty of De Bruyne.

7. And who should win the award for Manager of the Year?

James Ducker: Guardiola. Sean Dyche has done a superb job with Burnley, Chris Hughton and Rafael Benitez the same at Brighton and Newcastle respectively and David Wagner has worked wonders keeping Huddersfield in the top flight but Guardiola's achievement, both in terms of the number of points and goals, and the way City have been plundered has been quite brilliant.

Oliver Kay: I wrote a column about how, despite the brilliant performances by Dyche at Burnley and Wagner at Huddersfield, Guardiola should be manager of the year. The responses were unsurprising: "Look how much he's spent," "Could he do what Dyche has done?" And yes he has spent fortunes and, yes, I would have certain doubts about whether he could take a more limited squad to seventh in the table, when his way of working is so much about elite performance. But let's flip the question. Could Dyche or Wagner or indeed Pochettino or Mourinho or whoever else do what Guardiola has done – even with that transfer budget? I doubt it. If anyone looks at City's performance this season and cannot see the impact of the coaching, individually and collectively, well, they must be wearing blinkers.

Sam Lee: Pep

Mark Ogden: Sean Dyche – on the basis that he massively over-performed with a Burnley team that works with the lowest budget in the Premier League.

Pep has met expectations at City – you could be harsh and say that he has maybe under-delivered because of the Champions League exit – and I think you have to put Dyche's achievement into context.

To get Burnley into the Europa League is astonishing.

Simon Mullock: City (and Liverpool) fans should not be too disparaging about what managers like Dyche, Benitez, Wagner and Hughton have achieved this season. But after taking a wrecking ball to so many Premier League myths, it has to be Guardiola, hasn't it?

8. As a journalist, what has been your best personal experience of the season?

James Ducker: I enjoyed interviewing Benjamin Mendy in September, the derby at the Etihad was crazy and chaotic in the way you want football to be and City's 7-2 win with Stoke sticks with me, not least because it's remarkable Fernandinho could stick one in from 30 yards and the goal still not make the top three in the game. Liverpool's 5-2 over Roma was some game to be at.

Oliver Kay: If there was a stand-out occasion, then I'm tempted to say Liverpool v Roma in the Champions League. A stand-out performance? That would be any one of about a dozen from City. But one thing I really regret is that I didn't go to Accrington Stanley for the match when they secured promotion from League Two. I was close to going, but I couldn't make it. It sounded amazing. I love nights like that.

Mark Ogden: Being in Milan for Italy v Sweden on the night that Italy failed to qualify for the World Cup was a good one – not that I wanted Italy to miss out.

It was just one of those weird nights when you felt that you were witnessing a real moment.

The silence of the San Siro in the final 20 minutes, and the way the crowd left in silence and just drifted away, was the opposite of what I expected.

Simon Mullock: Liverpool's blitzing of City and Roma at Anfield in the Champions League were both mightily impressive.

9. And your worst?

James Ducker: The ever increasing number of hoops you have to jump through as a journalist. Oh for the days when reporters could pitch up at a training ground and talk to any player they want.

Oliver Kay: Nobody wants to hear a football writer moaning, do they? I don't think we would get much sympathy.

Mark Ogden: Denmark v Rep Ireland in Copenhagen. 0-0, freezing cold, nothing happened and no Ubers or taxis after the game, so had to walk three miles back to the hotel at midnight.

First World problems and all that, but that was a particular low point...

Simon Mullock: Press officers and the growth of club media. Not all press officers, by any means, but many of them see it as their duty to put up as many barriers as possible in the belief that fans are happy to be spoon fed sanitised, monotonous, cringe-worthy crap from in-house media platforms.

10. The World Cup - how excited are you? And who will be the contenders?

James Ducker: Excited probably isn't the word but I'm definitely intrigued. I'll be based in the south of Russia - Sochi, Rostov. I think any one of Germany, Spain, Brazil or Belgium will win it. If Messi is at his absolute best, Argentina will have a chance. If he's not, I think it would be a tall order for them to lift the trophy.

Oliver Kay: Am I allowed to say that I'm not quite as excited as I have been in the past? I think that's for two reasons. One is that it's part of growing older (though 2010 and 2014 both had a certain exotic appeal in South Africa and Brazil respectively). The other is that club football is so all-consuming now. Is international football the pinnacle of the game? I like to think so, but deep down it's hard to convince yourself of that. As for the contenders, I'll say France, Spain and Germany. If I had to pick one, I'll default to Germany, like I usually do.

Sam Lee: I'm a bit apprehensive about it - 2010 was awful, 2014 started off well but was pretty hard going by the end. I think most teams will be too defensive, and VAR will probably ruin it. I'm looking forward to going and covering it as an event, but I'm not sure about the overall quality/enjoyment of the tournament.

Mark Ogden: I wouldn't say I'm excited by the World Cup. You lose that child-like enthusiasm, sadly, and there is a real lack of mystery these days because virtually every team or player is known or familiar.
I just hope that surprises emerge and a new generation of players and coaches take over.
Contenders? The usual suspects – Germany, Brazil, France, Spain.

Simon Mullock: I'll be based in Kazan, Saransk and Samara. So I'll let you gauge my level of excitement just in case the Russian Embassy reads this and decides to revoke my visa. It'll be the usual suspects: Germany, Spain, Brazil, France, Argentina. I'm going for Brazil to win it now they have realised that sometimes in football you have to defend.

11. Do England stand any chance of progressing to the latter stages of the tournament?

James Ducker: I never expect much from England because history suggests it's daft to. I'm pretty certain (I think) they will get out of their group but, after that, who knows. The biggest concern for me is they don't really have much in central midfield and aren't particularly strong at centre half either.

Oliver Kay: They do – largely because the draw is favourable. They have some good players, talented players, but I don't feel they've developed into anything resembling a cohesive team yet. If they had had a tough draw, as they did in 2014, I would be all doom and gloom. But the draw gives them a strong chance of getting the group and a decent chance of making the quarter-finals.

Sam Lee: No

Mark Ogden: They should get out of the group, but a second round game against the likes of Colombia, Senegal or Poland could be tricky. The draw has them meeting either Brazil or Germany in the quarter-finals and I just can't see how they could beat either of those.

Simon Mullock: We should get through the group – and if that happens then the optimist in me would expect us to get past one of either Poland, Senegal, Colombia or Japan in the last 16. Beyond that? Nah.

12. Next season - should Liverpool now be seen as Manchester City's main contenders for the title? And what can Mourinho do to catch up? (essentially, how do you see future seasons panning out at the top?)

James Ducker: I've not seen much of Naby Keita but he's supposed to be pretty good so maybe he will improve Liverpool. They still need more in defence. If they get that in the summer and gain more strength in depth then perhaps they will mount a more sustained challenge. I don't really know where to start with United and what to expect from them next season. City will still be the team to beat.

Oliver Kay: I would expect the main challenge to come from United. I haven't exactly been blown away by Mourinho's work so far at Old Trafford, and Liverpool and Tottenham show much more encouraging signs in a lot of ways, but United have improved. They will have a big budget again this summer and if he has got a clearer vision of what he wants to do with the team, then they should make a more serious challenge. The encouraging thing for United and the rest is that it will be hard for City to produce this kind of unrelenting quality next season.

Sam Lee: Yeah I think Liverpool will be closer, but they still need to do a lot to match City's level - as long as City don't drop back. If City improve then nobody has any chance. United need some full-backs and probably another midfielder but Mourinho needs to get more out of them as a unit and it's the same case as Liverpool really - they need some more players but they also need to cut out the disappointing performances, and I'm not sure either Klopp or Mourinho can do that. It all depends on whether City get better or worse.

Mark Ogden: I think we need to see what happens this summer first. Will Real Madrid make a £200m bid for Salah? Will City's players be knackered after the World Cup – their squad will be hit hard because they have Brazilians, Spaniards, Germans etc?
United will also spend, but will they lose somebody like De Gea or Pogba?
But as it stands, it's between City, United and Liverpool for me.

Simon Mullock: I think the challenge to City will come from Anfield and Old Trafford, because Chelsea and Arsenal need a reboot, and it looks like Mauricio Pochettino is realising that Tottenham are probably as good as they are ever going to be.
As we've seen, Liverpool on their day are a team capable of beating City over 90 minutes. I am excited by their capture of Naby Keita, and Klopp will have a big budget after selling Coutinho and reaching the Champions League Final. But unless they make three or four really top signings I still think they are a couple of years away from having a squad that can do it over 38 games.
Mourinho will do what Mourinho does: spend money on players at their peak in the belief that if you have 11 world-class footballers and a manager who is a proven winner then you can't go wrong.
But what I am also confident about is that City are still nowhere near the level that Guardiola will take them to. And that's a frightening prospect

13. Very briefly - VAR - what future should it have?

James Ducker: I agree it needs more testing. If they can get to a point where it's as effective as the goal decision system then it will be a force for good.

Oliver Kay: I can't quite make my mind up about it. I had an instinctive dislike of the idea, on the purist basis that football should be the same from the Champions League to Sunday League, but by the time the trials started, I thought I was probably just about ready for it. But … it's not great, is it? All that faffing about and still nobody is happy with the decisions. It should become quicker and slicker as the refs and the VARs get used to it, but, unless there's a big improvement, I could live without it.

Sam Lee: Bin it.

Mark Ogden: A big one. Let's not forget, this season has been a trial run designed to test it and identify flaws. It was also going to be beset by teething problems.
Fans need to be more aware of what is going on in stadiums and the decisions have to be resolved much quicker – maybe have a 30 second time limit.
But it's here to stay, so get used to it.

Simon Mullock: I didn't want it introduced because I've always thought that football is like life – and sometimes you just get the shitty end of the stick. Once it came in I assumed that it would be rolled out right across the game, but UEFA and the Premier League aren't convinced so maybe not. It will be interesting to see how VAR operates during the World Cup and whether showing the replays on big screens in the stadiums will help to reduce the problems we've seen so far.

14. Finally, Safe Standing - will we ever see it in the Premier League? Is this simply a government blocking issue?

James Ducker: I think we'll see it one day and I hope we do but it could be many years yet.

Oliver Kay: I'm in favour of It, but I've never been convinced that clubs (with a few exceptions) or the football authorities are quite as enthusiastic about it as they suggest. It would be quite a U-turn after years of actively chasing the corporate market, pricing long-standing fans out of the game. I would love to see it happen, but I'm yet to be convinced that it's something that the clubs (again, with a few exceptions) are prepared to push hard for.

Sam Lee: I hope we do but it's obvious there is a lot of opposition. I don't hold out much hope for the government discussion in June to be honest, so if it does come in I don't think it will be any time soon.

Mark Ogden: Yes, it will happen. It makes no sense that you can have in Scotland, but not in England. If it's safe at Celtic, why is it dangerous at the Etihad?
Somebody in football once told me that no government would sanction it because it would be like raising the speed limit and then being blamed for more accidents at 80 mph. They just don't want to engage on it, but they will sooner or later.

Simon Mullock: The suggestion that the majority of Premier League fans aren't interested made me think that whoever conducted that particular poll had massaged the result by targeting supporters who wouldn't want to stand even if they had the option. In a way, I think the utter stupidity of expecting fans to swallow that kind of crap will actually help the safe standing campaign.

The City Podcast Family Q & A

After the dust has settled, how satisfied are you with the season?

Ste Tudor: Satisfaction became a mere dot in the rear-view mirror by late September. Then came astonishment. That was travailed by Christmas. Amazement honed before me then went in a flash by February. I will never experience another season like this because even if City improved next year – an incredulous proposition – I am now inured to their brilliance. This was all new. This was losing your virginity to a supermodel.

Steven McInerney: Very, very satisfied. I never thought I'd see City play this way, ever. Yes, we could have gone further, but this has been exceptionally fun to watch week in week out. Statistically speaking, at very least, this is the greatest Premier League league performance ever. And we got to watch that - how could I complain? The breathtaking football, the intelligence, the desire - it was all there. Watching City win at Wembley and then clinch the league title in such fashion will never be forgotten.

Lloyd Scragg: Incredibly satisfied. It's been a season beyond compare. We've broken almost every record there is to break, have cracked 100 points and all whilst playing the most outrageous football. Going out to Liverpool was a disappointment, as was the loss to United but I'm loathed to criticise Pep too much. He has masterminded arguably the most dominant season in Premier League history and certainly my most enjoyable season as a City fan - and for that, I cannot thank him enough.

Mark Meadowcroft: Yes, yes, yes. To not be satisfied would be astonishingly entitled.

David Mooney: It's hard not to be satisfied with the season, frankly. Having watched City destroy the previous Premier League records, it's impossible to be disappointed with how it's gone. The consistent level of quality that the team has put in has been nothing short of extraordinary and, while there are one or two moments or matches where they could have done better, the team has generally been so far ahead of the their opposition it's been a canter. Of course, the defeats to Liverpool in the Champions League and Wigan in the FA Cup leave a feeling of what might have been - but against a backdrop of a League Cup win and a title that's better than any other team has achieved in a single season, they're minor blips of the campaign.

Keri Collins: Very, but I do have a pang of regret of what happened during that week of losing to Liverpool and United. It could have been a perfect season, but if you'd offered me this season last August I'd have bitten your hand off!

Russ Cowper: Very satisfied. Winning the PL was crucial, the Carabao Cup the bonus.

What does Pep need to do in the next couple of years to truly make his mark in City's history?

Ste Tudor: Apologies for the brevity of the response but the answer to this is to simply keep on keeping on. Champions league success will ultimately define this side and the great man himself but in terms of cementing legendary status within the club itself he is all but there already.

Steven McInerney: Win, and then win again. I truly believe Pep has it in him to win a couple more league titles, and maybe get a lot closer to that elusive Champions League success. Even if we don't pick up the Champions League trophy, if we win the Premier League a couple more times people will rightfully talk about this City team as being the greatest we've seen over here potentially, at least in the modern Premier League era anyway.

Lloyd Scragg: Maintain a relative dominance in the Premier League, (probably) win the Champions League, but most importantly for me - he needs to properly bring through some of the youth players. In order to build a dynasty, Pep needs to see that some of this incredibly talented 'next generation' establish themselves as bonafide first team players. That's what will properly cement his legacy à la Cruyff, in my opinion.

Mark Meadowcroft: Defend the title, win the FA Cup, win the Champions League, identify a successor and oversee the renaming of the CFA as Guardiola Park.

David Mooney: I think he already has with this season. He'll be remembered as the man who gave the City fans their best ever campaign and rightly so. But if he's to cement a legacy, then he needs to win the title again next year and become the first City boss to win back-to-back championships. If he can progress further than he has done in the Champions League (is a final too greedy?) then he'll have made his mark, too - though no doubt he'll have eyes on winning it.

Keri Collins: He already has made his mark in our history due to how many records we have smashed. However, if he wins the Champions League he'd be having a statue. To be fair though even if we 'just' win the Premier League again he will be our most successful manager ever I think?

Russ Cowper: Retain the Premier League first and foremost - winning it three years in a row will be legendary.

Are you concerned that Pep has an Achilles Heel regarding the Champions League?

Ste Tudor: The problem is much higher up than his heel. Pep has been guilty three times now in the last five seasons of over-thinking his approach to key Champions League clashes. My concern is that there is no member of the back-room staff who can get through to him on this issue. We need a Hollywood scene just before a film's climax where a father-figure tells the protagonist to stay true to his ideals.
In this instance that would be Brian Kidd and, well, he's not going to do that is he?

Steven McInerney: Yes and no, but in general I just think the way we play is set up to be in control. A team that runs a marathon, not a sprint, and Champions League success is built towards great cup teams. Take Real Madrid's success. They win it often, but not necessarily the league alongside it, and Liverpool have been miles off in the league this year, and now they're in the final. Maybe we have to be a little less pragmatic and take a more blood and thunder cup approach to it next year? Or maybe we just need to avoid Liverpool... we'd probably be in the final now if we had!

Lloyd Scragg: Yes. Unfortunately, I do think he has a propensity for overthinking things in the very biggest games. He's been guilty of it before with Bayern and I think the Liverpool game at Anfield was another example. Hopefully it's something that he can learn from, but I've got a feeling that that's not how he will see it. Another thing that I think has gone very under the radar this season is Klopp's decision to rest his best players in the early-to-mid season. It was a decision met with much skepticism at the time but I think it has really payed dividends for Liverpool in the final furlongs of the season. It's something I'd like to see Pep do next year as a lot of our best players played way too much football over the winter months.

Mark Meadowcroft: Yes. There are still challenges to be met and his recent record cannot be denied.

David Mooney: Yes and no. Yes - because it seems to be the club's big aim and the competition they truly want to win. That's not to say Guardiola is likely to be sacked in the short term, the club was set up for him in its entirety when he was brought in, but he'll never be able to escape that criticism if he doesn't win it. But also no - because I'm just not that fussed about what is, essentially, a knock-out competition with all the best teams around. There's a big stroke of luck in who you draw and what form they're in at the time of the matches, which doesn't test how good a team is. That's why the league campaign takes precedence for me.

Keri Collins: With a proper referee we could have beaten Liverpool. Still mad about that!

Russ Cowper: I really struggle with the Champions League, personally it's a competition I don't like and I am apathetic towards it. It's a cup competition and to win it needs luck. Probably an unpopular answer but I would rather win the Charity Shield.

What parts of the squad need strengthening in the summer?

Ste Tudor: The two most pressing requirements are apparently being prioritised in an alternative to Fernandinho being sought (purely due to his age and our over-reliance on the Brazilian) and an attacking wide player who can play central.
Less pressing but a concern nonetheless is our reliance on Kyle Walker. A Mendy-style absence for him and the team is significantly weakened so a young, mobile, intelligent right-back would not go amiss either.

Steven McInerney: I think the obvious additions would be bringing in Fernandinho's long term successor and perhaps another versatile forward to offer support to our wingers and Jesus and Aguero. Other than that, I'm not really convinced we need major surgery. I suspect we'll look at signings that we don't really want to pass on though, even if we don't need them. De Ligt springs to mind - someone who could possibly the best CB in the world one day. Do we need him? No, but if we don't sign him now, we never will. That kind of signing.

Lloyd Scragg: A holding midfielder as an heir to Fernandinho. The Brazilian has been peerless across the league this season and is absolutely crucial to how we play both with and without the ball, but we need to start thinking about a succession plan. He's 33 now and will struggle to make 30+ league starts again next season. Another forward is also a must as we only have four (admittedly excellent) options for three forward positions.

Mark Meadowcroft: Not so much strengthening as succession planning. Fernandinho, Kompany, David Silva and Aguero will all leave between 2019 and 2021 at the latest. We need to have replacements in post before they depart. I wonder if we will see Ferna and Kun's successors arrive imminently. The only area that possibly needs strengthening is back-up goalkeeper, but even then, when we really needed him, Claudio Bravo delivered.

David Mooney: This is a tricky one. Personally, I think he might need another centre-forward option as it's clear that Gabriel Jesus is still developing - but it's hard to argue they're not that strong up front off the back of a season where they've broken the record for top flight goals. I think another centre-midfielder is important, as Fernandinho is such a key figure and is no spring chicken, while it may be wise to look at left-back options. Mendy and Delph are perfectly fine, but one's had a long injury and the other is injury prone.

Keri Collins: Forward and centre-midfield. Will be interested to see what happens with Kompany.

Russ Cowper: A new centre forward and centre mid would be nice. Not overly concerned though.

If you could buy any one player in summer, price irrelevant, who would you go for?

Ste Tudor: As much as I love Aguero and Jesus if you place Mbappé into City's forward line then maybe Duncan Castles would be prescient in suggesting the need for a second league title for the others.

Steven McInerney: Well, it'd have to be Messi wouldn't it? The greatest player ever, but even with the limitless boundaries it still feels unrealistic. Him aside, I'm really happy with who we seemingly have on our list, and Jorginho would be a perfect addition to this squad to ease in as Fernandinho's successor.

Lloyd Scragg: Kylian Mbappé

Mark Meadowcroft: Sensible answer – Mbappé. For the lolz – Salah (would be very, very funny).

David Mooney: I hate these questions because I don't really know a lot about transfer targets until I've seen them play for City. In light of my last answer, it'd have to be a central midfielder... Maybe someone like Casemiro or Verratti?

Keri Collins: Mbappé. Pace, power and ice in his veins.

Russ Cowper: We already have him – Leroy Sane.

Do you see City dominating the league for years to come?

Ste Tudor: It is impossible to say with any degree of certainly beyond the immediate future but it will be immensely surprising if City don't replicate their superiority again next term and still be the team to beat in 2019/20. The only potential hindrances would be of our own making.

Steven McInerney: We're certainly setting up to do that given the average age of our squad, which will no doubt drop further too. While Pep is here I have no doubt that we will continue to suffocate teams and I think we'll win the league for the next couple of years. Tactically, England is well behind Pep's ideas and I don't expect the rest of the league to catch up any time soon. Hubris and a lack of understanding being the main reasons.

Lloyd Scragg: Yes. It's been almost 10 years since a team retained the Premier League which proves just how difficult it is to dominate in this modern, uber-competitive era. City will dominate though, I'm sure of it. The average age of the squad is a massive factor. Most of these players aren't even close to their 'peak' yet.

Mark Meadowcroft: Depends on the hunger of the playing and coaching staff. The disappointment in the Champions League (we had a huge opportunity and even though we were terribly unlucky, we blew it) may prove a blessing in disguise in that it may keep everyone highly motivated and with a point to prove.

David Mooney: It's a strange question because I didn't see them dominating the league like they have done this season. That being said, I don't see anybody in particular closing the gap significantly next year - Liverpool and Tottenham both have the style to do it, but both will drop silly points again. Will Manchester United improve again under Mourinho? That's another debate and one I'm not sure would have the answer United fans would be after, frankly...

Keri Collins: Depends on how long Pep stays. I like the chatter of us spending up to £200m this summer & hope it's true as we didn't do that after our last title wins and suffered for it.

Russ Cowper: No. English football is cyclical. We have raised the bar, others will catch up.

What was your favourite match of the season?

Ste Tudor: Every truly great side who achieved sustained dominance over their peers and made an era their own have exceptional games that showcased their brilliance more than the rest. I believe in years to come the Stoke 7-2 will be one of ours. The otherworldly standard of football was new enough to amaze. Everything clicked. The goals were nearly all contenders for goal of the season. An unbelievable ninety minutes of showboatery.

Steven McInerney: Chelsea away. The current champions, and they barely had a single touch throughout the game. They looked like a relegation threatened team sitting incredibly deep, fearful of what we could do. That was the game, as most blues would attest, where I knew we'd win the league that year. It was sheer class.

Lloyd Scragg: The win away at Napoli. That's when I really thought 'right, this team is special'. Napoli were flying under Sarri, playing some ridiculous two-touch football, Silva and Walker were both out, but we still won - and did so by coming from behind. It wasn't out most dominant performance of the season in a footballing sense, that was Chelsea away, but it felt like the biggest turning point in terms of the team's mentality for me.

Mark Meadowcroft: I'll choose one nobody else will (and that's not to say the obvious answers are wrong). We were brilliant away at Leicester. We hammered a good side that we were playing well at the time. Wonderful team goal from Jesus and a signature De Bruyne goal. Add to that an excellent performance from Kompany after a very early and slightly fortunate yellow card and a great goal-line clearance from Walker. And Fernandinho, Silva, Sterling and Sane were all brilliant and Delph played to his usual very high standard. The only reason I haven't mentioned Ederson is that we defended too well for him to make a mark.

David Mooney: Napoli 2-4 City: It had everything - both sides with spells of pressure, City's fantastic counter-attacking football, set-backs, set-pieces, and a Sergio Aguero record-breaking goal.

Keri Collins: At the time, Napoli away for the performance level, but also United away and Liverpool at home for shutting their insufferable fans up for a bit. Beating Watford away by such a margin was the moment I thought this could be a special season.

Russ Cowper: Spurs at Wembley. Banished the spectre of Ricky Villa forever.

What was your favourite single moment?

Ste Tudor: City's third against Arsenal at the Emirates was when reality hit home for me. This wasn't a dream. This wasn't a temporary burst of magical superiority that could come undone at any point. This was who we are now. We reduced rivals to neurosis while playing football so sculptured and beautiful it stole the breath from our lungs.

Steven McInerney: The derby at Old Trafford, purely for the shithousery on show. Watching Bernardo and KDB absolutely humiliate Ashley Young over near the corner flag as the clock ticked down, and then Ederson allegedly throwing milk at Jose, as well as Mendy bringing confetti and celebrating loudly in the dressing room. It was the icing on a pretty blue cake.

Lloyd Scragg: Sterling's goal against Southampton. Absolute scenes in a bar in Colombia when that went in...

Mark Meadowcroft: Sane's goal at Arsenal and Vinny's goal at Wembley are neatly contrasting highlights. Hugely difficult to choose one and I could choose twenty more.

David Mooney: It has to be Kevin De Bruyne's through ball for Leroy Sane against Stoke. Watching him beat about nine players with one through pass that only needed a first time finish - I just don't know how he saw it.

Keri Collins: Raheem goal v Southampton.

Russ Cowper: Sterling winner against Southampton.

Your lowest moment or match?

Ste Tudor: Concentrating on the league, then my genuine answer would be that there wasn't one. Seriously. The 3-2 loss to United should have been so deflating given that we could have secured the title and had a two goal lead but after the game my head was spinning with how City comprehensively bossed them for the most part. We were a cat toying with a mouse who got so bored that it prompted a ten minute yawn and in that time the little critter legged it back to its mouse hole and celebrated in the dark with a tiny piece of cheese. Considering all of the wallopings they used to dispense upon us that is only something to be frustrated by, not despondent.

Both ties against Liverpool in the Champions League quarter finals however are a very different matter. They hurt like hell.

Steven McInerney: The way I felt after the derby at the Etihad. Liverpool. Champions League. So much promise, then so much pain. A genuine sinking feeling, promptly followed by the chance at perfect redemption, winning the league against our rivals. Only to totally throw that game away and lose so dramatically. Walking back from the Etihad that day hurt badly. Two absolute sucker punches back to back. It left a really sour taste.

Lloyd Scragg: The United loss at home. It was probably the worst feeling I have experienced as a football fan. From pure elation to devastation, the reverse-93:20. I actually missed both of Pogba's goals as I was still on the concourse having beers and celebrating our title triumph... That taught me a lesson.

Mark Meadowcroft: Half time at Liverpool in the Champions League. The derby defeat didn't bother me as much. You've got to throw them the odd bone and I have sympathy for their fans. While they are effective in their own way, they are painful to watch.

David Mooney: It would have been the third Liverpool goal in the Champions League tie at Anfield. At 2-0, there was a chance City could have rescued something if they got their heads together - instead they just fell apart.

Keri Collins: Liverpool Champions League games and the derby. Still can't believe we lost them.

Russ Cowper: Wigan – reminded me of the old days.

Your player of the season?

Ste Tudor: It's difficult to look past Kevin de Bruyne. He was everything to this incredible side: it's conductor, creator, and Pep's ears and eyes on the pitch. That he lost out to a goal-machine for the Player of the Year proves once again that Blighty will forever be stuck in the Eighties. Kev's football was futuristic.

Steven McInerney: Kevin De Bruyne. At one point he reminded me of Zidane. Truly and utterly mesmeric and capable of things I've never seen a City player do. I've witnessed some great passers in a blue shirt. Toure, Silva, Steve Lomas...ahem... but none of them had that same ability to split a defence perfectly from 60 yards almost seemingly at will. KDB's growing into a future Man City captain and he'll thoroughly deserve it when he steps into the roll full time.

Lloyd Scragg: Kevin De Bruyne.

[If you want an answer as opposed to just a name: 'He's been the standout and has cemented his status as one of the best players in the world, never mind the Premier League, but David Silva and Sterling haven't been too far behind. Silva's had another ridiculously consistent season, which is all the more impressive when you consider the personal problems he's suffered, whilst Sterling has taken his game up yet another level under Pep. He was the guy who got the game by the scruff of the neck in so many of our key moments and full credit to him.]

Mark Meadowcroft: Could give to so many, but David Silva (I now feel guilty that KDB has come second in a beauty contest yet again).

David Mooney: Raheem Sterling - everyone will pick out Kevin De Bruyne for his impact and he has been sensational, but I think the improvement Sterling has made is phenomenal. He's scored so many vital goals at vital times, too.

Keri Collins: Kevin De Bruyne.

Russ Cowper: Fernandinho.

Finally, away from City... who will City's main challengers be next season?

Ste Tudor: Liverpool will push, especially with the addition of Keita and an expected upgrade between the sticks. Their ferocity is unsustainable though over a 38 game season and there will inevitably be costly defeats and draws to inferior fayre who stick ten men behind the ball.
United will spend heavily but to my mind they are rotten to the core and no amount of expenditure will address that while Mourinho is in charge.

Steven McInerney: Ourselves? We're by far the best team in the league, and the only reason we won't it is if we take our eye off the ball and act complacent. No summer signings for United, Chelsea, Liverpool etc can make up a 20+ points gap. If I had to choose, i'd go for Liverpool. Keita coming in will improve their midfield a lot.

Lloyd Scragg: Liverpool, unfortunately. Van Dijk has made a big difference for them already, they've already got Keita coming in and no doubt they'll sign a few others. Add a world-class goalkeeper into the mix and they could be a real force.

Mark Meadowcroft: If Liverpool keep their front three and Keita is the player I think he might be, then they should finish above United, but whatever happens in the Champions League, they have 20 points to make up on us, so our level will need to fall as well as theirs to rise if it's to be a serious contest. I don't see United doing much better or worse – their level is what it is. The same is probably true for Spurs. Arsenal and Chelsea are wild cards but have a lot of ground to make up. It will be fun to see what Arsenal do post-Wenger. Could go either way. I fancy Crystal Palace to play the Burnley role.

David Mooney: I don't think it will be particularly close, but I think it'll be Liverpool if they can bring in the quality they need defensively.

Keri Collins: Liverpool. I just hope they continue the inconsistency against lower teams.

Russ Cowper: United.

Who will win the World Cup?

Ste Tudor: The familiar names demand respect and due attention but France and Uruguay have easy groups and should progress. From there they have the firepower to get through four one-off games very conceivably. If they click I'm backing France.

Lloyd Scragg: Brazil (if Neymar's fully fit). If not, then Spain.

Mark Meadowcroft: Spain, Germany and Brazil look very strong. France need to find a way of playing Greizmann and Pogba together or make a big decision. With the right coach, Belgium would be in the argument.

David Mooney: Toss a coin... let's say Germany.

Keri Collins: Germany.

Russ Cowper: Not bothered, it bores me, but Belgium will do well.

Dark horse in World Cup?

Ste Tudor: As mentioned above Uruguay are a great shout for a last four spot. So much depends on their experienced players stepping up to the plate but if they do le celeste are outstanding value at 33-1.

Lloyd Scragg: Uruguay.

Mark Meadowcroft: Serbia will get a lot of local support in Russia and have some decent players. Colombia, Uruguay and Egypt also interesting.

David Mooney: In a bizarre way, England - they won't win it, but I reckon they'll do better than most expect and get further than they have done for a while.

Keri Collins: England (ha ha).

Russ Cowper: Have Madagascar qualified?

Goodbye Yaya

This is (almost) the final article of the season review book. I write immediately after the end of the season, the Southampton match, as thoughts turn to the summer and beyond. At the time of writing, Yaya Toure is still an employee of Manchester City football club. But at the start of next season, he will not be, Pep Guardiola confirming that he will leave this summer, eight years after joining the club from Barcelona.

So with his exit imminent, my thoughts are chronicled below on a player that changed the club he played for. Thanks for reading this book, and have a great summer.

Football fans can argue, and thus disagree about, anything. In the past, I've seen City fans dismiss Kevin De Bruyne as useless, after all. Raheem Sterling is both England's greatest young(ish) talent and just a speed merchant who can't even shoot straight. Don't get me started on John Stones. Many other players at other clubs provoke similar divides in opinion. However, has any player attracted the level of debate as Yaya Toure?

The answer's no by the way.

And I reference the debate over Yaya not as he is now, but the player of years ago, the player that helped win the club trophies. Even then, it was a rocky ride for player and fans at times, and it's puzzling in a way.

He's lazy, he's slow, he's overpaid. No he's not, he's misused, he's misunderstood, he's capable of genius like few others. He's untouchable. Leave him alone. He's arrogant. He's a scapegoat. He should be sold. We're less of a team without him. Debates admittedly that timed themselves around our least successful seasons. As the team's fortunes dipped, so did Yaya's perceived worth.

City have, and have had, plenty of players that split opinion. It used to be easy of course – there was a certain consistency in our players, which is not necessarily a good thing, but now the bar has been raised so, so high, and so have expectations. There's no time for a £50m player to bed in. But no one can dispute that Yaya Toure was excellent value for money, so why does he attract so much attention?

Yaya Toure is a player with magnificent ball retention skills, almost impossible to tackle, world-class passing skills, a deadly long-range shot, a footballer with pure power and poise who has a knack of scoring crucial goals. He is a destructive not a restrictive player. Or he was. That is how I will remember him.

For a moment, let's widen the net. Just take a minute and consider how thankful we as City fans should be to have witnessed so many Premier League greats in the past few years. Vincent Kompany, Sergio Aguero, David Silva, Yaya Toure – they are all giants of their time. And inevitably when considering such players many feel the need to compare and contrast, rank and pick their own favourite.

I hate doing that. Hey, if I *had* to, it would be David Silva, but whilst Sergio Aguero knocked in THAT goal and a couple of hundred more for good measure, it was Yaya Toure that scored some of City's most important goals, and from midfield.

I probably don't have to remind you of them, but I will anyway. This is a *homage*, after all. The winning goal against United in the FA Cup semi-final, the match when City truly arrived. The winner in the FA Cup final, the photo of which is immortalised on my wall at home, securing City's first trophy in a generation.
Just as important for me was that late double at Newcastle that allowed the QPR match to matter. And boy did it matter.

And then there was the 2013/14 season. The season that prevented Liverpool from winning the league, an achievement that should merit knighthoods, castles made entirely from gold and a lot more. Let's break down just what Yaya, a 31 year old midfielder, achieved that season. Twenty goals from midfield, a feat only matched by Frank Lampard in 2009/10, and his goal tally included ten penalties. Yaya himself scored 6 penalties, but also 4 free kicks from 7 attempts. Add to that nine assists, the 2nd highest for a midfielder that season, and his impact is clear.

Toure set up a goal in each of the last four games, that crucial run-in that saw City overtake Liverpool to capture the title. That goal at Palace, preceded by an assist for Dzeko. That ridiculous, almost impossible goal at Wembley that started the comeback against Sunderland.

The rampaging runs. The inability to dispossess him. The nonchalant curled 25 yard shots into the corner. The ease with which he controlled matches. With his long, gangly legs, it seemed almost effortless when prime Yaya glided across the pitch. An unstoppable force, an immovable object.

That Yaya has gone of course. The bursts have decreased, remaining mostly in our shared memories, match highlights are desperately sparse. It's been this way for a while now, bar last season's purple patch that saw him get a 1 year contract extension. At his prime it seemed impossible that City could replace Yaya, that his demise would leave a gaping hole in the City team. But the team has moved on, breaking records as he watches on from the side lines.

City don't rely on Yaya Toure now. That's the truth of the matter. It is the cyclical nature of football that the man that contributed more than anyone to our success in the past six years is no longer a vital cog in the machine. He'll move on this summer, and so will we. He still has a role to play somewhere, but it won't be in Manchester. It is perhaps a shame therefore that he leaves long after he starred regularly for the team – perhaps it is better to let players leave when they still have plenty to offer, rather than watch them wither in club colours.

Perhaps City held on because he was so many midfielders rolled into one. The feeling was that he was irreplaceable, and whilst there is an element of truth in that, in so much as City have not bought a player since with a similar skillset, like any team that loses a big player, City have moved on and done just fine.

Of course if you evaluate Yaya's time at City, then sadly that must include off-pitch events and not just those on the pitch. I'll not hold any grudges or resentment against the antics that became known as #cakegate as his younger brother was dying, and I couldn't even begin to imagine how horrible that period of his life must have been. We know his agent likes to shoot off with whatever drivel pops into his mind that particular day, but Toure was never going to dispose of a man who is a close friend and after whom Toure's son is named.

We must assume, though it is just that – an assumption – that anything Dimitri Seluk says has gone through Toure first –it's Yaya's drivel, so to speak. Do you really think he lets his agent freely say whatever he wants? We must also assume therefore that Toure is the most precious of footballers. He's not alone in that respect of course. He and his peers demand recognition for their feats beyond wealth and trophies – hence the pointless Ballon D'Or ceremony every year. Getting rid of his agent as many demand will not only never happen, it would change nothing. Then we'd have a new agent saying the same things. And do you care? Apart from a tiresome transfer saga every summer, it's not highly relevant to fans how precious a player may or may not be. Except, for some it taints a legacy, and it will taint his place in the club's history of legends if things are said after his departure, a departure where the club and its fans have rightly feted him as an icon of the club.

I had a modicum of sympathy for Yaya's grumblings. African football is not always appreciated, Yaya himself, as we have all seen, is not always appreciated. He's done it all, but you wouldn't know this if you perused online for a few minutes. He wanted his place in history. Even this week he has commented on how perhaps he will be respected more after he has retired. Hey, get used to it Yaya – City's senior players don't get player awards, as we are still seeing to this day.

And it will be a shame if when the time arrives for Toure to leave, it is not done in a friendly manner. Something deep inside tells me it won't. My hunch tells me that Seluk will have plenty to say again once ties are cut, considering Yaya's limited playing time this season and Pep's barbed answers as to why this was the case. It will be a shame because whatever happens in the future, we shouldn't forgot for one moment what happened in the past.

He's a club legend, and he always will be. Possibly our most important player ever. So thank you Yaya, for helping make all this possible. A unique footballer that helped change my club's history forever.

As Pep said prior to the Huddersfield match, "we cannot forget what this guy has done for the club."

And we won't forget, Yaya. We won't.

To recap:

Manchester City have broken the record for most points won in an English top-flight season (100) – even if two-point era records are changed to three.

Manchester City have broken the record for most wins in an English top-flight season (32).

Manchester City have broken the record for most consecutive wins in an English top-flight season (18).

Manchester City have broken the record for most away wins in a Premier League season (16).

Manchester City have broken the record for most goals scored in a Premier League season (106).

Manchester City have broken the record for best goal difference in a Premier League season (79).

Manchester City have broken the record for biggest title-winning margin in a Premier League season (19 points).

Manchester City equalled the record for earliest top-flight title win (with five games remaining).

Manchester City are the tenth team to have beaten all other teams in a single English top-flight season, and the first since 2010/11. Manchester United became the 11th later in the season.

Manchester City became the first Premier League side to ever attempt more than 1,000 passes in a game against Swansea in April.

Manchester City have broken the record for most passes in a Premier League game three times this season.

Manchester City completed more passes in the first half of their 5-0 win over Swansea in April (542) than 247 of the 507 players to have played in the Premier League this season have attempted all campaign.

Pep Guardiola is the first manager to win the Premier League Manager of the Month award four consecutive times.

Pep Guardiola has been named Premier League Manager of the Month more times this season (4) than Jose Mourinho has in his career (3).

Manchester City have accrued more Premier League points this season (100) than eight clubs have in their entire Premier League history – including Oldham (89).

Manchester City have accrued as many Premier League points this season (100) as Brighton (40), Cardiff (30) and Swindon (30) have in their combined Premier League histories.

Manchester City have won as many Premier League matches this season (32) as Reading, Sheffield United and Wolves ever have.

Phil Foden is the youngest player to receive a Premier League winner's medal.

93:20 Monologue - Book Epilogue.

As the dust settles on another season, and thoughts turn giddily towards the prospect of Russia v Saudi Arabia, Egypt v Uruguay, Morocco v Iran and steroid-enriched Russian hooligans battering Dave from Luton as he attempts to sing German bomber songs, it is time to look back at the nine months that us blues have just experienced. Nine months of ups, downs, and a lot more ups. With some extra ups for good measure, and then another up just in case you were short of ups.
What I'm basically saying is that it was quite a good season to be a City fan.

Even the most optimistic of City fans, who truly believed that Pep was the messiah and not just a naughty boy, surely had some creeping doubts after his first season. The naysayers that wanted Pep to fail, that wanted the English game to show this cocky upstart that he couldn't just waltz in and win everything going, whilst looking dapper on the side-lines, were wet with joy after Pep's toils with ageing full backs, a goalkeeper allergic to leather and a myriad of other problems.
We wanted to believe, and I still did, but I think we'd hoped that after that initial winning run at the start of the 2016/17 season, it was all going to be a breeze. Only City could reduce Pep to his first trophy-less season as a manager.

And the start of this season did not hint at what lay beyond. An opening day victory at Brighton was satisfactory but not that enthralling, and the home draw against Everton suggested nothing had changed despite a second half dominance with ten men. Refereeing incompetence would certainly remain a theme throughout the season, a constant reminder that this team could achieve even more if knee-high, studs-up tackles were considered out of order by match officials just once in a while.

Slowly things took off though. The win at Bournemouth certainly wasn't the launch pad, but putting 15 goals past Liverpool, Feyenoord and Watford certainly was. Another 7 goals past Crystal Palace and a skilful Shakhtar Donetsk team, followed by that statement at Stamford Bridge, and now it was clear that this team was the one to beat, and Pep's blueprint and philosophies were stamped all over it.

From there on, City just kept on going, like a Duracell-powered bunny, though I am legally obliged to point out that other brands are available. Records were being broken before Christmas and after. There are multiple ways to win a league title – Leicester did it with consistency, Chelsea had run of victories last season that took them away from the pack. I'd say that City went for both options, because if you win virtually every match over 9 months, it is more than just a "run". Whichever way you look at it, the statistics are astonishing. There are only 114 points to play for in a league season, and City got 100. Any claims that this team is not one of the Premier League greats, one of the top flight greats, comes entirely from bitterness and club rivalry. On virtually every metric apart from Salah's goal-scoring record, City are first. Virtually every one – wins, points, passes, chances, away wins, home wins, assists, and on and on. Some of those records refer not only to this season, but all-time. Since football began. Which, contrary to general opinion, was not 1992.

And whilst I never truly believed the league was won until a 2-0 win at Stoke on a Monday night, it's probably fair to say that the title was effectively won by early December, City's victory at Old Trafford taking them 11 points clear of United. A packed Christmas schedule couldn't derail them, and it was pretty much in the bag. All the while, the team had reached a cup final without even trying that hard, and the eventual Carabao Cup victory was a nice icing on the cake, or as I said on a podcast earlier in the season, the fish sauce that made a meal much nicer even though on its own it had little merit.

The season wasn't perfect of course. The scintillating wins over Napoli counted for little in the end, as Jurgen Klopp, Pep's kryptonite, ended dreams of this season being far and away the greatest in our history. The FA Cup defeat was annoying as City had the squad to take that cup seriously as the league was already in the bag. And of course winning the league against United would have provided a story only second to Aguero's biggest moment. Ah well, we have been spoiled as fans this season, and the possibility of everything being perfect proved to be wishful thinking in the end. In the end, with the last kick of a momentous season, Gabriel Jesus gave us a pretty good story anyway. Our saviour, a Pep disciple.

That bad week in April hurt big time, but is should not diminish from what this team achieved, and what it still can, and as I watched Vincent Kompany lift a 3rd Premier League trophy, all was well in the world again. My football team, your football team, is the best team in the land and all the world. We probably need a new song.

When rival fans are counting empty seats, and when rival fans suddenly take up a profound interest in global human rights that is the moment that you know your team is better than their team. And our team can get better, that much is clear to me.

Did I see this season coming? No. I would say that Pep was under big pressure and the league title was needed. But I could never expect the chasm in quality and points that slowly developed. My basic expectation was that City should, perhaps must, contest for the title. The absolute minimum requirement was to narrowly miss out on a title, and even that would have been disappointing, but progress of sorts, as United fans are currently trying to claim. The summer acquisitions greatly excited me, though I knew little of Ederson and knew Bernardo Silva would need time. We still seemed to be missing a forward player, and still do, and I had some misgivings about other positions too, such as defensive midfield and central defence too. This team was just too good for any gaps to prove that costly though. With fine tuning this summer, the team, scarily, can be even better. I get the feeling that Pep only sees a squad that is 80% complete, and is not the finished product just yet.

As for the current crop, Kevin was the best though David Silva makes me think about how I will cope once he leaves. I don't think I will. Our new keeper, a Bond villain with gloves was a revelation, though Pep's brand of possession football means we still can't truly rate him as a shot-stopper. We've got another 7 years to judge that. Sane and Sterling truly came of age and Fernandinho just keeps on going, quietly fixing everything with little aplomb. A new full back roster was as key as anything else though, despite the terrible injury to Mendy.

So what do City need to do this summer? The answer is, not a lot. The need remains for another attacking player, and whilst all the talk is of another wide forward, I would still prefer an out and out striker, someone deadly in front of goal. Either way, someone is needed, and will no doubt be acquired after previous attempts at snaring the likes of Sanchez and Mahrez. The other area is back up or competition for Fernandinho, and Jorginho is the most likely arrival, even if he is not identical to Fernandinho when comparing skillsets. Otherwise, the only other area is central defence, and Pep's decision on how much he can trust our captain. More important is keeping the existing squad fired up for next season, maintaining the intensity and overcoming the psychological issues that come with a title defence. Do not expect a push at 100 points again. Then again, don't be surprised if we go close.

Everyone seems to expect Liverpool to be the main rivals next season, but I am yet to be convinced that the team can be consistent enough over a long period. I'm not convinced the squad depth is there either, unless the front three can largely avoid injury for nine months again.

United should not be dismissed however. Mourinho's brand of football may wipe the smile off a hyena and has halved global rates of insomnia, but it can still accumulate points. Add another £200m to the summer war chest and a powerful, functional team may still emerge at some point that doesn't lose many games. Spurs will be Spurs, Arsenal's new manager could be a mix between Pep Guardiola and well, Pep Guardiola and he'd still need a couple of years to sort that mess out, and you just don't know with Chelsea, who might be a threat because they alternate between good and really bad. Essentially they're probably not good enough though, especially if Hazard exits stage left.

The future is bright, the future is blue. City will not have everything their own way, they never will, but this team has the opportunity to dominate the league, to reduce Stan Collymore and Duncan Castles to tears at the thought of how we killed the beautiful game forever. We have a set of top class young players who will only get better, supplemented with a splattering of club legends still performing, a base of top class players who reached new heights, all led by the greatest manager in world football.

Feels good to support football's centurions, doesn't it?

And for everyone else – do mind the gap.

And one final addendum for the 2nd edition – United lose the FA Cup final, we all had a good laugh at Liverpool as they lost the Champions League final in hilarious circumstances, Pep got manager of the year then signed a new contract and David Silva got to take his son home. What perfect endings to a generally magnificent season.

36139991R00180

Printed in Great Britain
by Amazon